M000290069

CHARGING AHEAD

This book is the first comprehensive treatment of credit cards in the global economy. The topic is timely not only because of the attention focused on cards as a contributor to the substantial rise in consumer borrowing, but also because of the role of cards in the recent retrenchment in the U.S. bankruptcy system. Relying on data from the United States, the United Kingdom, Canada, Australia, and Japan, *Charging Ahead* includes a careful statistical analysis of the relation between the rise of credit card use and broader macroeconomic phenomena such as consumer borrowing and bankruptcy. It also provides a broad narrative of how credit cards have come to be used so differently around the world. Finally, it sets out a detailed and coherent program for regulatory intervention grounded in both empirical analysis and the existing theoretical literature.

Ronald J. Mann received his J.D. from the University of Texas where he graduated first in his class and was the managing editor of the *Texas Law Review*. After graduation, he clerked for judges on the United States Court of Appeals for the Ninth Circuit and the United States Supreme Court. After three years in private practice, he worked for the Justice Department for four years as an Assistant to the Solicitor General. Before joining the University of Texas faculty in 2003, he taught for six years at the University of Michigan and for three years at Washington University in St. Louis.

Charging Ahead

THE GROWTH AND REGULATION OF PAYMENT CARD MARKETS

Ronald J. Mann
University of Texas School of Law

CAMBRIDGE UNIVERSITY PRESS
Cambridge, New York, Melbourne, Madrid, Cape Town, Singapore,
São Paulo, Delhi, Dubai, Tokyo, Mexico City

Cambridge University Press
The Edinburgh Building, Cambridge CB2 8RU, UK

Published in the United States of America by Cambridge University Press, New York

www.cambridge.org
Information on this title: www.cambridge.org/9780521711487

© Ronald J. Mann 2006

This publication is in copyright. Subject to statutory exception
and to the provisions of relevant collective licensing agreements,
no reproduction of any part may take place without the written
permission of Cambridge University Press.

First published 2006
First paperback edition 2007

A catalogue record for this publication is available from the British Library

Library of Congress Cataloging in Publication Data
Mann, Ronald J., 1961–
Charging ahead : the growth and regulation of payment card markets / Ronald J. Mann.
p. cm.
Includes bibliographical references and index.
ISBN-13: 978-0-521-86611-8 (hardback)
ISBN-10: 0-521-86611-1 (hardback)
1. Credit cards. 2. Credit cards – Law and legislation. I. Title.
HG3755.7.M36 2006
332.765 – dc22   2006005052

ISBN 978-0-521-86611-8 Hardback
ISBN 978-0-521-71148-7 Paperback

Cambridge University Press has no responsibility for the persistence or
accuracy of URLs for external or third-party internet websites referred to in
this publication, and does not guarantee that any content on such websites is,
or will remain, accurate or appropriate. Information regarding prices, travel
timetables, and other factual information given in this work is correct at
the time of first printing but Cambridge University Press does not guarantee
the accuracy of such information thereafter.

Contents

Figures and Tables

FIGURES

TABLES

Acknowledgments

The gratitude I owe my wife Allison Mann cannot be overstated. If this book has succeeded in providing any insight that is deep or compelling, there can be no doubt that it is attributable to her vision and persistence.

I owe a special debt to my friend Kinami Atsushi, who first saw the inherent interest of this project and arranged for my time spent studying this subject at the Institute of Monetary and Economic Studies at the Bank of Japan.

For assistance in collecting data, I am grateful to the National Bank of Belgium, the Department of Finance of Canada, the Institute for Monetary and Economic Studies at the Bank of Japan, the Bank of England, and the Federal Reserve Bank of New York. I also thank Morgan Stanley and Euromonitor for the use of proprietary data they kindly have provided to me.

Allegra Young deserves special thanks for reading the entire manuscript with great care and insight. For assistance with statistical analysis, I thank Dr. Dan Powers, Tracey Kyckelhahn, and Abe Dunne. For comments on earlier versions of various portions of this project, I thank Oren Bar-Gill, Terry Sullivan, Elizabeth Warren, Mark West, Jay Westbrook, and anonymous reviewers on behalf of Cambridge University Press. I received useful comments on a presentation of an early version of this work as the 2003 John C. Akard Distinguished Lecturer at the University of Texas School of Law, and on presentations of part of this work at the University of Michigan Law School and the CEGLA Center at the Tel Aviv University Faculty of Law. For particularly useful editorial assistance, I thank Andrew Brasher and Nick Bunch. For assistance with data collection, I thank Travis Siebeneicher, Tammy Macy, and Aimie Cryer.

Finally, I owe special thanks to Jeff Lehman and Bill Powers (my deans at the University of Michigan and the University of Texas, respectively) and to the Marlow Preston Fellowship for funding my work on this project.

Introduction

I start in 2003 at a parliamentary hearing in London. The witnesses are an impressive group, the CEOs of most of the large issuers of credit cards in the United Kingdom. The topic is the concern of a select Treasury Committee about the high cost and excessive use of credit cards. From the perspective of the media, the high point of the hearing was a sound bite from an exchange with Matthew Barrett, Chief Executive Officer of Barclays Bank. In the course of questioning Mr. Barrett about the high interest charges on the cards that Barclays issues, one member of the committee jests that "you probably have a Cahoot card in your wallet," referring to a low-cost card issued by a British Internet bank. In Washington, you could predict with great certainty that the CEO of Citibank would respond tartly that he of course carries a CitiCard and uses it everywhere he goes. In the more casual British atmosphere, however, Barrett offers us a lapse of apparent sincerity:

> I do not borrow on credit cards; it is too expensive.
>
> * * *
>
> I have four young adults in my family, and I give them advice on "don't get too much debt on credit cards" and they are very literate and fluent and extremely well informed because of who their dad is, but it does not matter a w[h]it; they still run their credit cards.[1]

The British press, as might be expected, filled stories for weeks with amused commentary on Barclays' admission that credit cards are too expensive. But the second statement is what intrigues me. What are we to think about this financial product, marketed around the globe by the world's leading financial institutions? In his capacity as a parent, Mr. Barrett (like many of us) is filled with trepidation at the thought that *his* children would use the product frequently. And if that is not enough, he tells the committee that despite the expressed fears of a sophisticated, informed, and apparently concerned parent, his children nevertheless use the product excessively. How can such a product be so successful? Why do we tolerate it? Why have so many of the world's largest economies allowed it to flourish?

The pages that follow provide a broad overview of my answers to those questions. In brief, the product is successful because it is one of the most effective mechanisms ever devised for retail purchasing and borrowing. Thus, we tolerate the product because efforts to ban it would do much more harm than good. At the same time, the problematic aspects of the product that motivate Mr. Barrett's trepidation cannot be ignored. Rather, they demand policy responses that allow the card to do what it does well, but limit the harms from excessive spending and debt that afflict many of those that use the card.

The problems have not escaped the attention of governmental policymakers. Australia and the United Kingdom have been investigating card markets for a decade. More recently, initiatives have appeared in the European Union, Spain, Mexico, and Argentina. Even the United States – where the credit card was invented and has been most warmly welcomed – has begun to consider major market interventions. At the same time, the legislative desire to protect the credit card's place in the American economy was one of the most important motivations for the Bankruptcy Abuse Prevention and Consumer Protection Act of 2005.

Academic contributions, by contrast, have largely missed the hard problem – the mix of values and costs that card use offers an economy. That is not to say that academics have ignored the card entirely. On the contrary, prominent critics like Robert Manning, George Ritzer, and Juliet Schor all have decried the contribution of the credit card to the increasingly consumerist society in the United States. From a wholly different perspective, David Evans and Richard Schmalensee have focused on the structure of the networks that dominate modern credit card markets, arguing that antitrust concerns about those networks have been seriously overstated. Finally, populist supporters of recent U.S. bankruptcy legislation have argued that the laxity of the consumer bankruptcy system in the United States paved the way for widespread abuse of the freedom that the credit card offers.

To make sense of the phenomenon from a global perspective, it is important to situate the rise of the credit card in the general shift from paper-based to electronic payments. Part I of this book explains the importance of that shift. Among other things, it shows how the United States, despite its affection for the plastic card, is far behind other developed countries in moving away from the wasteful use of traditional paper checks as a device for retail payments. Given the resources the United States wastes – about one-half of one percent of its gross domestic product – on processing paper checks, the United States is the *last* place in which it would make sense to stifle card-based payments as a retail payment system.

Part II of this book provides an empirical understanding of the costs and benefits of the card. The plastic card brings substantial benefits as an effective device for payment and for borrowing. To the extent consumer spending, consumer borrowing, and entrepreneurial activity are important drivers of economic growth, the card is an important component of a modern healthy economy. At the same time, the convenience of the card – in particular, the credit card – is uniquely associated with an increase in financial distress. The social costs of financial distress offset the benefits of convenience if they do not in fact outweigh them.

To some degree, this should come as no surprise. Academics for more than a decade have noted simple and apparent correlations between increased debt and consumer bankruptcy filings. And there can be no doubt that the rise of the credit card has been associated with a general rise in consumer borrowing. My work here extends the existing work in three important ways. First, the credit card is a global phenomenon, and I analyze data not only from the United States but also from other developed countries in which the card plays an important role in the economy. Second, I quantify the specific effects of credit card debt, as opposed to consumer debt in general. That analysis supports two premises: increased card spending leads to an increase in overall consumer borrowing; and increased credit card debt leads to an increase in consumer bankruptcy (even when I control for overall borrowing levels). Third, I emphasize the social costs of consumer financial distress, something of which previous writers have lost sight. Nearly everyone loses when consumers are mired in debt. Taken together, those points suggest a classic base for regulatory intervention: credit card borrowing as it exists in the globalized West imposes substantial external costs on the economy, not internalized by the networks, issuers, or cardholders.

Part III of the book takes that concern as the basis for a critical examination of global card usage and the circumstances that have led to its oddly varied pattern. I write from the perspective that regulators dealing with a global phenomenon like the credit card cannot sensibly design policy responses without some understanding of the reasons for the wide variations in usage patterns around the world. As I explain, fortuitous features of the post-war institutional setting in the United States – a fractionated banking system, the interstate highway system, the lack of serious data protection – made the United States uniquely suited to a rapid uptake and adoption of the card. Those circumstances have left the United States dependent on a credit-centered cards market to an extent unmatched in any other economy.

In countries less dependent on the credit card, the forces of globalization are pushing toward markets in which lending and payment functions are more segmented. That norm – epitomized by the United Kingdom and Commonwealth members like Canada and Australia – is characterized by common use of the debit card as a payment device, coupled with rapid increases in credit card borrowing and consumer bankruptcy (albeit at much lower levels than in the United States). Resisting that global norm is a third pattern, epitomized by the continental European Union. There, the coincidence of strong norms of data protection and resistance to consumer debt has hindered the development of the plastic card, forfeiting the benefits of the card but avoiding its costs.

The natural question, then, is what policies will be useful to confine the problems related to credit cards without creating undue inefficiencies in retail payment systems. Parts IV and V consider that question. The most obvious solution would be to push the United States toward debit cards for paying and credit cards for borrowing. But what policies encourage debit card use? Should the government police the price the card industry charges merchants ("interchange fees") or the prices merchants charge customers (credit card "surcharges" or cash discounts)? Should the government conduct a press campaign enlisting Oprah or Dr. Phil?

Unfortunately, those initiatives range from counterproductive to ineffectual. Any serious effort must focus on the heart of the problem: the relation between the issuer of the card and the cardholder. That relation, in turn, can be understood only in the context of the unusual contracting practices that dominate the modern cards industry. My analysis builds on the premise that firms use contracting and marketing techniques that focus the attention of myopic consumers on the more favorable parts of a relationship. Where those techniques are effective, consumers will give inadequate attention to the less favorable aspects of a relationship. In this context, sophisticated card issuers have learned to exploit the boilerplate terms of their agreements to produce a set of obligations that even the most sophisticated cardholder could not master. What does a government do about this? Should regulators then invalidate agreements that disadvantage cardholders? I conclude that regulatory standardization of cardholder agreement makes a great deal of sense. At a minimum, a strong case can be made for regulatory stabilization of terms, to bar the frequent post-hoc amendments that make it difficult for cardholders to understand their obligations.

The complexity of the relationship combined with the tendency of issuers to exploit consumer shortsightedness suggests that the existing system of agreement-based disclosures is at best ineffectual. I recommend a ban of all marketing aimed at minors and college students. I also suggest a revamped disclosure strategy – one that focuses on the critical times, the points at which purchasing and borrowing decisions are made. If one of the major causes of limited borrowing in Japan is the need for consumers to make their borrowing decisions at the point of sale, there is some reason to think that disclosures at that point might lead to more careful cardholder behavior. Finally, the most direct response would prohibit the rewards programs that issuers currently use to give cardholders such a strong incentive to use their cards as their regular spending device and the teaser rates that encourage them to borrow.

As the data presented in Part II suggest, consumer financial distress is rising rapidly even in the countries that use the credit card much less pervasively than the United States. Thus, even if the reforms discussed earlier could shift the United States toward the less credit-dominated global norm, they would not solve the problem entirely. Accordingly, Part V closes with a discussion of broader reforms directed to consumer credit markets in general. Starting again from the premise that the issuer/cardholder relationship imposes social costs, I show how modern technology gives the issuer a ready capacity to limit financial distress through actions designed to limit borrowing by distressed cardholders. The natural implication is that a sophisticated regulatory policy would harness that capacity by giving credit card issuers a monetary incentive to limit borrowing by the financially distressed. If that lending is privately profitable only because of the lender's ability to externalize the consequent costs of distress, the natural response is to inhibit lending. Among other things, that rationale supports mandatory minimum payment requirements, a tax on distressed credit card debt, and the subordination of payments to credit card lenders in bankruptcy.

* * *

I have a great belief in the ability of the market to drive behavior, and an abiding skepticism in the ability of the government to improve on the results produced even by flawed markets. Thus, it has been most unsettling as the evidence that I have collected and the theoretical frameworks built on it have steadily driven me to the interventionist conclusions presented in the closing parts of the book. As you read forward, I hope you can sense the atmosphere of inquiry and the quest for understanding that has motivated my long work on this project.

PART I

The Basics of Payment Cards

1 Paper or Plastic? The Functionality of Payment Systems

We live in a world of choices – sometimes seemingly endless choices. Some are important and some are meaningless. It is rational to make irrational choices some of the time, particularly in our capacity as consumers. In the grocery store, for example, after making "important" choices about what to cook in the coming week or whether to indulge the children with the new Star Wars cereal, we have to decide trivial things like how we want our groceries packaged and how we want to pay.

Merchants have some say in how we pay, and sometimes their choices limit our choices as consumers. Even so, merchants often accept payment forms that have distinctively different advantages to themselves and to their customers. What could be an advantage to a merchant could be a disadvantage to a customer and vice versa.

Plastic cards are one of the many different payment forms that are common in developed economies. To understand their importance, it is helpful to discuss some of the distinctions between different types of payments and payment transactions. For present purposes, the most important distinctions are between cash and noncash payments, paper and electronic payments, in-person and remote payments, and universal and networked payments.

Cash and Noncash Systems

Payments can be cash or noncash systems. The benefits of cash are obvious. It is widely accepted as payment. In the United States, creditors act wrongfully if they refuse to accept U.S. coins or currency when offered to

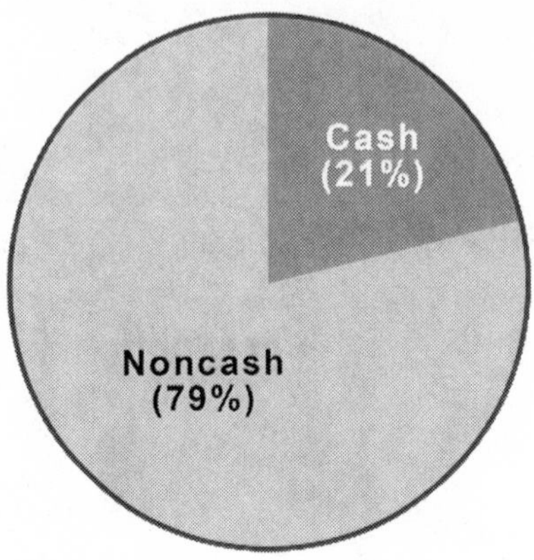

Figure 1.1. Value of cash and noncash retail transactions. Values for the United States in 2003. *Source:* Nilson Report 823.

discharge an obligation.[1] Sellers generally like cash because when a purchaser pays with cash, the seller receives immediate and final payment in a form that the seller can immediately use to make other payments without further processing or transformation.

Cash is also anonymous. It usually leaves no trail from which investigators or data marketers can track the payment. The privacy benefits of cash have led technologists to devote substantial efforts to provide similarly anonymous electronic payment solutions, but those efforts have not been successful to date. The anonymity feature raises a concern that people will use cash when they wish to avoid the notice of law enforcement for tax purposes or other reasons. Because of those concerns, some governments affirmatively discourage cash payments.

Cash is used for little more than one-fifth of the value of retail transactions in the United States (Figure 1.1). The reasons are obvious. It is difficult to transport and to use securely.[2] In addition, the finality of cash induces some purchasers to use noncash payment systems. Although it is difficult to quantify the effect, some purchasers use checks or credit cards solely to obtain the "float" that we gain when we can purchase an item today in return for a withdrawal from our deposit account that occurs some days later. Similarly, although less common, strategic purchasers should use credit cards when dealing with merchants of dubious reliability because of legal attributes of the credit card system that give purchasers a right to withhold payment that is not paralleled in other modern systems. Finally, in some cases, a merchant or individual may wish to leave a paper trail that proves the payment has been made. Few of us, for example, use cash to pay reimbursable expenses.

Noncash payment systems provide payment from a reliable third party, usually a bank or other financial institution. A check, for example, offers the hope – certainly not a promise – of payment from funds the purchaser has deposited with a bank. A credit card offers payment from the financial institution that has issued the card. The key point, however, is that all noncash payment systems depend for their success on credible arrangements to facilitate collection of claims in a timely and inexpensive manner.

Paper and Electronic Systems

Another important fault line lies between paper-based and electronic systems. In the United States, after depositing funds in a checking account a consumer can make payments through the largely paper-based checking system or through the mostly electronic automated clearinghouse (ACH) system that facilitates direct debits and direct credits to banking accounts. More commonly, the traditional, paper-based checking system is used. Even now, the procedures for using and collecting on checks center almost exclusively on the tangible object. Compared to procedures that manage information electronically, check collecting procedures are quite costly, in the range of several dollars per check (including the costs of handling the item by the payor, the payee, and the various banks that process it). Because of the large number of checks that are written in the United States, about 0.5% of the gross domestic product is spent in creating and processing paper checks.[3]

The procedures are slow, typically requiring days – not hours – for the merchant to be sure that the bank on which the check is drawn ultimately will pay it. Such delays hinder the efficiency of the system. Just as seriously, the procedures increase the potential for fraud. The delay between the time of deposit and the time at which the depositary bank discovers whether the check will be honored presents an opportunity for a variety of creative schemes to steal the money.

Responding to the high costs of paper-based processing, the American banking industry has supported several efforts to foster the use of electronic technology as a means for controlling and reducing costs in the checking system. Most recently, the industry has supported the Check Clearing in the 21st Century Act of 2003 (commonly known as Check 21). The principal purpose of this statute is to foster check truncation, in which electronic systems replace the need to transport the paper check through the normal check collection process.

By contrast, payment card transactions (at least in the United States) are processed electronically. The settlement process has been electronic since the early 1970s. In the 1990s, the industry dispensed with the use of paper credit card slips at the checkout counter. The result is that the cost of processing and collecting payments has fallen with the increase in the efficiency of electronic information systems. The ability to transmit information electronically also facilitates more rapid transactions at the checkout counter, which lowers labor costs for the merchants, and might even attract customers who value the shorter wait in checkout lines. To quantify the effect, empirical evidence suggests that card transactions already are about thirty seconds faster than check transactions.[4] Moreover, early studies indicate that as contactless cards are deployed in the next few years they will be even faster at the retail counter than cash.

Payment card transactions are not just faster but are also increasingly safer than paper-based transactions. Because the information on the card can be read electronically, the system can verify the authenticity of the card in real time. The terminal that reads the information on the card transmits that information to the issuer while the customer is at the counter, so that the issuer can decide whether to authorize the transaction. Although that system is not impervious to fraud (especially with the rise of identity theft), it plainly is more efficient than the checking system, which relies for verification primarily on a manual signature or presentation of a photo-bearing identification card. To be sure, the payment card system depends on a reliable and inexpensive telecommunications infrastructure, but the United States has had such an infrastructure throughout the relevant period.

Countries have moved from older paper-based payment systems to modern electronic payment systems at significantly different rates. For

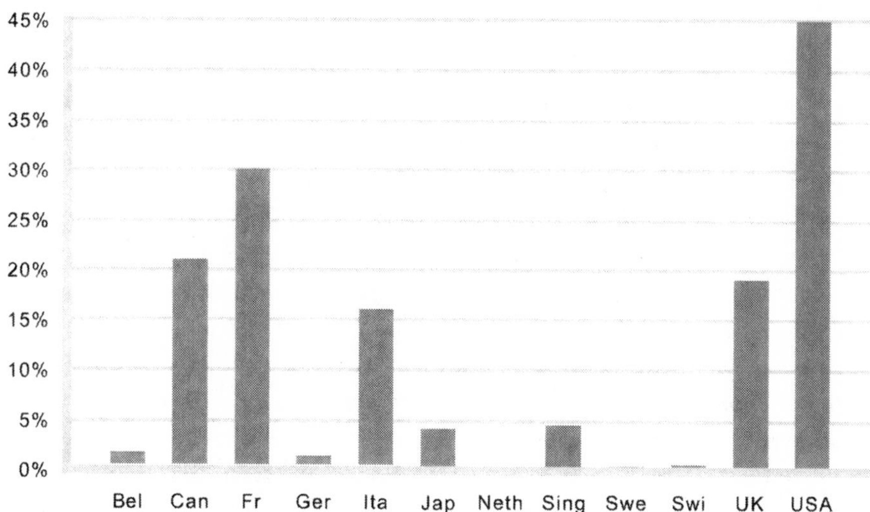

Figure 1.2. Share of value of checks in noncash transactions in 2003 values. *Source:* 2005 Red Book.

example, where the United States has moved farther toward noncash payment systems than many other countries (such as Japan and Italy), it has not made as much of a move from paper-based to electronic systems. As Figure 1.2 shows, most of its trading partners make relatively little use of the check, which Americans still use about fifty billion times a year. Check-use patterns continue to shift rapidly, as cost savings move countries toward electronic payments. The existing use patterns, however, are something of a puzzle – one that cannot be readily explained by any single factor. Chapter 10 revisits this subject, emphasizing the difficulty of discerning whether the growth of debit cards comes from a reduction in the use of checks, as opposed to a decline in the growth rate of the use of credit cards.

The shift from paper-based to electronic systems also has a substantial policy component, because at least in the United States it is a shift from the government-subsidized systems, provided exclusively by pervasively regulated financial institutions, to wholly private systems. Those systems are provided by entities less subject to the control of public authorities and for whom profitability is a primary motivating factor, so that users bear a much greater portion of the costs of the system.

In-Person and Remote Payments

A third way to think about payment systems is to consider the difference between face-to-face and long-distance transactions. The rise of Internet retailing, in particular, focuses attention on the advantages of the payment card in long-distance transactions. The preexisting Visa and MasterCard networks, and the widespread distribution of cards to consumers in the United States, gave credit card issuers a built-in nationwide payment network available when Internet commerce began. Other payment systems that existed at the time were not useful in the Internet setting. For example, cash is entirely impractical in a remote transaction unless the consumer has some reliable way to send the cash to the merchant. Even if some consumers were willing to mail cash for an Internet purchase, the merchant would not receive the cash for several days. Similarly, a commitment to pay by check gives the merchant nothing for several days (except a promise that "the check is in the mail") while the merchant waits for the check. Finally, when Internet commerce began, online retailers could not accept ACH transfers. A system for such payments now exists, but the move to ACH Internet payments is happening only after the credit card was entrenched as the predominant system for payment on the Internet. Thus, the most perceptible shifts in the payments patterns for maturing Internet retailers are not from credit cards to wholly separate systems, but from credit cards to debit card products that clear through the incumbent Visa and MasterCard networks.

The success of eBay's auction business had the rare effect of creating a market for a new payment product. Because a large number of sellers whose businesses were too small to make it cost-effective for them to accept conventional credit card payments populated eBay at that time, suddenly there was a large market for making payments quickly in remote transactions. The poor state of the institutions at the time was shown when I had to make several trips to local drugstores to purchase money orders to acquire items my niece was purchasing on eBay. With any concern at all for the value of my time, the transaction costs of acquiring the money order far exceeded the cost of the underlying object (in each of her transactions less than $20). Typically, sellers waited to ship products until they received the paper-based payment device in the mail.

From a flood of startups offering competing products, PayPal (now owned by eBay) has emerged as the dominant player in the industry, processing hundreds of millions of payments each year. According to eBay's 2004 10-K, PayPal was used for about $18.9 billion of transactions in 2004. One interesting aspect of that development is that it does not present a new payment system, but relies on existing systems (credit cards, debit cards, checking accounts, and ACH transfers) to make payments. Essentially, it uses the technology of the Web site to facilitate the use of conventional payment networks. Still, because of its nimble development of that technology, PayPal has emerged as a player that can compete directly against Visa and MasterCard as the currency of choice that an eBay-based merchant will accept. There is nothing on the horizon, however, that presages a similar realignment of the competitive forces in face-to-face retail transactions, where plastic cards steadily consolidate their dominance as the check fades from use.

Universal and Networked Payment Systems

Cutting across all of the functional categories discussed earlier is the question of whether a payment system is universal or limited to members of a network. Checks and cash are functionally universal in the sense that they can be presented to almost any person or business. To send the check, you must know the address to which you wish to send it. To collect the check, the person who receives it need not even have a bank account. They do not have to be a merchant approved by a credit card network or have a contract with a member of the ACH network or some other collection system. To be sure, a number of people do not have bank accounts, which makes it somewhat harder to collect a check, particularly if an individual rather than a business writes it. In particular, persons without bank accounts are almost certain to pay fees to collect a check, even if they go to the bank that issued the check (a task that will be inconvenient for most people). Yet, with respect to in-person transactions, a larger number of payees accept checks than other noncash payment systems. For example, almost all individuals will be compelled by social custom to accept a check in payment of an obligation. To succeed in that market, a new payment system must devise some method of collection that is generally available to payees. PayPal, for instance, was successful in developing an Internet-based payment system that depends on payees having a combination of an e-mail address and a checking account into which PayPal can disburse funds.

By contrast, payment cards are not universal payment systems. Rather, they depend directly on networks of participants, economically motivated by the structure of the system to make a voluntary decision to join the network. The banks that issue the cards do so because they believe they will profit from the fees and interest that they can charge. The customers that use the cards think they are a better vehicle for payment or borrowing than the alternatives available to them – the central focus of this book. The merchants that accept them believe that customers will make additional and larger transactions with cards, the profits from which will more than offset the fees they must pay. The institutions that acquire the transactions and process them from the merchants believe that the fees they charge the merchants will exceed the costs of their processing. Persons or entities that do not make those decisions do not participate in the network.

The distinction between networked and universal payment systems is important as a policy matter because of the need to maintain a menu of payment systems that includes at least some universal payment systems for most important payment transactions. Because the later chapters of this book will discuss policies designed to stem credit card use in favor of other systems, it is important to keep this distinction in mind.

Developing Payment Systems

Payment cards in the United States surpassed the use of cash more than a decade ago and then surpassed checks by 2003 (Figure 1.3). The use of cash sinks lower each year as noncash payment systems penetrate the markets of merchants with smaller and smaller transactions. The departure of McDonald's from the list of cash-only merchants presaged the desuetude of that category for substantial chain merchants. Use of checks drops each year as more consumers use debit cards and Internet banking systems for transactions that formerly would have required a check.

I expect that, eventually, some wholly new electronic payment system could reorder the traditional markets. For instance, electronic

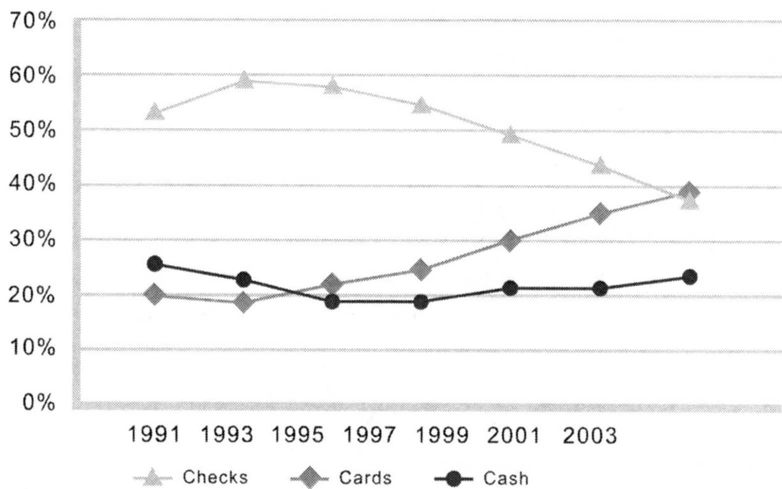

Figure 1.3. Consumer payment systems over time. Data on value of U.S. payments, in billions of U.S. dollars. *Source:* Nilson Report 761, 823.

storage gives rise to a number of options. That feature would obviate the need for a contemporaneous authorization confirming the availability of funds – a central feature of the dominant credit and debit card networks today. Rather, the transaction could be completed entirely based on an interaction between the merchant's terminal and the card itself. One example would be a portable currency, capable of being stored on a card or other device (such as a cellular telephone or a personal digital assistant). Gift cards and payroll cards also show promise.

In the hybrid model deployed in the United Kingdom, cards include authorization information – the limit on the card and some information to allow the merchant to verify that the card is being used by the accountholder – and the system approves most transactions without real-time authorization by the issuer. Surprisingly, despite the abandonment of real-time assessment by the issuer, that system probably is more secure than the existing U.S. system.

Stored-value cards also have the potential to limit the risk of violent crime against cardholders, at least if they are deployed broadly enough to lower the amount of cash that cardholders are carrying. If the thief that steals the card is unable to use the value on the card for the thief's own purposes, there is little point in stealing the card. Finally, stored-value cards are not tied to a bank account or line of credit, and thus individuals that do not have bank accounts can use them. For that reason, they have been a persistent object of government policymakers attempting to develop cheaper – that is, electronic – methods of disbursing benefits to the unbanked.

Likewise, despite a series of market disappointments that continues through the date of this writing, there is good reason to believe that some form of electronic currency will have a significant role in commerce in the decades to come. On the Internet, a wholly electronic currency promises advantages of higher security, lower costs (especially for low-value "microtransactions"), and greater user privacy. To date, however, electronic currency systems have foundered, generally because there has not been sufficiently broad deployment to make the product cost-effective. At bottom, there has been relatively limited consumer interest in the privacy and security benefits of electronic money, and thus it seems unlikely that electronic money will dominate Internet commerce in the foreseeable future. It is almost certain, however, that entrepreneurs will continue to search for niches in which to promote the use of electronic money. For now, however, PayPal seems to be filling that niche effectively. (Witness its acceptance at the iTunes Music Store!)

The last major electronic product on the horizon is the bank transfer or the giro, which is common in many foreign markets (particularly Japan and countries in continental Western Europe). Functionally, this is the equivalent of the ACH transfer that is used in the United States to make direct debits (for recurring payments such as mortgages or car loans) and direct credits (for recurring income items like salary). Bank transfer systems – account-to-account or A2A payments in the conventional terminology – result in a payment directly from one bank account to another. A2A payments have not been important in Internet commerce to date, largely because until 2001 the ACH network did not permit consumers to authorize nonrecurring transactions on the network. Yet the search for new market niches, coupled with continuing merchant dissatisfaction about the high costs of accepting credit cards, led NACHA (the main proprietor of the ACH network) in 2001 to permit a new type of entry (a "WEB" entry in NACHA terminology) that permits such payments. At this writing, that product has begun to gain a substantial market share, with about one billion payments in 2004 worth about $300 each. The likely success of the product was bolstered by the prominent decision of Walmart.com to start accepting it in 2005. Given the common use of bank transfers in so many countries, it seems likely that this product or something like it will play a substantial role in Internet retailing in the years to come.

* * *

From this list of distinctions, one thing is clear: Whatever the benefits of payment cards might be, they do not include the anonymity, universality, and unquestioned finality associated with the older, paper-based forms of payment. This means that when we think of ways to influence consumer payment choices, we need to keep in mind that it always will be important to have some payment options that have those features.

2 The Mechanics of Payment Card Transactions

The distinctions among automated teller machine (ATM) cards, charge cards, credit cards, and debit cards are largely invisible to the ordinary user. Still, those differences are critical to informed policymakers. To set the stage, this chapter discusses the mechanics of credit and debit card transactions, providing basic information on the economics of payment cards, primarily from the perspective of the merchant.

The Credit Card Transaction

Most credit card transactions involve four participants (depicted in Figure 2.1): a purchaser that pays with a credit card, an issuer that issues the credit card, a merchant that sells goods or services, and an acquirer that collects payment for the merchant. The acquirer is so named because it acquires the transaction from the merchant and then processes it to obtain payment from the issuer. In American Express and Discover transactions, the entity that issues the card also acquires the transaction. That arrangement is called a three-party or closed-loop system.

Although the purchaser, issuer, merchant, and acquirer are the nominal parties to the transaction, the network under which the card has been issued (usually Visa or MasterCard) is also involved. The networks (associations of member banks that issue Visa or MasterCard branded cards) provide information and transaction-processing services with respect to the transaction between the acquirer and the issuer. For example, when an acquirer has transactions involving Visa-branded cards, it

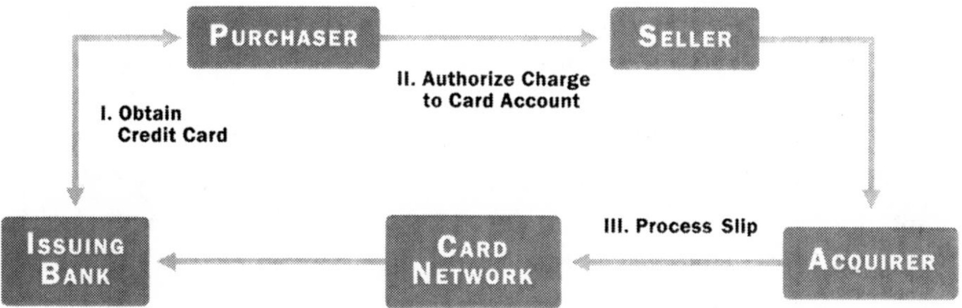

Figure 2.1. Payment by credit card.

will use VisaNet to communicate with the issuer of the card to obtain authorization and payment for the transaction.

Perhaps more importantly, Visa and MasterCard (and the other network providers) establish and enforce rules and standards surrounding the use of cards carrying their brands. Those rules, in turn, govern the contract between the acquirer and the issuer. Instead of negotiating a separate agreement with each issuer, each acquirer simply joins the relevant network and agrees to comply with the network rules for all transactions on that network. For example, the network rules specify for all entities in the network the fees that the issuer will deduct from each transaction when it forwards payment to the acquirer. Although the network rules are central to the operation of the system, they are proprietary documents, owned by the networks, and thus not readily available.

The key to any credit card transaction is the relationship between the cardholder and the card issuer. The typical relationship is familiar. The issuer commits to pay for purchases made with the card in return for the cardholder's promise to reimburse the issuer over time. That relationship is the opposite of the common checking relationship, where the customer normally must deposit funds *before* the bank will pay checks.

The buy-first, pay-later aspect of most credit card relationships alters the underlying economics of the system. Banks that provide checking accounts can earn profits by investing the funds that customers have placed in their accounts. A credit card issuer does not have that option, because most cardholders do not deposit funds before they make purchases on their cards. Indeed, at least in the United States, the cardholder often does not even have a depositary relation with the card issuer. Traditionally and predominantly, the profit for the typical card issuer comes from the interest that the issuer earns on the balances its cardholders carry on their cards from month to month.

The business models have become more diverse in recent years. Some major full-service issuers like Bank of America, Wells Fargo, and JP Morgan Chase, for example, use relationships to create synergies among a broad portfolio of products. The centrality of this strategy is epitomized by Wells Fargo's annual report, the theme of which is its corporate commitment to have seven of its products in the hands of each of its customers. For these issuers, the profit comes from creating switching costs so that the banks can charge higher fee levels without losing customers to competitors.

A second group of issuers, banks such as MBNA (recently acquired by Bank of America), Providian (recently acquired by Washington Mutual), and Capital One, focus on cards as individual profit centers. Those issuers often are called monolines because they typically do not offer depositary accounts or other traditional consumer banking products. Monolines rely on interest and fees for a large part of their income. Even among those issuers, though, there is a considerable amount of specialization. MBNA, for example, uses sophisticated data mining to profit in a market niche for loyalty cards, attractive to upper middle-class card users. Those cards and other premium-brand loyalty cards typically carry a substantial annual fee. By contrast, Providian and Capital One traditionally have emphasized cardholders of considerably lower credit quality. Still other issuers focus entirely on highly risky subprime cardholders.

As a matter of industry structure, the monolines are important because they give each potential cardholder multiple issuers from which to select credit cards. This is not true in other countries. For example, in England and France, the majority of cards are issued by banks that hold deposit accounts for the cardholders. It is fair to say that the card industry in those countries has not shown as rapid a pace of product innovation or as aggressive a competition on price as the U.S. card industry.

That structure has been in considerable flux. In 2005, large mainstream financial institutions acquired several of the prominent monolines. Although the ultimate competitive implications of those mergers are difficult to assess, it seems clear that one of the dominating motivations was the need of monoline issuers to lower the cost of their

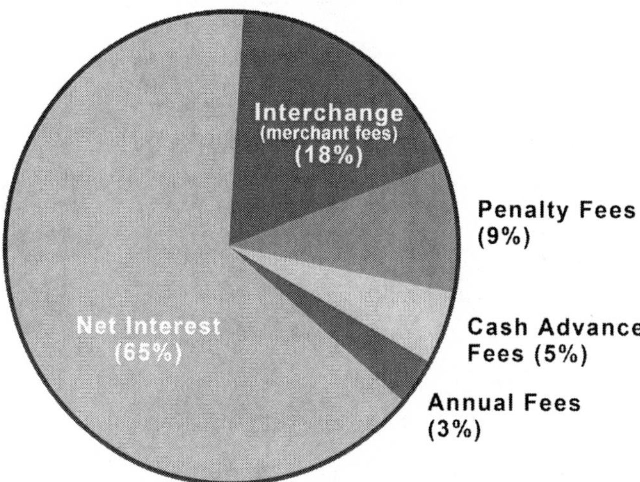

Figure 2.2. U.S. card issuer revenue sources (2004). *Source:* Credit Card Management, May 2005, at 27.

funds. It is clear from the annual reports of the acquired entities that these acquisitions would increase the profitability of the monolines even if the acquiring entities made no changes in business operations and were unable to create any synergies with their existing customer bases. To give a sense of the overall revenue structure of the industry as it currently exists, Figure 2.2 displays the sources of the $100 billion in 2004 revenues for U.S. bank card issuers.

The credit card serves two distinct functions. It is a device for both payment and borrowing. That juxtaposition is both a major reason for the card's value and the source of many of the problems that can be traced to the use of credit cards. On the first point, credit card payment transactions are successful primarily because they are fast and convenient, an attribute that is attractive to both customers and merchants. The seeming ease of the transactions hides a complex and thoughtfully ordered authorization and collection process. As the credit card is swiped at the merchant's counter, the terminal captures information from the magnetic stripe on the back of the card and transmits that information through the relevant network to the issuer. Among other things, as Figure 2.3 illustrates, that information makes it easy for the merchant's terminal to route the transaction to the correct issuer. The

By the Numbers

Although phone companies, gas companies and department stores have their own numbering systems, ANSI Standard X4.13-1983 is the system used by most national credit-card systems.

What the Numbers Mean

Illustration by Rosaleah Rautert

The front of your credit card has a lot of numbers -- here's an example of what they might mean.

Here are what some of the numbers stand for:

- The first digit in your credit-card number signifies the **system**:
  - **3 - travel/entertainment cards** (such as American Express and Diners Club)
  - **4 - Visa**
  - **5 - MasterCard**
  - **6 - Discover Card**
- The **structure** of the card number varies by system. For example, American Express card numbers start with 37; Carte Blanche and Diners Club with 38.
  - **American Express** - Digits three and four are type and currency, digits five through 11 are the account number, digits 12 through 14 are the card number within the account and digit 15 is a check digit.
  - **Visa** - Digits two through six are the bank number, digits seven through 12 or seven through 15 are the account number and digit 13 or 16 is a check digit.
  - **MasterCard** - Digits two and three, two through four, two through five or two through six are the bank number (depending on whether digit two is a 1, 2, 3 or other). The digits after the bank number up through digit 15 are the account number, and digit 16 is a check digit.

Figure 2.3. Credit card numbers. *Source:* www.howstuffworks.com. Reprinted by permission.

issuer (or more commonly an agent processing transactions on behalf of the issuer) examines that information to determine if the transaction is within the cardholder's limit, and also to assess the likelihood that the card is legitimate (rather than a forgery), and that the transaction is being conducted by the cardholder (rather than a thief). If the issuer's computer approves the transaction, it sends back an authorization message a few seconds after the merchant's terminal contacts it.

After the cardholder leaves the merchant's place of business, the merchant collects payments by transferring the data for its transactions (usually at least once a day) to the acquirer for the appropriate network. As the earlier discussion emphasizes, a merchant cannot obtain payment for any card transaction unless it has an agreement with an entity that acquires transactions for that network. Credit cards are not like checks, which can be presented to the issuer by any party that receives them. Rather, a merchant cannot accept Visa cards unless it has an agreement with an entity that is a member of the Visa network. Although this is not true in all countries (Japan is a conspicuous counterexample), merchants in the United States ordinarily can contract with a single entity to process most if not all of their credit card transactions. Originally, all acquirers were banks, but in recent years, the market has become dominated by technology companies that specialize in efficient processing. Thus, First Data Corporation now processes about half of all general-purpose credit card transactions in the United States.

When the merchant sends the transaction data to the acquirer, the acquirer credits the merchant for the total amount of the transactions, reduced by a discount, which the acquirer charges for the service of collecting the transactions. The amount of the discount varies with the type of transaction, network, and characteristics of the merchant, but in the United States, it is rarely less than 1%, and for conventional brick-and-mortar merchants, not often more than 3%. Although the market is increasingly concentrated, the market for acquisition is competitive, in the sense that a large number of acquirers compete for merchants based on the price that they charge. As of 2004, more than eighty acquirers were processing transactions worth more than $1 million per week. First Data's increasing ascendancy seems to be attributable almost entirely to its size. It has economies of scale and investment that allow it to serve merchants more effectively and cheaply than smaller competitors do.

To put it more pointedly, you do not hear merchants complaining about First Data's market power. The only industry players that complain about First Data's growing power are the large credit card networks (especially Visa) whose market positions are threatened by First Data. For example, Visa recently promulgated a rule requiring all transactions using Visa cards to be processed over VisaNet. Although Visa offered other justifications, press reports suggested that the purpose of the rule was to prevent First Data from bypassing VisaNet to process (at a lower fee than Visa) the growing number of transactions for which First Data is the processor for both the issuer and the merchant.[1]

The acquirer, in turn, processes the transactions by sending to each issuer the transactions that involve that issuer's cards. Generally, the acquirer sorts all of the transactions it has received into batches for each of the networks in which it participates and sends each batch through the switch for that network. Each switch then will distribute the transactions to the issuers in the network. Each issuer, in turn, pays each acquirer the total amount of the transactions the acquirer has sent, reduced by an interchange fee set by the network. As noted earlier, the interchange fee is set for the entire network and is not negotiable on a case-by-case basis. Fees vary depending on the type of merchant and the specific card, but fees for most classes of Visa and MasterCard transactions currently are between 1% and 2%, with fees for American Express and Discover somewhat higher. For acquirers to be profitable, the discount fees that they charge merchants generally must be slightly higher than the interchange fees that the acquirers must pay issuers. In recent years, the spread between the interchange fees and the discount that merchants pay has become increasingly thin, as acquirers compete vigorously to retain market share.

The issuers, in turn, sort the transactions reported to them, post them to the separate accounts, and bill their cardholders on a monthly basis. When the process is complete, the cardholder has been charged for the total amount of the transaction. The issuer has a receivable for the total amount of the transaction. Yet, the issuer has paid about 98.5% of that amount to the acquirer. From the 1.5% spread (together with interest and other fee income), the issuer must cover the costs of its operations and losses from cardholders that do not pay their bills in a timely manner.

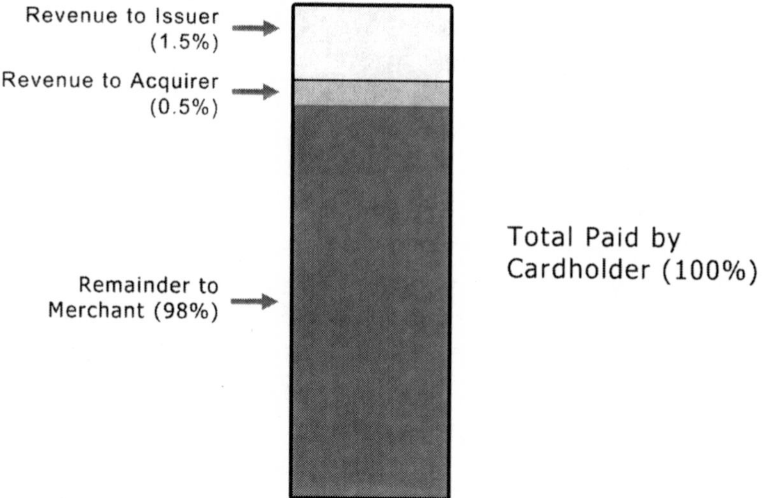

Figure 2.4. Dividing the credit card dollar.

The acquirer has received about 98.5% of the transaction and has paid the merchant about 98% of the value of the transaction. Its spread (0.5% in this example) must cover the costs of its operations. The merchant has received about 98% of the value of the transaction and has sold the good to the customer. It must be able to make a profit at that price. Figure 2.4 illustrates a typical allocation of funds from such a transaction.

One distinctive feature of the credit card system is that in the United States (and many other legal systems) a consumer has a right to cancel a credit card payment that is broader than the consumer's rights with other payment systems. Standing alone, that right would wreak havoc with the credit card system, because it would put issuers to the thankless task of addressing their customers' complaints about remote merchants. The card-issuing networks solve that problem by the simple expedient of adopting rules that pass the losses (known as chargebacks) back to the merchants. Thus, when a cardholder challenges a charge that appears on a credit card account, the issuer can charge the transaction back to the acquirer. This is done by notifying the acquirer of the claim and withholding funds equal to the claim from the daily transmission of funds paying the acquirer for the day's transactions. The acquirer, in turn, charges the transaction back to the merchant by withholding payment from the merchant equal to the claim. Visa and MasterCard also impose fees (generally about $25) for each chargeback processed through their networks. Merchants that have a large number of chargebacks often are obligated to deposit funds with their acquirers as a reserve to cover anticipated future chargebacks. Merchants with too many chargebacks eventually are evicted from the networks.

In addition to the right to withhold payment, American law, through the Truth in Lending Act (TILA), protects the cardholder from card theft by limiting the cardholder's liability for unauthorized charges to a maximum of $50. That $50 limit is absolute: It applies even if the cardholder knows that the card has been stolen and fails to notify the issuer of the theft. Thus, the issuer generally cannot shift losses from unauthorized transactions to the cardholder. Moreover, within the network, credit card issuers in ordinary face-to-face retail transactions retain the risk of unauthorized transactions. Although merchants bear responsibility when customers complain about the quality of goods and services that they have been sold, the issuer bears the loss when the cardholder contends that he or she did not in fact engage in the transaction. Such a system puts the incentive on the issuer to develop technologies to minimize the risk of loss from unauthorized transactions.

The Debit Card Transaction

Unlike a credit card, a debit card does not reflect an independent source of funds. Rather, it allows a customer to draw on funds that are already in the customer's checking or savings account. At first glance, that difference might seem insignificant, particularly in an era where both products can reside on a single piece of plastic. That difference, however, has important economic and legal consequences.

Debit cards have two primary uses. The first is for depositing and withdrawing money from an account at an ATM. That functionality has little macroeconomic significance because it does not involve use of the card as a payment device. Thus, for present purposes, the use of debit cards in point-of-sale (POS) transactions is much more important. Point-of-sale transactions work much like credit card transactions. The customer (or the merchant) swipes the card at a terminal, the terminal conducts an online authorization transaction to verify the authenticity of the card and the availability of funds in the account, and the transaction is completed a few seconds later.

American law draws a firm distinction between a credit card and a debit card. Because debit card transactions do not involve a substantial extension of credit, the TILA protections described earlier do not apply. Rather, the transactions are treated as electronic fund transfers and are subject to the less robust protections offered by the Electronic Fund Transfer Act (EFTA). Therefore, if your debit card is stolen and you do not report this promptly to the issuer, you might be liable for up to $500 of the unauthorized transactions, where in the same situation a theft of your credit card would expose you to a maximum liability of $50. In addition, if you purchase a plane ticket with a debit card and the airline becomes insolvent and cancels the flight, you have no remedy except against the airline. If you had used a credit card to make that purchase, TILA would permit you to refuse to pay the portion of your credit card bill attributable to the plane ticket. Systemically, the advantages should make debit cards less attractive to consumers, but more attractive to merchants, than credit cards.

Those distinctions might seem arbitrary. However, there are also important policy distinctions between the two kinds of cards. In particular, as discussed in Chapter 4, there is good reason to think that debit cards are less likely to contribute to the excessive spending and financial distress that makes credit cards so troublesome. Accordingly, policies that push consumers from credit cards to debit cards could have a salutary effect on the net costs of payment systems.

There also is an important distinction between two classes of debit cards: personal identification number (PIN) based (online) cards and PIN-less (offline) cards. PIN-based cards require the customer to enter a PIN to complete the transaction. PIN-based cards are issued by one of a number of regional or national networks of banks that clear transactions in much the same way as Visa and MasterCard. The networks have consolidated over the last few decades. The largest remaining networks are Star (with more than half of the market), NYCE, and Pulse (each with about 10% of the market). The use of a PIN lowers the risk of fraud by a factor of about fifteen (about one-tenth of a cent per transaction in PIN-based transactions versus 1.6 cents per transaction in PIN-less debit transactions).[2] In addition, the charges to merchants for PIN-based transactions are much lower than the charges for conventional credit card transactions, rarely more than 35–50 cents per transaction. PIN-based cards were introduced several decades ago but gained market share very slowly, largely because of the costs to merchants of obtaining terminals into which customers could enter their PINs. Only in the late 1990s did the cost of terminals fall sufficiently (they now cost less than $100) to make it cost-effective for ordinary merchants to obtain them. Coupled with the legal advantages to debit card transactions discussed earlier, merchants have strong incentives to accept debit cards. As of the end of 2003, there were about four million terminals in the United States.

PIN-less debit transactions are authorized just like credit card transactions, solely by presentation of the card and the cardholder's signature. PIN-less debit transactions are cleared through the Visa and MasterCard networks (VisaCheck and MasterMoney, respectively) precisely like credit card transactions, except that the issuer removes funds from the deposit account when a debit card transaction is posted, instead of posting the charge to an open account for which a bill will be sent. Generally, PIN-less debit transactions cost the merchants about 1% of the transaction amount, considerably less than credit card transactions, but much more than the PIN-based transactions.

The PIN-less debit cards are crucial to the history of the market because their deployment in the mid-1990s was the event that spurred the rapid growth of debit card use in the United States. For two reasons, PIN-less debit cards started with a much larger set of acceptance points than the PIN-based products. First, merchants could accept PIN-less transactions on the terminals they used for conventional Visa and MasterCard credit transactions. Second, merchants were obligated by Visa and MasterCard's "honor all card" policies to accept the debit cards if they accepted the Visa and MasterCard credit products. Thus, the strong market position that Visa and MasterCard have had for decades gave their debit products a substantial advantage when they were introduced in the mid-1990s. Because all merchants accepting Visa and MasterCard credit cards immediately accepted the debit products, it was not surprising that consumers began to use those products much more rapidly than the similar PIN-based products that had been introduced decades earlier.

Currently the debit card market is unstable. Among other things, it is still adjusting to successful antitrust litigation by major retailers that gave retailers the right to refuse Visa and MasterCard debit cards even if they accept Visa and MasterCard credit cards. The retailers had claimed that Visa and MasterCard's "honor all cards" rules amounted to an illegal tying arrangement. A settlement just before trial resulted in an agreement by Visa and MasterCard to abandon those rules and substantially lower the interchange fees for their PIN-less debit products.[3] It is too soon to tell whether this ultimately will lead to a decline in market share for PIN-less debit products (because merchants are no longer obligated to accept them) or to an increase in market share (because the fees have fallen). To the extent the large market share rested on the "honor all cards" rule, there is reason to think that the superior features of PIN-based products might cause them to gain market share.[4] The lower interchange fees attract merchants. Policymakers should be attracted by the much lower fraud rates. And consumers might be attracted by the security that the PIN provides. It is worth noting that outside the United States, the PIN-based product is much more widely deployed than the PIN-less product.[5]

The relation to the check complicates pricing for debit card products. As discussed in Chapter 1, the debit card can be viewed as a substitute for the check. From that perspective, banks should be paying their customers to use debit cards because debit card transactions are so much cheaper to process than check transactions. If, however, they are viewed as substitutes for credit cards, the pricing should be much higher because the banks would need to cover the processing costs solely out of transaction fees. Unlike credit cards, debit cards do not generate interest revenues.

Debit cards (PIN-less debit cards in particular) also are gaining a substantial foothold on the Internet. In the early days of the Internet, credit cards had an appreciable advantage over debit cards largely because debit cards were relatively uncommon at the time. Debit cards, however, have made major advances in the United States since 1999, so that they now are used in face-to-face retail transactions almost as frequently as credit cards. Moreover, because about 20% of American consumers do not have a credit card, retailers that accept both credit cards and debit cards have access to a broader customer base than retailers only accepting credit cards. As a result, a rapidly increasing share of Internet retail transactions are paid with PIN-less debit cards rather than credit cards. Here, as in the brick-and-mortar context, PIN-based debit cards have lagged behind. Despite their unquestioned advantages in security, system operators have not yet come up with a way to collect PINs in Internet payment transactions that is sufficiently user-friendly to attract mainstream Internet merchants.

Consumer Confusion

The leading credit card products and the leading debit card products in the United States now use the same technology. The cards have the same appearance. They have the same antifraud features. They bear the same logos on their faces (Visa and MasterCard). They are cleared through the same network switches. Their transactions are verified in the same way (by signature). And, they are issued by the same entities. What this means is that even the most sophisticated consumer often cannot tell whether the card pulled from the wallet is a credit card or a debit card. Few understand the different legal protections associated with the cards.

Although it would be easy to overstate the point, press reports suggest that both issuers and networks are contributing to consumer confusion. Visa's avowed strategy for the debit card is to make it resemble its successful credit card product as closely as possible, so that consumers will not know the details that distinguish the products by design.[6] Similarly, the pervasive advertisements for the PIN-less debit card products emphasize the convenience of the products as compared to the check. However, they do not point out the difference in legal consequences between using the debit card and either a credit card[7] or a check (where, at least technically, the consumer's right to stop payment extends until the check-clearing process is complete).

An analogous problem arises from the dual-use cards that banks commonly issue to their depositors, which contain two distinct debit products: a Visa or MasterCard PIN-less product and a PIN-based ATM network product. Indeed, about 85% of debit cards now carry both of those products.[8] Because both products are debit products, no transaction with the card is entitled to TILA protections. Yet, under the dominant existing technology, a consumer's choice at the point of sale is made in a misleading way. When the typical terminal asks the consumer to select whether the consumer wishes to pay by credit or debit, the customer who chooses credit reasonably would think the transaction was a credit transaction (with attendant legal protections). In fact, however, the buttons labeled "credit" and "debit/ATM" are asking the consumer to pick between the Visa and MasterCard debit products (chosen with the "credit" selection) and the PIN-based debit products (chosen with the "debit" or "ATM" selection). Whichever button the consumer chooses, the funds promptly will be removed from the consumer's account and the EFTA (not TILA) will apply, to the consumer's peril.

PART II

Easy Money

The payment card is perhaps the most important financial innovation of the twentieth century. Like many other innovations, it developed gradually, resulting from a series of cumulative advances. Accident also played a significant role, as explained in detail in Part III. The benefits of the payment card are obvious. In essence, it provides easy money. As a payment device, it is faster and cheaper to use than paper-based payment systems. As a lending tool, it can be used to borrow indefinite amounts for a broad range of purchases without providing security or even stepping into a bank. Those features are the focus of Chapter 3.

The credit card, however, is not an unqualified success. Broader social costs arise from increases in credit card use. Specifically, the credit card is associated with increases in spending, borrowing, and financial distress. It is not clear why that is the case, although academics have suggested it may be due to any number of factors: cognitive impairments, compulsive behavior, excessive or unfair advertising, or fraudulent contracting practices. Chapters 4 and 5 discuss that problem. Specifically, I examine the quantitative relations between credit card use and consumer borrowing and also between credit card borrowing and financial distress. I sidestep temporarily the question of why those relations exist. Setting the stage for the comparative discussion in Part III, the analysis also shows that the effects of credit card use are not unique to the United States.

3 In Defense of Credit Cards

Policy analysis of the credit card has focused on two topics. The first is a series of works criticizing the contribution of the credit card to the consumerist ethos of the United States.[1] A second topic, researched mainly by economists such as Lawrence Ausubel, on the one hand, and David Evans and Richard Schmalensee, on the other hand, debates whether the structure of the credit card industry has led to collusive and above-market pricing.[2] What is missing, however, is a serious and critical assessment of the benefits that credit cards provide to society. Without a fair acknowledgment of the benefits, analysts cannot hope to provide a credible accommodation of the concerns the critics of credit cards articulate.

Paying with Credit Cards

Credit cards assumed their place as the dominant payment system in the United States largely without a credit feature. They had functional advantages over competing systems, and credit card companies paid more attention to information technology.

As Chapter 7 explains, the credit card rose to prominence because it was a more effective device for business travelers making payments to merchants away from home. From the perspective of the cardholder, it is easier to carry a credit card than it is to carry cash. From the perspective of the merchant, it always has been easier to verify the creditworthiness of a person holding a credit card than a person offering to pay with a check. Conceptually, this is an institutional use of information technology. The core idea is that a token can serve as an authentication device and can bear a number that identifies the appropriate cardholder.

However, the dominance of the credit card rests more directly on its rapid deployment of electronic technology and the vision to pursue new markets facilitated by that technology. To be sure, through the 1960s, credit card processing depended on paper for the most part, with little advance over the paper-based, check collection system. In 1970, however, Visa's national network provided a computer system that could process transactions on a national basis. Given the state of computer technology at the time, this was a bold and risky step. The success of that investment earned Visa the dominant market position that it has held or shared with MasterCard through the intervening decades.

Oddly enough, the decision to create and deploy that network did not rest on a rational calculation of the costs and benefits. Rather, it must be attributed to the forceful (if eccentric) personality of Dee Hock, who (by his own account and Lewis Mandell's) was largely responsible for convincing the major banks to participate in an endeavor that at the time seemed unlikely to succeed.[3] (A sense of Hock's eccentricity is evident from the title of his autobiography – *The Chaordic Age*. That work sets forth a philosophy of organizational management – chaordism, a combination of chaos and order – that, in Hock's view, is exemplified by his successful career at Visa.)

Continuing to press at the forefront of innovation, the major networks starting in the early 1990s moved to eliminate the last vestiges of paper-based processing, shifting the American credit card system for the most part to an electronic processing system, in which transactions are collected and billed to cardholders without any paper document to reflect the transaction. Among other things, that advance has given the credit card an additional advantage as the most convenient device at the point of sale. The increasingly rapid online authorization process makes the credit card superior on that point to checks and in some contexts almost equivalent to cash. A recent Federal Reserve study, for example, suggests that credit card transactions are about thirty seconds faster than check transactions.[4]

With the rise of Internet commerce, the industry has pressed its exploitation of technology even further, largely abandoning the physical token of the card. Thus, in online transactions, only the card number and accompanying authentication information are needed. That move solidified the role of the credit card as the dominant Internet payment device. More recently, attempting to exploit small-dollar markets in which time is of the essence, the industry has developed verification technologies sufficiently reliable to justify abandoning signatures even in face-to-face contexts. As this book is written, large issuers are beginning mass deployment of contactless cards, in which the verification is completed by waving the device near a terminal at the checkout counter.

Many readers will find those technological achievements pedestrian in an era of wireless Internet access and online retailing, but electronic processing has saved billions of dollars in transaction costs. Any business that has struggled through a full-scale upgrade of a legacy computer system to a more modern system will look with envy at the successful transformation twenty-five years ago of the already-deployed networks of Visa and MasterCard from traditional paper-based processing to electronic processing.

Consider the checking system, which would have been the strongest competitor to the credit card if banks had not so thoroughly squandered the advantages of the dominant market position the check held among noncash payments when the credit card was invented. Even now, in the twenty-first century, when more than 95% of credit card transactions in the United States are authorized online by the issuer in real time and collected electronically, policymakers in the checking system can look forward with great excitement to a time – still in the future – when 10% of checking transactions will be processed electronically. Moreover, in the checking system, electronic processing will not include any real-time communication with the bank on which the check is drawn, and in most cases still will involve the costs of transporting a paper check from the point of sale to the bank of first deposit. Even now, as check usage declines, in the United States about one-half of one percent of the GDP (some $50 billion) is spent each year creating and processing paper checks.[5] The savings in resources attributable to the electronic processing of credit card transactions must be at the center of any serious policy analysis of the credit card.

To be sure, as Robert Hendrickson recognized thirty years ago, electronic processing poses a privacy concern to the extent that it facilitates the collection of personally identifiable information about the systems' users. Although this book does not discuss privacy in detail, it is a serious issue. The best response may be to have a menu of payment choices including some that are payor-anonymous. That is easy enough at the store counter, where cash provides a payor-anonymous option, at least for smaller transactions. In the remote context, however, the concern is more difficult to accommodate.

Borrowing with Credit Cards

Most authors that have written about credit cards have failed to accept what strikes me as the indubitable genius of the credit card as an efficient lending mechanism. To make the point more bluntly, if it is easy to see that the credit card surpasses the competing paper-based, bank-issued payment product – the check – it is difficult even to see the competition between the credit card and the competing paper-based, bank-issued lending product – the conventional closed-end bank loan.

Again, the basic distinction is one of transaction costs. The closed-end loan from a bank typically starts with one or more visits to a banker's office, an interview, and the completion of forms in the banker's presence. For decades, however, the process of obtaining a line of credit on a card has been as streamlined as can be imagined: filling out and mailing a short application received in the mail or picked up at a merchant's place of business. Have you ever heard of somebody driving to a bank to apply for a credit card? Related to that, consider the task of applying for an increase in a line of credit. That is a cumbersome and challenging task for a conventional loan, but an easy task for a credit card lender, often one that can be fulfilled directly through a Web site.

A related advantage is the use of information technology to assess the risk of transactions. Once transaction processing and account management becomes electronic – something that has been true in much of the credit card industry for thirty years – it is possible to aggregate and analyze accounts electronically, using statistical analysis to discern creditworthiness. In the credit card industry, this has led to an ever-advancing differentiation of customers based on risk. What that means is that with each passing year, sophisticated lenders can subdivide their customers into ever-smaller groups, differentiating prices into more and more gradations, so that the price the lender offers each customer comes ever closer to a hypothetical "true" assessment of that customer's particular risk.

That level of sophistication undoubtedly has led to concentration in the industry. Thus, it is not surprising that the market for credit card lending has concentrated rapidly in the last decade. In the United States, the market share of the top ten issuers has risen from 55.5% to 87.9% since 1995.[6] Still, the total number of issuers is remarkable. As of 2005, Visa and MasterCard each had thousands of issuers.[7] Nevertheless, the technological sophistication required to price risk in this highly differentiated manner is subject to substantial learning-curve efficiencies and economies of scale. Lenders with larger portfolios – or a willingness to invest in development of larger portfolios – have substantial advantages competing against lenders with smaller portfolios and less sophisticated risk-differentiation strategies.

The advantages are perhaps most telling when it comes to small-business lending. Once the exclusive province of unregulated finance companies and commercial banks, credit card lenders have deployed the tools described earlier to take much of the market share from commercial banks. Small businesses, it seems, just as much as consumers, prefer the ease of credit card borrowing to the hassle of traditional bank lending. It is difficult to get current data, but even by 1998, 49% of small businesses were borrowing on a personal credit card, and an additional 34% were borrowing on a business card.[8] There is a reason why such a large percentage of small-business lending is on credit cards – and it is not price.

A natural question to ask is why banks have not integrated cost-saving and pricing techniques into conventional lending. They could learn much from the credit card system and their efforts would make their products more effective. Bank lenders in many contexts now rely pervasively on credit scoring and doubtless close loans with much lower transaction costs than they did before. Nevertheless, the advent of credit scoring has not made bank loan pricing as sophisticated as credit card pricing. Even now, banks typically set a market price for each of their products, make loans to the borrowers that are sufficiently creditworthy to make the product a prudent investment, and deny loans to borrowers that are not sufficiently creditworthy for that product. To be sure, there is some price differentiation, but not to the extent of spreads of 10% or more per annum that credit card lenders use to distinguish between the most and least creditworthy to whom they extend a functionally identical product.

Moreover, the closed-end bank loan has made few strides in lowering transaction costs to match the credit card loan. Scholars often puzzle about the irrational nature of credit card borrowing, relying solely on comparative studies of interest rates to argue that most borrowers could use conventional bank loans to obtain funds at lower prices. That might be true if bank lending had the functionally nonexistent transaction costs of credit card borrowing, but in the real world the transaction costs remain a dominant part of the competitive terrain. A borrower that uses a high-interest rate credit card but avoids a high-transaction cost bank loan often is making a rational decision.

To be fair, however, the problem with the closed-end bank loan as a competitor to the credit card is not solely sluggishness in taking advantage of technological advances. A more fundamental distinction is inherent in the products themselves. A closed-end loan typically requires consumers to borrow the entire amount up front, incurring the interest costs even if they do not need the entire amount. That works well for large purchases of cars and houses, but a closed-end loan does not work well for the contexts for which credit cards commonly are used – future expenditures on items not yet selected, for prices not yet known, on dates that cannot yet be determined.

By contrast, the open-ended credit card line offers flexibility that is most useful for the day-to-day expenditures of cardholders, smoothing the irregularities in income and expenditures that typify middle-class life in a developed country. Similarly, a small business is much better off with a credit card on which it can charge all of its daily purchases and make a monthly decision about repayment amount than it is with a bank line against which it would take periodic advances – each of which probably would require conversation and documentation with the banker. Most importantly, the consumer or business with the open-ended credit card need not worry that the lender will decline to advance funds at the first sign of financial difficulty. Even in the current climate of close attention to credit events, a layoff is much more likely to lead to termination of a bank line of credit than a credit card, where the need to borrow will be welcomed as an event motivating the borrower to carry a larger monthly balance.

A bank could make an open-end loan and allow the consumer to access the funds in some way other than using a card. Banks for centuries have offered line-of-credit products that charge interest only on the amount outstanding from time to time. In practice, however, that product has not been standardized in a way that permits the mechanization of process that characterizes everything about the credit card transaction. Thus, for example, the line of credit is likely to require a substantial maintenance fee even if no funds have been advanced.

That advantage at last might be receding. Open-ended home equity loans have become increasingly common in recent years, at least in part because of the deductibility of the interest payments. If that product continues to develop, it eventually might take the place of a substantial part of credit card lending, particularly for large-dollar borrowing (like business borrowing) where the security of a mortgage might be necessary to supplement the unstable income of the borrower as a plausible source of repayment.

It is worth noting that a shift from credit card lending to home equity lending would not solve the spending and borrowing problems outlined in Chapters 4 and 5. Home equity lending might be even more troublesome for consumer borrowers. For example, it is likely that borrowers are even less likely to appreciate the consequences of a failure to repay a home equity line of credit – loss of their home – than the consequences of failure to repay a credit card debt. The adverse consequences of a home mortgage default – unlike the consequences of a credit card default – are not so readily capped by a bankruptcy discharge. Unfortunately, the recent provenance of substantial home equity lending makes it difficult to collect data that would support that intuition.

Similarly, many countries in which the credit card has not taken hold rely on the bank account overdraft as an open-ended consumer-lending tool. By separating the point of the borrowing agreement from the decision about consumption and repayment, this solves many of the problems outlined earlier, but in terms of efficiency, its desirability is more difficult to assess. On the one hand, as a practical matter a consumer can obtain an overdraft product only from the consumer's bank of deposit. That limits the ability of lenders to compete for the consumer's business that has driven so much innovation in the American market. On the other hand, as we will see in the discussion to follow, a product that limits the free accessibility to credit that American competition has engendered has at least some redeeming qualities.

For present purposes, however, the central point is that, from the joint perspective of the borrower and lender contemplating a loan, the credit card is plainly the lowest-cost way for a lender to advance the funds. When those loans have positive spillover effects – through increased employment or other economic activity, they are valuable not only to the parties that engage in them but also to society. About what, then, can anybody reasonably complain?

4 The Psychology of Card Payments: Card Spending and Consumer Debt

The problem with credit cards is that they are not just easy to use, but too easy. The idea that credit card debt might contribute to a broad increase in financial distress in an economy is not a new one. Diane Ellis at the FDIC first brought the idea to mainstream attention almost a decade ago in a 1998 paper noting some straightforward correlations between credit card debt and consumer bankruptcy filings in the United States.[1]

Although that idea has a commonsense appeal, it has not gained a great deal of attention from policymakers. It is not difficult to articulate public-choice explanations for the failure of policymakers to take the problem seriously. It would be easy enough to claim that policymakers have been unduly attentive to the interests of the credit card issuers who have focused so much attention on control of the federal legislative process.[2] In truth, however, the existing literature has not examined the relation between credit card use and financial distress with the rigor that would justify taking seriously any claimed connection between the two. This chapter and Chapter 5 take up that question in two parts. First, this chapter considers the relation between plastic card use and overall consumer borrowing. Then, Chapter 5 closes this part of the book by considering the relation between credit card use and consumer bankruptcy.

Cards and Spending

The first concern over credit card use is the possibility that the credit card – as distinct from all other payment devices – is associated with prodigal spending. Is there something about the credit card that makes us spend more than we would with a checkbook? Although it is not easy to unravel the psychology of the spending phenomenon, it has an intuitive and anecdotal appeal.

Let us start with the point that is easiest to see: a distinction between paper and electronic systems – cash and checks versus plastic cards. Slot machine designers, for example, understand that gamblers will gamble more with a card that they insert into a machine than they will with cash that they must drop into a slot.[3] Similarly, at the pizza/entertainment chains that attract young children, a parent can see the dissipation of resources proceeding much more effectively at the venues that issue simple stored-value cards than at the venues that issue quarter-sized tokens to meter use. Part of it is the pure ease of the transaction. The ease obscures precisely what is occurring, so we notice less if a particular game costs 25, 50, or 75 cents than we would if we deposited three separate tokens.

Similarly, in part as a marketing tool to persuade merchants to accept the cards, the card industry has generated a variety of studies designed to show that customers who pay with cards are likely to spend more than those who do not. For example, the decision by McDonald's to begin accepting credit cards appears to have led to both higher average checks and faster checkout times.[4] A Visa study (at Sonic restaurants in Oklahoma) argues that the average expenditure per customer is 30% higher when customers are permitted to pay with cards.[5] Yet another study, looking at vending machine use (conducted, to be sure, by a payment technology provider), suggests that average purchase amounts more than double at vending machines that accept cards.[6] The persuasiveness of those studies is demonstrated by their effect on merchants, bitterly opposed to paying card fees, but turning to cards at a "lightning pace," convinced by evidence that customers spend more when they pay with cards than when they pay with cash.[7] By all accounts, the rise of contactless cards appears likely to contribute to the effect.[8]

Ease of use, however, does not capture the entire point, for even among plastic cards there is a cognizable, albeit subtle, difference in the psychology of payment. As Chapter 9 discusses, there is good reason to think that American consumers, at least, react differently to payments with a debit card and payments with a credit card. The tie between a debit card and funds already on deposit in a checking account helps to maintain a reality and appreciation for the pain of payment that a credit card dissipates by its separation of the point when the purchase is made from the point when the consumer must decide when (or even whether) to pay for the purchase.

The marketing efforts of the major networks have buttressed the spending effect by using colorful logos and schemes associated in the minds of their customers with increased gratification and financial empowerment.[9] The American Express logo – a Roman centurion in full regalia – has obvious connotations of mastery and control. For a current example, a variation on MasterCard's notable "Priceless" campaign is set in a Willy Wonka-themed candy store full of consumer products, playing on the theme that MasterCard is the best tool for realizing personal fantasies.

However vague this discussion seems, psychologists have substantiated the relationship between card use and spending. Although others have contributed important papers,[10] the work of Richard Feinberg is illustrative. The central question for him is the extent to which credit cards provide a "spending facilitating stimulus." He starts with a variety of empirical projects to test the relation between the choice of payment system and the amount of spending. The most interesting is a study of tipping practices. Although the data are limited, they suggest that individuals that purchased with credit cards left tips that were significantly larger (16.95% on average) than individuals that had purchased with cash (14.95% on average). With respect to the possibility that payment system choice is related to the size of the check, Feinberg shows that a substantial spread is evident in each quartile of purchase size. (The most interesting point for the student of tipping behavior is that credit card purchasers pay higher tips by percentage when the checks are smaller; cash purchasers pay lower tips when the checks are smaller.)[11]

Recognizing the small size of his data set, Feinberg relies more heavily on four experiments designed to assess the extent to which credit card cues affect spending behavior. Generally, the experiments involve undergraduate students who are asked to examine books that contain information about consumer products. The students then are asked to answer questions about how much they would spend to purchase particular items. For one group of students, a stimulus in the form of a credit card logo of some kind was placed near the book. The students were told that the materials related to another experiment and not the survey in question. In each of four related experiments that Feinberg reports, the presence of credit card stimuli had a substantial and positive effect on the amount the subjects were willing to spend and on the speed with which they decided to spend. One of the experiments involved a researcher that entered the room and asked for United Way donations while students were reviewing the books. Again, the amount, frequency, and speed of donations were affected by the presence of credit card stimuli.[12]

The most telling real-world experiment comes from a paper by Drazen Prelec and Duncan Simester. They auctioned Celtics and Red Sox tickets, and showed that bidders offer substantially more when sellers accept credit cards.[13]

For a variety of reasons, that research cannot be regarded as definitive. For one thing, other researchers (and Feinberg himself) have had difficulty replicating or extending the results.[14] For another, even after his experiments, Feinberg found it difficult to understand the mechanism by which credit cards affect spending responses. He suggested, quite tentatively, that they operate to condition consumers to spend. Generally, the idea is that the cardholder comes to associate the Visa and MasterCard logo with spending, so that the presence of the logo triggers spending activity – much like Pavlov's dog salivated at the sound of a bell.

Joydeep Srivastava and Priya Raghubir offer a somewhat different explanation. In their view, the problem is that the availability bias causes consumers to do a poor job of recalling past expenditures on cards. Because cash and debit card expenditures are associated with the immediate pain of disbursement, spenders readily recall and account for them in future budgeting and spending activity. Credit card expenses, by contrast, are associated with the lesser and deferred pain of a statement received some weeks after the expenditure.[15]

Yet another possibility, based on research by Dilip Soman and Amar Cheema, points to the credit limits that come with the cards. Their experimental research suggests that consumers base their borrowing on current estimations of future likely ability to pay, and that consumer estimates of future ability to pay are influenced by the credit limits banks bestow on them. Thus, consumers reason: "If a bank is willing to loan me this much money, there must be good reason to think that my salary will increase in the future sufficiently to permit repayment." An intriguing series of matched experiments about propensity to spend when told that a bank has offered high and low credit limits on a credit card suggests that such a line of reasoning is common.[16]

The distinction is an important one. The latter explanations suggest that consumers are more likely to spend indiscriminately on credit cards than on debit cards. On the other hand, the focus of Feinberg's conditioning explanation on the Visa and MasterCard logos themselves suggests that the spending response might be associated with plastic cards more broadly (or at least with the cards of those networks). If so, then the spending response would occur on both debit cards and credit cards. For reasons explained in Chapter 9, I am inclined to think the credit/debit distinction is more powerful.

The policy implications of a connection between cards and spending are profound. For instance, we might expect to find a connection between credit card use and the growth of consumer borrowing. Furthermore, excessive credit card spending or debt might lead to a reduction in savings. Depending on your perspective and the point in the economic cycle at which you are considering the question, this might trouble you. Thus, as Table 10.1 illustrates, it is noteworthy that a country like Germany – with a high savings rate and low card use – also seems to have one of the lowest rates of consumer borrowing among highly developed countries.

Cards and Financial Distress

More broadly, excessive credit card spending or debt might lead to financial distress, which imposes substantial costs on third parties – costs that are not considered by the parties to the credit transactions. Such externalities include the costs imposed on debtors' family members. Among other things, children and spouses suffer substantially in the event of financial distress of a wage-earning spouse.[17] Although we might hope that distressed borrowers will give adequate attention to the costs that distress imposes on their dependents, writers like Tom Jackson have recognized that we cannot always expect this to be the case.[18] The dependency problem is exacerbated if financial distress is likely to lead to a decline in mental and physical health, as some have argued.[19]

Financial distress also burdens the welfare safety net. Eric Posner has suggested that the socially costly behavior of taking excess credit risks justifies price restrictions on credit.[20] If those in financial distress make greater demands on the existing safety net, and if they make lower contributions to defray the costs of payments made to others, then their distress has substantial ramifications for the rest of society.

Another category commonly noted is the loss to the economy of the diminished productivity of people in financial distress.[21] To the extent economic activity generally creates positive spillover effects, the decline in economic activity by the financially distressed is harmful to the economy at large.[22] Again, in a perfectly competitive market, the wage rate might be equal to the marginal social value of an employee's labor. Previous writers have noted, however, that this will not always be the case. The most that we can say with confidence is that in a reasonably competitive market the economic activity of an employee will be worth at least as much as the wage that is paid for it.[23] Whenever it is worth more, society loses from the loss of the employee's efforts.

Finally, there are the costs that debtor default imposes on other creditors. If excessive borrowing from one creditor leads to financial distress, it is likely that all creditors will lose, not just those who made improvident loans. Those costs raise concerns when lending by one creditor results in losses borne by other creditors, especially when the other creditors are not well placed to adjust their prices to account for the risks related by the improvident borrowing and lending.[24] In other cases, where the losses shift to adjusting creditors, improvident lending in one sector will lead to higher interest rates and less favorable credit terms for borrowers in other sectors. Finally, debtor insolvency may lead to creditor insolvency. Thus, in severe cases, debtor insolvency can threaten the entire financial system. Here, consider the example of South Korea in Chapter 10.

To be sure, it is easy to see institutions that mitigate the risk of financial distress: insurance, savings, and the bankruptcy process itself being the most obvious. Insurance is available to cushion the downside risks of many of the adverse events that lead to financial distress. Similarly, deferred consumption and savings can provide a backup cushion against risks for which insurance is not available. Finally, the bankruptcy process itself can mitigate the losses financial distress imposes on third parties, particularly if it is sufficiently accessible to provide a swift return to productivity on the part of consumer borrowers. Even collectively, it is difficult to believe that such institutions can remove all (or even most) of the externalities of financial distress.

A Look at the Data

To examine the relationship between credit card use and aggregate consumer borrowing, I collected a time series of data from five countries: Australia, Canada, Japan, the United Kingdom, and the United States. Germany and other continental European countries were excluded from the quantitative analyses in this study because I was not able to locate sufficient data about credit card use in those countries. In any event, it would be difficult to compare data from countries like Germany, where checking overdrafts provide easy access to consumer credit that in some ways parallels traditional credit card use.

For each country, I collected information about the use of credit cards and overall levels of consumer borrowing (excluding mortgages). In each case, the analysis uses data on credit card use as far back into the past as is available from the most reliable source.[25] This results in sixty-two observations for the five countries. With a single exception,[26] I use data on consumer credit from the central banks of the respective countries. Miscellaneous data on savings rates, population, gross domestic product, unemployment, and exchange rates come from the World Bank's proprietary database of World Development Indicators (WDI). All currency figures were converted to U.S. dollars and normalized to 2002 values.

The selection of the five countries does not reflect any particular view about their relative importance or representativeness. Rather, they are the only countries for which the necessary data were available. The likelihood of sample bias seems minimal, however, because the countries collectively amount to about two-thirds of the overall share of global credit card spending. Although a broadened data set from more countries might produce different results, the poor availability and possible unreliability of data might diminish the value of the data set analyzed

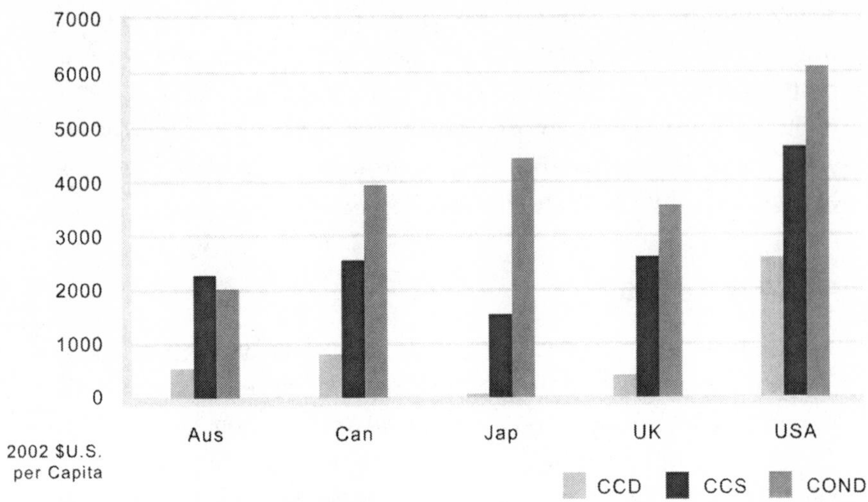

Figure 4.1. Credit card debt (CCD), credit card spending (CCS), and consumer debt (COND).

here. In addition, there is little likelihood of improving the reliability of the data by extending the data set back in time, because outside the United States the effects of credit card spending and debt are unlikely to have been significant much before 1990.

Card Spending and Consumer Debt Levels

I am interested in isolating the effect of credit card spending because credit card spending might increase credit card debt. It might also increase overall consumer debt. Thus, I included data on consumer debt (meaning nonbusiness debt other than home mortgages), credit card debt (meaning money people borrow on cards), and credit card spending. The level of those variables differs considerably among the countries. Figure 4.1 displays the data, in 2002 U.S. dollars per capita, for 2001 (the latest year for which I have data for all five countries).

The analysis starts with the easiest and most obvious question, whether there is a relation between credit card debt and total consumer debt. Put simply, do people borrow more when they use their credit cards? The dependent variable was consumer debt. Credit card debt was the sole explanatory variable. To ensure that the causal relation runs from credit card debt to consumer debt, I lagged the credit card data alternatively by one, two, and three years. Table 4.1 (in the chapter appendix) reports the technical details of that analysis, which suggests the commonsense result that there is a strong and significant relation between credit card debt and consumer debt.

The relation between credit card debt and consumer debt is interesting, but not particularly provocative. If the convenience of a credit card lowers the transaction cost of borrowing, you would expect that it would result in an increase in the total amount of borrowing, just as a decrease in the cost of gasoline might result in an increase in driving. To be sure, it does contradict the argument of Todd Zywicki that increased use of credit cards has not led to an increase in consumer debt, but that is clear even from the figures he uses, which plainly show a major increase in total consumer debt between 1993 and 2003.[27]

A more provocative question, suggested in the opening pages of this chapter, is whether there is a connection between credit card spending alone (apart from borrowing) and consumer debt. Turning to that question, the results (summarized in Table 4.2) suggest an even more significant relation between credit card spending and consumer debt than between credit card debt and consumer debt. Specifically, each dollar per capita increase in credit card spending is associated (after a lag of one year) with an increase in consumer debt per capita of about $1.15.

Those relations suggest a more central question, whether credit card spending and credit card debt have independent effects on overall consumer debt levels. After all, given the obvious correlation between credit card spending and credit card debt, it is not surprising that both variables show similar relations to consumer debt. As Table 4.3 summarizes, the results indicate that when both credit card spending and credit card debt are combined in a single model, only credit card spending continues to be significant.

That result was surprising at first. I expected that credit card debt would have a more direct effect on consumer debt levels than credit card spending and ran the analysis wondering whether credit card spending would have a smaller secondary effect. It seemed odd that credit card debt does not have an effect separate from the effect of credit card spending.

On reflection, however, there is a good explanation for the results. To put it in a narrative form, at least in recent years in these countries, the best indicator of consumer debt levels is whether credit card use has been growing rapidly. That is true because once credit card use grows, the growth of consumer debt is inevitable. It is just easier – psychologically and physically – to spend.

We can imagine circumstances in which credit card spending might remain constant, but an increase in credit card debt would lead to an increase in consumer debt. Similarly, we can imagine circumstances in which credit card spending rises but overall borrowing remains constant. The data suggest, however, that such scenarios are implausible, at least within the confines of this data set. Total debt does not generally rise without a preceding increase in credit card use, and credit card use does not generally rise without a subsequent increase in total debt.

Yet could there be another, more general explanation – perhaps one explained by macroeconomic conditions? To investigate the possibility that the effects might be caused by general conditions in the economy, I added data on two macroeconomic variables (unemployment and GDP) and ran tests with consumer debt as the dependent variable and with the macroeconomic variables and the credit card variables as independent variables (all lagged one year). As Table 4.4 reports, neither test diminished the significance of the analysis. Because this is the model with the most variables, and the highest explanatory value, it is the one whose coefficients are most useful in understanding the relations. It suggests, holding all else equal, that an increase of $100 in per capita credit card spending is associated with an increase, one year later, in total consumer borrowing of $105.

A Note on Credit Card Use and Savings

The other side of the relation between credit card use and excessive debt is a relationship between credit card use and inadequate savings. There is a wide variation in savings from country to country. Figure 4.2 shows comparative data on savings for the five countries in 2001.

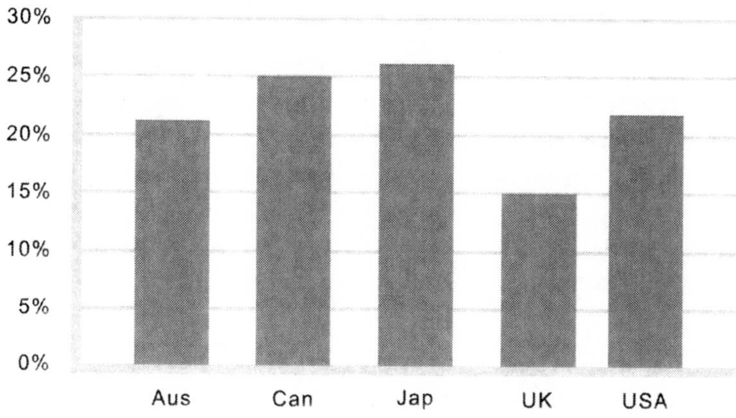

Figure 4.2. 2001 Savings rates.

To investigate the possibility of a relation between credit card use and savings rates, I ran a set of regressions parallel to the regressions reported earlier, using savings as the dependent variable. The regressions are much less provocative because they disclose no significant relation between savings and the two variables of credit card use. As Table 4.5 summarizes, about the most that can be said is that the signs on the coefficients suggest that any relation between credit card spending and savings would be negative. Pressing harder to find a relationship, I added data to account for general economic conditions (unemployment rates and changes in GDP) and added dummy variables for the separate countries. Those analyses suggested strong relationships (significant at the 5% level) – a negative relation between credit card spending and savings, and a positive relation between credit card debt and savings. Nevertheless, statistical diagnostics suggest that those results are unreliable.[28] Accordingly, I do not report them in detail.

The lack of significance does not prove that there is no relation, particularly with such a small data set. Moreover, comparative savings data have been criticized because they do not account for differences in state provision of health care, retirement income, transportation, protection of employment status, confidence in banking systems, and the like,[29] so there is good reason to think that the data do not accurately capture true differences in savings patterns. Thus, it may be that the absence of a relationship is an aspect of the data rather than an aspect of the underlying behavior. For now, however, it suggests that concerns about such a relation need some objective proof before they should be taken seriously. This is of little concern to my work, which relies on the connections among cards, borrowing, and bankruptcy without regard to any effect on savings.

Data Appendix to Chapter 4

A. CREDIT CARD DEBT AND CONSUMER DEBT

All of the analyses in this chapter use ordinary least squares (OLS) regressions, with robust clusters to control for autocorrelation in the time series. Scatterplots and cox-box estimators indicate that ordinary least squares regressions are appropriate without any log transformations.

The results in Table 4.1 are interesting for two reasons. First, the coefficient in each case is greater than one, which suggests a compounding relation between credit card debt and total borrowing. Thus, looking to the column for a lag of one year, the data suggest that a \$100 increase in credit card debt per capita is associated with an increase in consumer debt a year later of about \$147 per capita. Second, as in all the tables that follow, the coefficients steadily increase over time. This makes it most implausible to think that an increase in consumer debt is followed by an increase in credit card debt. On the contrary, it strongly suggests a causal relation between credit card debt (or some variable closely correlated with credit card debt), on the one hand, and total consumer borrowing, on the other.

Table 4.1. Credit card debt and consumer debt

	No LAG	LAG1	LAG2	LAG3
Coeff	1.397** (.137)	1.474*** (.135)	1.564*** (.141)	1.652*** (.153)
N	62	58	53	48
R^2	.71	.71	.71	.72

#p < .10; *p < .05; **p < .01; ***p < .001

B. CREDIT CARD SPENDING AND CONSUMER DEBT

The results in Table 4.2 are parallel to the results in Table 4.1. They show the same trend of coefficients increasing with increasing lags, together with a T-statistic suggesting an even more significant relation between credit card spending and consumer debt than between credit card debt and consumer debt.

Table 4.2. Credit card spending and consumer debt

	No LAG	LAG1	LAG2	LAG3
Coeff	1.050*** (.046)	1.146*** (.034)	1.254*** (.038)	1.400*** (.058)
N	59	55	51	46
R^2	.75	.79	.81	.83

#p < .10; *p < .05; **p < .01; ***p < .001

C. CREDIT CARD DEBT, CREDIT CARD SPENDING, AND CONSUMER DEBT

As a diagnostic for the possibility of undue multicollinearity, I calculated the variance inflation factor (VIF) for a model that included both credit card debt and credit card spending. As Table 4.3 illustrates, the mean VIFs were between 5 and 6, where 1.0 would indicate that the variables were wholly unrelated and 10 would indicate an unacceptable degree of multicollinearity. This model was successful, with adjusted R-squareds

Table 4.3. Credit card spending, credit card debt, and consumer debt

	No LAG	L1	L2	L3
CCS	.7639* (.189)	1.012* (.261)	1.084* (.215)	1.400* (.371)
CCD	.4101 (.318)	.189 (.396)	.241 (.278)	−.001 (.495)
N	59	55	51	46
R^2	0.76	.79	.81	.83
Mean VIF	6.66	7.08	6.02	6.75

#p < .10; *p < .05; **p < .01; ***p < .001

over 75%, and a consistent relation, significant at least at the 5% level for credit card spending. Again, as with the previous tables, the coefficient on credit card spending increases steadily as the lag increases, supporting the idea that the causation runs from spending to debt rather than the converse.

D. CARDS VARIABLES, MACROECONOMIC VARIABLES, AND CONSUMER DEBT

This is the most comprehensive model for this chapter, and thus the one on which I rely directly in subsequent chapters. Table 4.4 reports data from the one-year lags. Generally, it suggests a relationship significant at the 5% level for credit card spending, but not for credit card debt. It suggests a positive coefficient on credit card spending, consistent with an increase in per capita consumer debt of about $105 one year after a $100 increase in per capita credit card spending. Although I do not report them here, I ran similar models with country dummies, but VIFs in the range of 25 indicated an unacceptable degree of multicollinearity.

Table 4.4. Credit card spending, credit card debt, macroeconomic variables, and consumer debt

	UNEM	GDP
CCS	1.087* (.261)	1.027* (.244)
CCD	.1184 (.423)	−.0048 (.284)
UNEM	38.74 (51.71)	n/a (n/a)
GDP	n/a (n/a)	5.20e-11 (7.58e-11)
N	55	55
R^2	.80	.80
Mean VIF	5.42	5.93

#p < .10; *p < .05; **p < .01; ***p < .001

E. CARDS VARIABLES AND SAVINGS

As the chapter explains, models with country dummies were inconclusive because of the multicollinearity of the variables.

Table 4.5. Credit card spending, credit card debt, and savings

	No LAG	L1	L2	L3
CCS	−.0015 (.0035)	−.0025 (.0039)	−.0039 (.0038)	−.0043 (.0043)
CCD	−.0018 (.0048)	−.0007 (.0053)	0.0008 (.0050)	.0011 (.0056)
N	58	54	50	45
Adj. R^2	.27	.27	.32	.33
Mean VIF	6.84	6.44	5.38	5.66

#p < .10; *p < .05; **p < .01; ***p < .001

5 Over the Brink: Credit Card Debt and Bankruptcy

The relationships between credit card debt and spending, on the one hand, and consumer debt, on the other, show two things of policy import. First, credit card debt does not merely substitute for other types of consumer debt. Second, increased levels of consumer debt are financing discretionary consumption (represented by credit card spending). A substantial share of each credit card dollar spent is borrowed. Yet those relationships do not show that using credit cards increases the risk of financial distress. Thus, a more pointed question is whether the data support the perception that credit card borrowing leads to bankruptcy. This chapter explores that question.

Data Problems

It is difficult to obtain data that capture the possibility that credit cards foster a prodigal impulse that leads to financial distress. For example, data about delinquency rates on credit card accounts are readily available, and those data show that delinquency rates correlate with consumer bankruptcy filings.[1] That relation, however, is not surprising. Delinquency rates on automobile loans and home mortgages are also likely to correlate with consumer bankruptcy filings.

Moreover, the causal link evidenced by the delinquency data is not at all clear. It is, for example, at least as likely that the same economic conditions that lead to consumer bankruptcies also lead to credit card delinquencies as it is that delinquencies on credit cards *cause* consumer bankruptcies. Even if the data show that delinquency precedes bankruptcy, it would remain likely that the sequential rise in the two variables reflects a single pattern caused by other economic conditions.

We also know that people in bankruptcy are likely to have more credit card debt than people not in bankruptcy.[2] Those data, however, are consistent with the hypothesis that spurred the recent U.S. bankruptcy reform. In other words, people may borrow in anticipation of bankruptcy based on the expectation that they can discharge the debt in bankruptcy.[3]

The key, then, is to examine credit card debt owed by people that are not in financial distress to discern whether there is a relation between that borrowing and subsequent events of financial distress. Ideally, I would examine that question with a data set containing information about the financial position and borrowing practices of a large number of families over time so that I could trace patterns in how borrowing practices and financial health might relate to each other.

Unfortunately, it is not practical to obtain that kind of data. In the United States, the most obvious possibility is the Federal Reserve's Survey of Consumer Finances (SCF). At first glance, the work of previous scholars suggests that the SCF offers an intriguingly valuable data set. For example, Ian Domowitz and Robert Sartain used that data to show that families with high credit card and medical debts are overrepresented in bankruptcy.[4] Similarly, Joseph Lupton and Frank Stafford analyze a similar survey dataset (Michigan's Panel Study of Income Dynamics [PSID]) to show that a specific set of individuals became increasingly mired in credit card debt as they grew older.[5]

The problem with survey data, however, is that they are likely to be inaccurate for families that do not understand the significance of the amounts that they are spending and borrowing. Indeed, what little we do know about that data makes it clear that the families do understate their prodigality. For example, Elizabeth Warren and Amelia Tyagi report that a sample from the PSID understates the expected rates of personal bankruptcy by about 50%.[6] Similarly, a study by an independent research organization found that data from the SCF appear to understate credit card receivables by about 25%.[7] It would be imprudent to ignore the likelihood of selection bias in survey data that understate the true amount of borrowing by such substantial amounts, particularly for an analysis focused on tracing relationships between the variables. The survey problem is not limited to the United States. Martin Wolf reports pervasive problems with similar household survey data for countries other than the United States.[8]

Thus, I rely on nation-level aggregate data about credit card debt. To be sure, that evidence cannot be used to explain details of the problem. Different economies could have the same aggregate amount of credit card spending and debt. If it were distributed in a less responsible (more regressive) way, it would put more people at risk, and thus have a larger effect on bankruptcy rates. Conversely, if spending and debt appear in a more responsible (more progressive) pattern, the same amount of spending and debt might have no significant effect on bankruptcy rates. To look at it from the familial perspective, the problem is worse when the aggregate amount of credit card debt is concentrated on a smaller number of families who have borrowed to the brink than it is when it is spread more uniformly across a large number of families in more manageable amounts.

Another difficulty with relying on aggregate data to assess the conditions of individual family units is the large variation in the circumstances and behaviors of individual family units. For example, we know that a large number of families have both substantial amounts of liquid assets and substantial amounts of credit card debts.[9] Thus, it is not fair to assume that substantial credit card debt always indicates exposure to financial distress. It also is clear that the rate of adverse impact from credit card spending and debt might shift over time if (as seems to be true in the United States) the pool of credit card users becomes more risky as the market matures.[10]

There is also a more fundamental difficulty: separating the specific reasons why people might have large amounts of debt. Because the different ways in which people might have incurred the debt reflect differing roles for the credit card, and different degrees of prodigality, the problem of disentangling them with aggregate data is nearly impossible. The problem is exacerbated by the subjectivity of the prodigality concept: without some objective baseline as to what constitutes prodigal borrowing, it is difficult to be sure which family situations reflect a use of credit cards that a well-ordered society should foster and which reflect uses that a well-ordered society would regret. Yet, my approach is intended to be solely economic. I am interested in financial distress because of the social costs associated with it. My concern with credit card use focuses on the likelihood that card spending will generate financial distress.

Even from that perspective, however, it is easy to see a variety of scenarios in which the credit card plays a different role. At one end of the continuum, some irresponsibly spend themselves directly into bankruptcy, with credit cards being the vehicle. Although such cases might reflect excessive borrowing, they are not caused in any significant degree by the borrower's failure to appreciate the consequences of borrowing. The behavior suggests a calculated indifference to consequences, an indifference that is not related to the card with which the money is spent. As it happens, however, the available data suggest that the calculated indifference cases are not a major part of consumer bankruptcies, at least in the United States.[11]

At the other end of the continuum, some bankruptcy cases are associated with a catastrophic family crisis such as a divorce, loss of job, or medical event. Data from the Consumer Bankruptcy Project, for example, indicate that one of those three events is present in 87% of bankruptcies involving families with children.[12] A more recent study of related data provides further details about the pervasiveness of medical problems in consumer bankruptcies.[13] Similarly, the Griffiths Commission Report in the United Kingdom emphasizes a "trigger" scenario, in which a catastrophic event leads to a spiral of increasing borrowing and ultimate insolvency.[14]

There, the use of credit cards is ambiguous. First, high credit card borrowing might reflect rational post-crisis borrowing as a response to the tragedy. For example, data suggest that many families use credit cards to meet crisis-level medical expenses,[15] and the special features of credit card borrowing might have eased the difficulty. After all, a rational, closed-end bank lender faced with a loan application after the crisis might decline to extend credit that the family can obtain so easily from the existing credit cards. Moreover, there may be a large group of similar families that engage in heavy, crisis-related credit card borrowing but manage to turn things around and avoid bankruptcy.[16] Here, the credit card can be the lifeline by which the families pull themselves out of distress. That borrowing is not profligate in its failure to consider the future. It is a reasoned reaction to an adverse situation. To be sure, particularly for the families that fail, and perhaps for the group as a whole, the availability of credit card borrowing might delay refuge in bankruptcy beyond the point where the family's financial affairs would be restructured optimally. However, that seems to be a different problem, and the relation of the credit card to that scenario is at best ambiguous.

Another group of cases is the focus of Robert Manning's work and the scenario at the heart of Elizabeth Warren's book with Amelia Tyagi: People that use credit cards borrow enough to put themselves in an unstable position, leaving them unable to withstand a catastrophic event that they otherwise could have weathered.[17] That scenario is distinct from the trigger scenario because it involves spending that puts a family at a risk of financial distress that has costs that the family does not appreciate. When a family borrows to the hilt, they explain, it does not have any discretionary cash flow available to apply to respond to the adverse event. Moreover, because by hypothesis the family already has used the credit that a prudent lender would have extended to it while times were good, it will be difficult to obtain additional credit to respond to adversity.

Results

Using nation-level aggregate data from five countries, I examined the relation between credit card debt and consumer bankruptcy. There is a wide variation in the level of bankruptcy. At least in part, of course, this is caused by differences in the procedures from country to country, but it also surely reflects differing cultural attitudes toward borrowing and failure. Figure 5.1 shows 2002 bankruptcy rates (per million of population) in each of the five countries. The most obvious point is that the U.S. bankruptcy rate is more than twice the next highest rate (Canada's). Given the discussion in the preceding chapters, perhaps that is not surprising. What is more intriguing is the gap between Canada's filing rate of 2,000/million and the United Kingdom's filing rate of about 500/million. To some degree, those differences depend on differences in the bankruptcy systems that make them more or less hospitable to insolvent consumers, but the broad range of filing rates remains provocative.

My first runs used credit card debt as the lone explanatory variable, lagged by one year to ensure that I was tracking a relation that ran

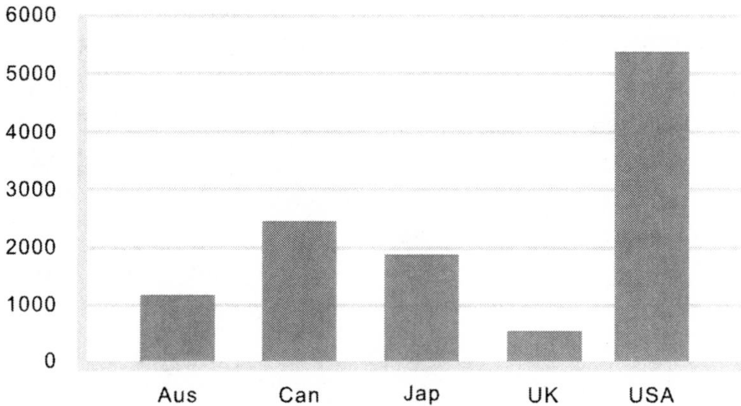

Figure 5.1. 2002 Consumer bankruptcy rates (per million). *Notes to Figure 5.1:* Australian statistics include personal bankruptcies only. Canadian statistics include bankruptcies, but not consumer proposals. Japanese statistics aggregate filings under the liquidation and rehabilitation proceedings. United Kingdom statistics include insolvencies and individual voluntary arrangements. United States statistics include consumer filings, as designated by the Administrative Office, that is, both Chapter 7 and 13 filings.

from credit card debt to bankruptcy filings rather than the reverse. As summarized in Table 5.1, the relation was significant at a 0.1% level, with an R-squared of 85%. Table 5.2 summarizes a parallel analysis, showing a similar relation between consumer debt and bankruptcy.

As I explained at the beginning of the chapter, my goal was to untangle the effects of credit card debt and consumer debt. I hoped to understand not only whether there is a relation between credit card debt and bankruptcy, but also whether the credit card simply facilitates borrowing or instead has a different relation to bankruptcy than other forms of borrowing. The crucial question, of course, is what separate effects credit card use and consumer debt might have on bankruptcy filings. As before, that question is a difficult one, because the strong correlations among credit card spending, credit card debt, and consumer debt make it challenging to isolate the effects of the three closely related activities.

To analyze the relationship, I used a multivariate model, including credit card debt, consumer debt, and credit card spending as explanatory variables in a model with bankruptcy filings as the dependent variable. Diagnostics like the ones I describe in Chapter 4 indicate that the data are adequate to distinguish the separate effects of credit card debt and consumer debt. As summarized in Table 5.3, the basic model with the one-year lag was highly significant, and the variables explained 93% of the variation in consumer bankruptcy filings. Most interestingly, all of the variables retained independent significance (at least at the 10% level in a two-tailed test). The results are relatively robust. As Table 5.3 indicates, the signs on the coefficients are stable, and the sizes of the coefficients steadily increase over time.

Finally, I ran an additional model incorporating unemployment and GDP as alternative macroeconomic independent variables. The addition of the macroeconomic variables (unlike the addition of unemployment data to the model in Table 4.4) improved the significance of the variables. That is not surprising, because it suggests that macroeconomic variables have an important effect on bankruptcy, where their effect on overall debt levels is more ambiguous. Including them in the model helps to reveal more precisely the effects of the financial variables studied here. As Table 5.4 summarizes (for a lag of one year), credit card debt and consumer debt are both significant at the 1% level in models with the macroeconomic variables.

To respond to the possibility that country-specific differences might be causing spurious correlations, in a final set of runs summarized in Table 5.5, I incorporated both the macroeconomic variables and dummy variables for all of the countries other than the United States. Even with the inclusion of dummy variables, and in a dataset so small, the credit card debt variables retained significance (albeit only at the 10% level for the GDP run). Given the small number of data points available, the results are striking.

The most important aspect of the results is the finding on credit card debt. Even if credit card spending and consumer debt are held constant, an increase in credit card debt – a shift of consumer borrowing from noncard borrowing to card borrowing – is associated with an increase in bankruptcy filings. The size of the effect is in the range of an increase of 165 bankruptcy filings per million for each $100 increase in per capita credit card debt. As Figure 5.1 shows, that effect amounts to about 40% of all filings in the United Kingdom and about 4% of all filings in the United States – a startlingly large effect for a debt increase of only $100 per capita. To be sure, the overall debt level also appears to be significant. Thus, the results in Table 5.3 suggest that even if credit card use remains constant, an increase in total borrowing of $100 per capita (new borrowing not on credit cards), will be associated, after a lag of one year, with an increase in bankruptcy filings of about thirty-five per million. That does not undermine the separate effect of credit card debt. Rather, it suggests that if other forms of borrowing are held constant, an increase of $100 per capita in credit card debt would increase bankruptcy filings by about 200 filings per million (the sum of the effects of increased credit card debt and increased overall borrowing). It is not surprising that the coefficient on credit card spending in Table 5.3 is negative. If total borrowing and credit card borrowing remain constant in the face of increased spending, we would expect bankruptcy rates to fall – this would suggest a generally positive economic climate.

Implications

For several reasons, the data are not definitive. The number of data points is small, and the number of years over which the time series run is short. Moreover, particularly with respect to the bankruptcy data, there is the possibility that the apparent relationships might be caused not by profligacy in the borrowing, but rather by practical features of credit card debt (such as its general lack of collateral, as compared to home mortgages, car loans, and other common types of consumer debt).

Still, if the relations that the data suggest are not spurious, the policy implications are intriguing. To understand why, consider first the relation between credit card use and consumer debt. Before conducting this analysis, I would have thought that the relation between credit card use and total consumer borrowing depended on the distinction between convenience users and borrowers: that the borrowers use credit cards to increase borrowing in the economy, while the convenience users use the cards only as a payment device. That view implies that policy responses to any concern about excessive borrowing should focus on the features of cards that facilitate borrowing.

As discussed in Chapter 4, however, the data indicate that credit card borrowing by itself has no separate significant effect on overall borrowing. Of course, given the small number of data points that I have (only about sixty), there could be a relation between credit card debt and consumer debt that the data do not reveal. Yet it seems unlikely that the true relation is more significant than the relation between spending and consumer debt that I do see. Thus, policymakers concerned with excessive borrowing justifiably might take steps to limit credit card use directly.

Furthermore, because the data are drawn from five different countries, they strongly undermine the idea that the problems with credit cards are limited to their use by Americans, infected by the consumerist values that so many decry here and abroad. If the relation between credit cards and borrowing was markedly different among the countries in the data set (admittedly, mostly countries that are culturally tied to the United States by their membership in the Commonwealth), the data would not disclose the powerful relationships that they do.

Finally, with respect to the data on bankruptcy filings, the use of a time lag in my model, suggesting that bankruptcy rates rise one or more years after the increase in credit card borrowing, is particularly instructive with respect to my inclination to infer something about causation from the results. Thus, I think it is plausible that an increase in credit card debt causes an increase in bankruptcy filings one year later. It is not plausible, however, to think that the causation arrow runs in the reverse direction, that an increase in bankruptcy filings causes an increase in consumer debt or credit card activity years earlier.

That point is particularly salient because of the prominent populist argument that the rise in bankruptcy filings since 1978 is caused by changes in the bankruptcy system in 1978 and by institutional responses to the changes.[18] There may well be some truth to the claim that legal changes in 1978 caused a rise in bankruptcy filings. As Chapter 16 explains, it is difficult to discern the relationship between the 1978 bankruptcy reforms and the deregulation of credit card interest rates that occurred in the same year. For example, it surely is the case that the bankruptcy system is both more efficient and more generous than it was before 1978, and it would be surprising if that did not have some effect on bankruptcy filing rates. I also expect that some of the tenfold difference in the level of bankruptcy filings between the United States and the United Kingdom is attributable to the relatively generous system for such filings in the United States. However, those points seem logically unrelated to the analysis presented here, which suggests that card use and borrowing have an effect on the filings made each year while the nature of the system is held more or less constant, as it is in each of the jurisdictions during the time periods examined.[19]

The most persistent counterargument is that credit card borrowing actually rises in anticipation of bankruptcy. From that perspective, families borrow excessively – they "load up" their credit card, as the literature has it – because they expect that bankruptcy will come and they know that they will not have to repay it.[20] Again, the data are inconsistent with that hypothesis because the time lag that produced the best correlations was a lag of a year – the bankruptcies lagged the increase in credit card debt and consumer debt by a year. The thesis would be more plausible with a lag of a few months at most. Moreover, the fact that the coefficients increase over time is much more consistent with my theory. Specifically, the contrary theory suggests that the effect should decrease as the lag increases (because the ability to predict bankruptcy should decrease over time). Yet my theory suggests that it should increase (as the borrowing has a longer opportunity to affect the financial stability of the borrower).

Summing Up

The data suggest a compelling picture of the relationship between the payment system that the consumer selects and the pattern of consumer spending, borrowing, and bankruptcy. Consumer spending depends largely on the income that is available to spend and on the individual's proclivities to spend and save. I present no new data on this point, but it is well recognized in the psychological literature that the credit card is associated with increased spending. At the second stage, consumer borrowing must be a function of income and spending choices. The data presented in Chapter 4 show, at least for those countries in which credit cards are widely used, that the increased use of the credit card as a payment system is followed by an increased level of overall borrowing. Finally, the greatest policy concern relates to the causes of consumer bankruptcy. The data presented in this chapterindicate that changes in the rate of consumer bankruptcy filings depend primarily on the aggregate level of consumer borrowing and the consumer's choice to

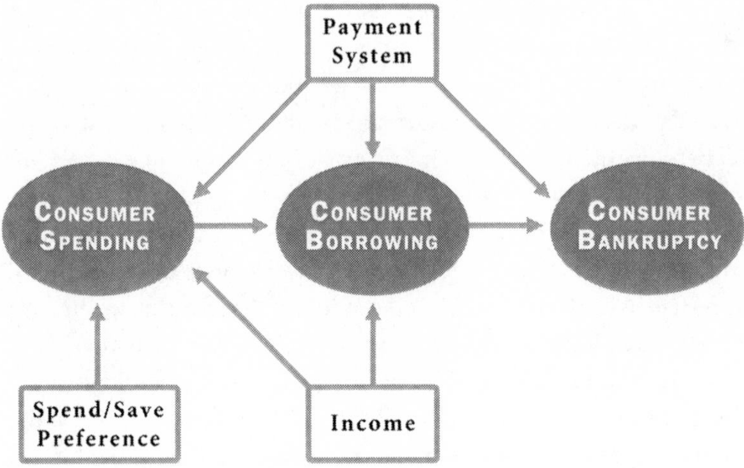

Figure 5.2. Payment choices and consumer finance.

use a credit card to borrow. Overall, as summarized in Figure 5.2, we see a picture in which the choice of the credit card affects each stage of the consumer consumption cycle.

DATA APPENDIX TO CHAPTER 5

A. CREDIT CARD DEBT AND BANKRUPTCY

As with the previous chapter, I use OLS regressions here, this time with consumer bankruptcies per million of total population as the dependent variable, and robust clusters to respond to the problem of autocorrelation in the time series.

Table 5.1. Credit card debt and bankruptcy

	No LAG	LAG1	LAG2	LAG3
Coeff	1.768*** (.090)	1.884*** (.093)	2.016*** (.105)	2.155*** (.120)
N	62	60	55	50
R^2	.87	.87	.87	.86

#p < .10; *p < .05; **p < .01; ***p < .001

B. CONSUMER DEBT AND BANKRUPTCY

Table 5.2. Consumer debt and bankruptcy

	No LAG	LAG1	LAG2	LAG3
Coeff	1.004** (.166)	1.079** (.181)	1.160** (.188)	1.257** (.181)
N	61	59	54	49
R^2	.77	.79	.80	.81

#p < .10; *p < .05; **p < .01; ***p < .001

C. CREDIT CARD DEBT, CREDIT CARD SPENDING, CONSUMER DEBT, AND CONSUMER BANKRUPTCY

As a diagnostic for the problem of multicollinearity, I calculated the variance inflation factor (VIF) for a model that included all three variables. Because the VIF in each case was less than ten, I concluded that the multicollinearity of the variables was not significant.

I also ran a number of other models that I do not report that mixed the lags, primarily to examine the effect of a longer lag for consumer debt than for the credit card variables. None of the models produced a notably higher R-squared or more significant variables than in the simpler runs reported in Table 5.3.

Table 5.3. Credit card use, consumer debt, and bankruptcy

	No LAG	LAG1	LAG2	LAG3
CCS	−.4484 (.353)	−.6984 (.403)	−.7044# (.303)	−.6841 (.372)
CCD	1.641* (.451)	1.804* (.438)	1.834** (.354)	1.801* (.420)
COND	.4917* (.141)	.6800* (.149)	.7228** (.071)	.7900*** (.066)
N	58	56	52	47
R^2	.91	.93	.94	.92
Mean VIF	6.57	6.28	5.40	5.97

#p < .10; *p < .05; **p < .01; ***p < .001

Table 5.4. Credit card use, consumer debt, macroeconomic variables, and bankruptcy

	UNEM	GDP
CCS	−.4724 (.453)	−.7415 (.434)
CCD	1.725* (.483)	2.031* (.457)
COND	.5758** (.094)	.7175** (.093)
UNEM	70.43# (28.4)	n/a (n/a)
GDP	n/a (n/a)	−6.65e-11 (3.72e-11)
N	55	56
Adj. R^2	.94	.94
Mean VIF	5.79	5.61

#p < .10; *p < .05; **p < .01; ***p < .001

Table 5.5. Final model (with dummies)

	UNEM	GDP
CCS	−.0933 (.221)	−.2791 (.275)
CCD	1.472* (.518)	1.882# (.857)
COND	−.3329 (.186)	.4140# (.172)
UNEM	60.62* (71.6)	n/a (n/a)
GDP	n/a (n/a)	−2.26e-10 (1.07e-10)
Australia	−204.9 (297)	−1429# (628)
Canada	268.4 (316)	−925.7# (404)
Japan	−80.39 (522.8)	−437.7 (535)
UK	−747.2 (450)	−1756* 480
N	55	56
Adj. R^2	.97	.97

#p < .10; *p < .05; **p < .01; ***p < .001

PART III

The Puzzle of Payment Cards

Although the spending and borrowing problems might be more serious in the United States than in most other countries, there is no obvious reason why payment cards should have more or qualitatively different adverse effects in the United States than they have elsewhere. Indeed, Part II suggests that the problem is not unique to the United States.

The comparative discussion that follows is central to explaining the United States card market. It shows that the early rise of the credit card in the United States has caused the United States to become overly dependent on a credit-dominant pattern of card use that is literally unparalleled in any other country. Without an understanding of the reasons why other countries have come to a different pattern, it is impossible to develop a coherent understanding of the card, its effects, and its resilience in the face of policy initiatives designed to shape its use.

6 Explaining the Pattern of Global Card Use

If you just looked at the plastic cards presented at retail counters, you might conclude that the credit card has spread throughout the developed world as uniformly as the products of Walt Disney and McDonald's. In fact, however, the credit card as used in the United States has no close parallel in any other country. Outside the United States, the card normally is used for far fewer transactions, with a much smaller share of borrowing. The story of how cards have come to be used so differently occupies the next five chapters of this book.

Variations in the Pattern of Usage

Even the casual tourist would expect the use of credit and debit cards to differ somewhat from country to country, if only because developed economies must use cards more than undeveloped economies. In fact, however, the pattern of usage is much more complex. Currently, among large and developed economies, card use differs substantially on almost any criterion one might care to offer.

Figure 6.1 shows the rate of card usage. The rate of card transactions per capita varies from low-use countries like Japan (with less than twenty transactions per person per year), to moderate-use countries like Australia and the United Kingdom (about seventy transactions per person per year), to high-use countries like Canada and the United States (about 115 transactions per person per year).

The differences in the types of cards people use are equally striking. The share of card transactions conducted on debit cards varies widely

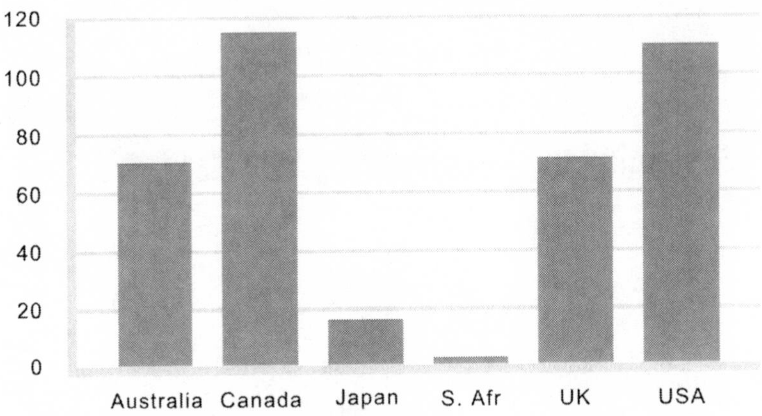

Figure 6.1. Card transactions per capita (2001).

from countries like Japan and South Africa, where debit cards are rarely used, to countries like Belgium, Sweden, and the Netherlands, where credit cards are almost never used. For countries that use both cards with some frequency (Figure 6.2), there is a variation between countries like the United States and Australia, where credit cards are used more frequently than debit cards, to countries like Canada and United Kingdom, where debit cards are used more frequently than credit cards.

As I discuss in the chapters that follow, the share of all card transactions conducted on credit cards is declining in many countries. Yet

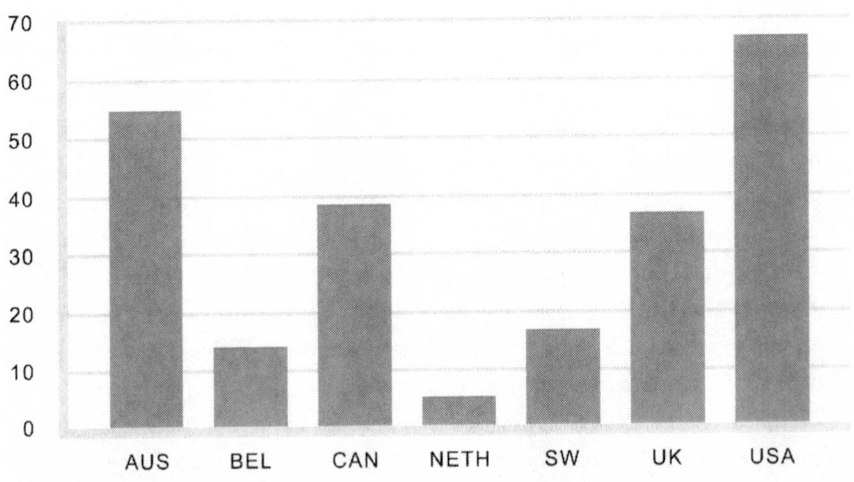

Figure 6.2. Credit card transactions/total card transactions (2001).

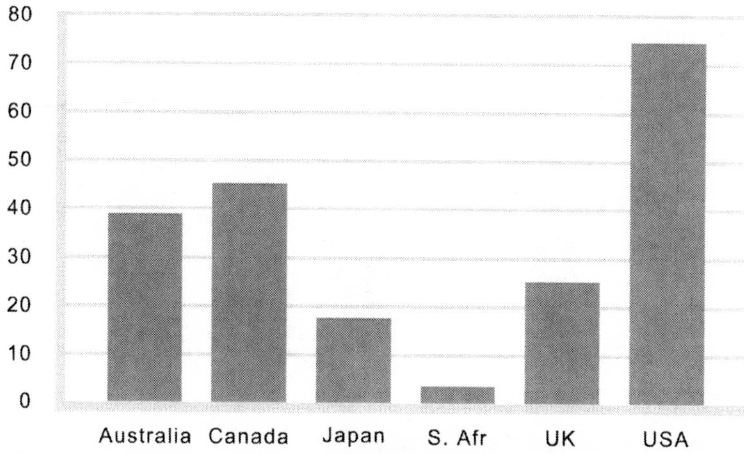

Figure 6.3. Credit card transactions per capita (2001).

the number of credit card transactions per capita remains high in many countries (Figure 6.3).

To understand the broader market effects of cards, it is important to look not only at the number of transactions, but also at the value of the transactions. Using card spending as a share of GDP equalizes the metric across various countries. As Figure 6.4 illustrates, credit card spending as a percent of GDP ranges from 13% in the United States to less than 2% in many European Union countries.

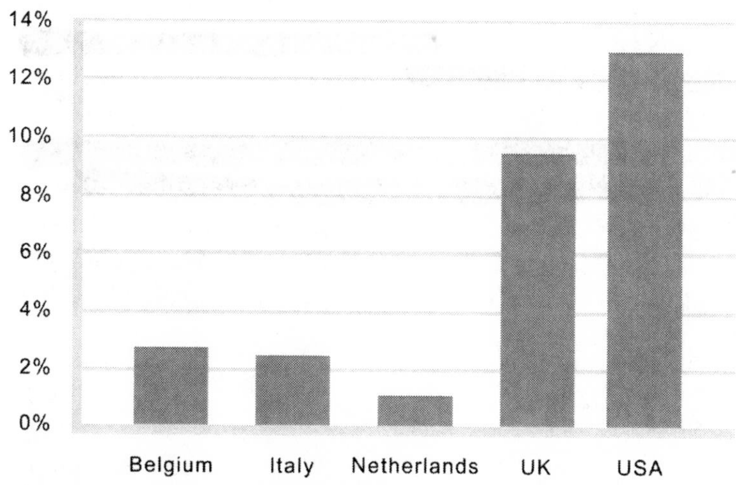

Figure 6.4. Credit card spending/GDP (2001).

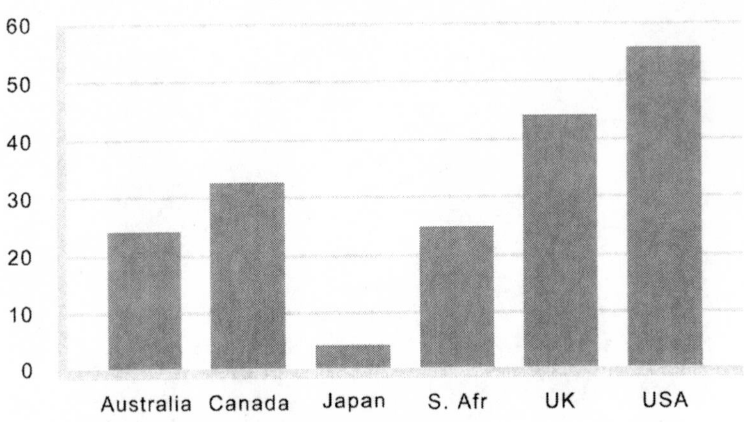

Figure 6.5. Credit card debt/credit card value (2001).

As Part II emphasizes, the relation between card use and debt raises the most troubling policy concerns. There is no standardized metric for assessing the extent of that problem. Media often report the share of cardholders that consistently pay off their bills each month. That metric has been falling steadily in the United States over the last several years,[1] but it is difficult to calculate for other countries. Accordingly, I use in this book a more replicable metric, the ratio of outstanding credit card debt to annual credit card volume. As displayed in Figure 6.5, that ratio varies even in highly developed countries from a high in the United States of more than 50% to a low of about 5% in Japan.

Recognizing some ambiguity in the distinction between credit cards and debit cards for this purpose, Figure 6.6 displays a parallel calculation of credit card debt to total card value. Even in that calculation, the United States stands alone with its dominant use of cards as a borrowing vehicle.

More broadly, it is also important to get a sense of the relation between credit card debt and other forms of nonmortgage consumer debt. As of 2002, credit card debt in the United States was about 40% of all nonmortgage consumer debt, while in other high credit card usage countries like the United Kingdom, Australia, and Canada, the share ranged from 20% to 30%.

Explaining the Pattern

There are many reasons that countries exhibit distinct patterns both in the use of cards relative to other payment systems, and in the use of

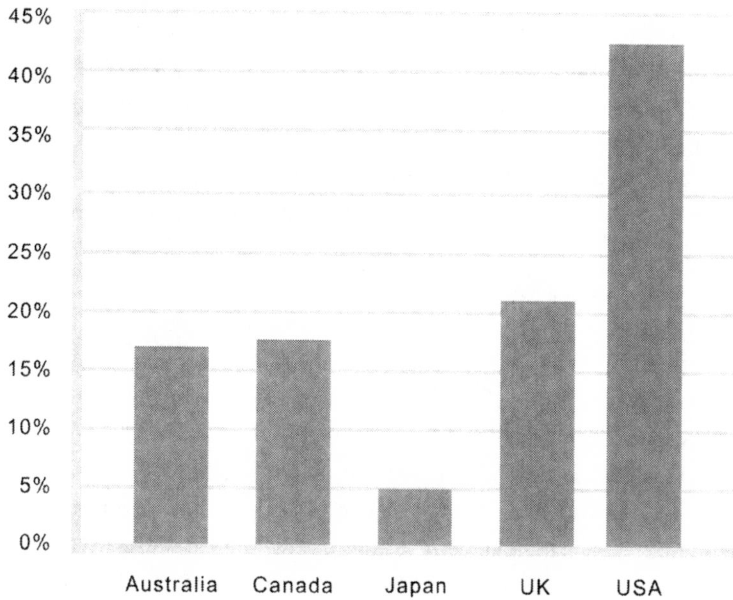

Figure 6.6. Credit card debt/total card value (2001).

debit cards relative to credit cards. The specific level of usage in any country is likely to be influenced by the functionality of other payment and lending products, the interplay among legal rules that foster or retard card usage, demographic trends, cultural norms that support or inhibit the practice of using cards, and other institutional factors that facilitate or block the development of a robust card market. Given the spending and borrowing problems discussed in Part II, and the wide variations in usage summarized here, it is astonishing how little effort previous writers have devoted to understanding or even describing that pattern.

It would require a much more ambitious effort to collect and analyze information (both qualitative and quantitative) about particular countries to explain the pattern in a comprehensive way. Fortunately, however, it appears that a great deal of the current pattern has little or nothing to do with institutional factors. That is not to say that the institutional factors are not useful. For example, I think that they have great explanatory power for predicting the potential size of the credit card market in different countries. With respect to the current patterns of usage, however, I think the institutional factors are largely irrelevant.

The best explanation of the current pattern of card usage is a path-dependent one. Thus, the basic outlines of the current pattern of card usage depend to a substantial degree on fortuitous events that occurred decades ago, when the credit card product first came to prominence in the United States. To tell that story, Part III of the book summarizes the path by which the modern payment card products have developed. Here, I draw on the historical work of a number of scholars who have studied the early American developments with considerable care.[2] My contribution here is to put the specific historical events in a broader global frame. My narrative emphasizes the features of the American story that differentiate the United States from other countries, and thus helps to explain both why the United States has taken the path it has taken and why other countries have not followed its lead.

In general, I see three major stages in the development of modern card products (the subject of Chapters 7 through 9). The first stage was the deployment of payment cards without a long-term extension of credit. The second was the development of the revolving credit product that historically has been the principal basis of the card's profitability. Networks and issuers have used the profits from that product to provide the incentives that have led merchants and consumers to accept and use the credit card with increasing pervasiveness. Finally, in the third stage, the availability of POS, PIN technology has accelerated the growth of a sophisticated debit card product. The growth of the debit card, in turn, is both lessening the relevance of credit in countries where it is important and limiting its rise in countries where it has never been important. Part III of the book concludes in Chapter 10 with a recapitulation and summary of the policies and institutions that may push other countries to converge on or diverge from a global norm.

7 The Introduction of the Payment Card

Credit cards as we know them today were introduced in the United States in the 1950s. The first product was the Diners Club card. Functioning much like the product we now call a travel-and-entertainment card or charge card,[1] the Diners Club card was marketed to high-salaried business travelers. It responded to a specific problem with the checking system as it functioned in the United States at the time.

Specifically, business travelers needed some way to pay remote merchants for food and lodging without having to carry large sums of cash. Merchants were reluctant to accept a nonlocal check, because it was difficult to make an informed assessment of the likelihood that the traveler's bank would honor the check. Creditworthiness problems were aggravated by the long clearance times prevalent for nonlocal checks before the Expedited Funds Availability Act. To quote the U.S. Supreme Court's assessment, until Congress's 1987 enactment of the Expedited Funds Availability Act, 12 U.S.C. §§ 4001–4010, "[T]he check-clearing process too often lagged, taking days or even weeks to complete."[2]

As a response to that problem, the payment card was a brilliant invention. For the first time, bills from diverse places such as hotels, restaurants, and airlines were consolidated, reimbursed by the issuer, and then billed to the customer to be repaid in full the next month. Among other things, this placed the billing function in the hands of an intermediary, so that alternative payment devices were unnecessary and the restaurant did not have to extend credit by invoicing a customer directly. Before that time, oil companies and department stores had issued cards. However, gas and store cards had a limited impact on payment markets at large because they were accepted only at locations affiliated with the issuer. Diners Club was the first to introduce a general-purpose payment card.

Still, the complex structure of the market for payment products made it doubtful that the payment card would succeed, given that payment cards are subject to network or bandwagon effects. Cards are more valuable to each person in the system when the number of people using and accepting them grows. Thus, network promoters faced a challenge in persuading initial players to take part, much like the inventors of the fax machine had trouble persuading initial users to buy a machine that was of little value until many people started to send and receive faxes.

The problem is exacerbated for payment cards because the system depends on the participation of three separate groups: issuers, users, and merchants. However much Diners Club wanted to deploy the technology, it could not make the product successful without persuading a critical mass of users and merchants to use and accept the product. To succeed, Diners Club had to insert itself as the sole issuer and convince a large number of merchants and users that the product was desirable.[3]

Diners Club was able to profit from the fees it charged to merchants for guaranteeing payment by cardholders as long as it could hold its bad-debt losses and overhead to 7% of transactions (the amount it charged merchants in the early days, having raised the charge from 6% shortly after the card was launched). Similarly, customers wanted to use the cards because they paid little or nothing for doing so – Diners Club instituted a $3 annual fee shortly after the system was launched to weed out cardholders that were not active users – and because the cards made the process of obtaining accommodations and other services in remote locations much simpler.

The value to merchants was more complicated, even debatable, presaging the persistent conflict between merchants and issuers that has plagued the industry periodically to the present day. Despite complaints about cost, many merchants were willing to accept the cards because the fees that they would pay to Diners Club were at most about equal to the costs that they faced when they accepted checks. A rational merchant would include in the costs of check acceptance not only delay in payment, but also losses from nonpayment and the costs (including the indignity and hassle) of credit assessment of their customers. As explained earlier, the merchant that accepts the credit card does not bear the risk of nonpayment as it does when it accepts a check.[4] The merchant's costs also included, of course, the profits lost when the merchant turned away a potential customer because it decided not to accept a check and no other payment system was available. Looking forward, that business model remained profitable and successful for decades, although leadership quickly passed from Diners Club to the better-capitalized hands of American Express.[5]

In context, the most important aspect of that business model is its direct dependence on two features of the U.S. economy that were not common elsewhere. The first is the significant amount of remote business travel. The relatively large geographic size of the United States afforded greater opportunity for lengthy cross-country business trips than in many other countries. Similarly, the rise of the interstate highway system and the postwar economic boom of the 1950s fueled a large number of business travelers at distances remote from their homes.

The second factor relates to the U.S. banking market. Although the interstate highway system fostered an unusually integrated economy, the banking market through which checks were processed was not integrated. The U.S. banking industry by comparison to the banking industries of other countries was (and is) highly fragmented. In 1952, for example, about the time of the invention of the credit card, the United States was home to 14,000 commercial banks.[6]

As Mark Roe explains, the geographic fragmentation of the industry rests directly on the United States' persistent populist suspicion of large financial enterprises. The regulatory system that governs financial enterprises in the United States from the earliest days has been structured to inhibit the growth of the large financial intermediaries that have flourished for some time in England, Germany, and Japan.[7] It is important to note that the fragmentation of the payments system is related to the World War I-era decision of the Federal Reserve to support the collection of checks at par.[8] Before intervention by the Federal Reserve, banks competed against each other in the prices that they charged for collecting checks drawn in remote locations. Had that competition continued unchecked, the obvious economies of scale involved in that process probably would have led to considerable consolidation in the market for check collection. In England, for example, a single entity ("APACS") controls substantially all check collection; APACS is an association of the major depositary institutions. However, the intervention of the Federal Reserve provided long-distance collection that at the time was essentially free. That action played a substantial role in the rise of checks as a common payment system in the United States, much more common than in most of its trading partners. Looking back to the beginning of the book, we can see how that World War I-era subsidy is a major cause of the United States' unfortunate commitment to paper-based payment systems. For present purposes, however, another effect of that subsidy is important: it limited the need for consolidation in the process, thus contributing to the limited concentration of the banking entities that provided that service to customers.

Another federal policy of great relevance is the institution of deposit insurance during the FDR era. That policy has had the particular effect of encouraging the survival of small local banks that would have been eliminated without the support of deposit insurance.[9] Of course, a less populist and more concentrated banking system might have avoided the need for insurance. In Canada, for example, not a single bank failed during the Great Depression.[10] With such a widely dispersed group of small and local entities, it is inevitable that a large portion of checks accepted by the types of merchants that deal with out-of-town business travelers would be drawn on banks that did not have a presence in the area in which the check was presented. The slow pace of clearance in the checking system exacerbated the problem, making checks a generally unsatisfactory payment system for merchants.

The integration of the economy and fragmentation of the banking industry are important in understanding the relatively early rise of payment cards in the United States, because they help to explain why payment cards were not used to any significant degree in any other country until much later. In other countries, it was less likely that a business traveler would go to a remote destination and use anything other than cash as a payment system. To the extent that they would, a concentrated banking system predictably led to procedures by which checks readily could be accepted for such transactions throughout the country.

Thus, in England a check-guarantee scheme was introduced in 1969 to compete with early British card products. Payment cards have been available in Britain since 1951 when Donald McCullough launched Finders Services after a trip to the United States.[11] (Finders Services merged with another company to become Diners Club in 1962. American Express opened a service in Britain the next year.) The check-guarantee card solved the same problem as the Diners Club card in the United States, but did not lead to the early development of a payment-card network. The key to that product was the concentrated banking system. England has only a small number of significant banks (six or less at all relevant times), all of which have some market presence throughout the country. Thus, a business traveler in a remote part of the country presenting a check for payment, backed by a check-guarantee card, had the benefit of a local bank assuring payment. American banks have tried repeatedly, and without success, to deploy such a product. Their failure has meant that business travelers in the United States have not had that kind of support for the acceptance of their checks.[12]

8 Revolving Credit

For current purposes, the turning point in the history of the credit card was in the 1960s when banks recognized the potential for profiting from the issuance of payment cards and began to offer products that competed with Diners Club and American Express. Bank of America created the BankAmericard in 1958, a product that eventually evolved into the Visa system. In 1966, a group of card-issuing banks, fearing the competitive ramifications of joining the Bank of America network, established their own network, which eventually developed into MasterCard.[1] The most interesting part of that story is that the credit card product went to market and was able to survive. In truth, the question is not why the revolving credit card has been slow to catch on outside the United States, but how it ever managed to succeed in the United States.

In thinking about the rise of the Visa and MasterCard networks, it is important to understand the dual-issuer system in which many banks for decades issued cards under both Visa and MasterCard brands. Dual issuance has diminished in recent years because Visa has enforced an exclusivity rule for debit cards. The government more or less unintentionally created the dual-issuance system in the 1970s when it decided not to permit Visa to exclude MasterCard members. Most observers believe that this decision led to relatively weak competition between what have become the two dominant networks.[2] Canada, for example, permitted the networks early on to insist on exclusive membership in one or the other and, by some accounts, has a considerably more robust competitive landscape as a result. By creating entirely separate groups

Figure 8.1. Chargaplate.

of banks in the two networks, it would be natural to expect that the Canadian system would foster more competitive networks.[3]

For present purposes, what is most important is what the banks did with the payment card. They rapidly transformed the product into a general-purpose card that could be used not only to make payments but also to access a substantial line of revolving credit.[4] Generally, the product and its introduction combined three distinct features of existing markets. The first was the proprietary store cards that large retailers had issued since the 1920s as a method for identifying customers with lines of credit, the most successful of which were the dogtag-like "chargaplates" provided by New York department stores in the early postwar era (illustrated in Figure 8.1).[5] The second was the combination of the line of credit (something with which banks were familiar) with a general-purpose payment card accepted by merchants of various kinds in various locations. The third – the mechanism for solving the initial startup problem – was the mass mailing, a technique used with success by oil companies for their cards earlier in the century.[6]

The resulting product used a business model that was distinct from the model of the older payment card. For the merchant, the cost in the early days was about the same. The potential benefit, however, was

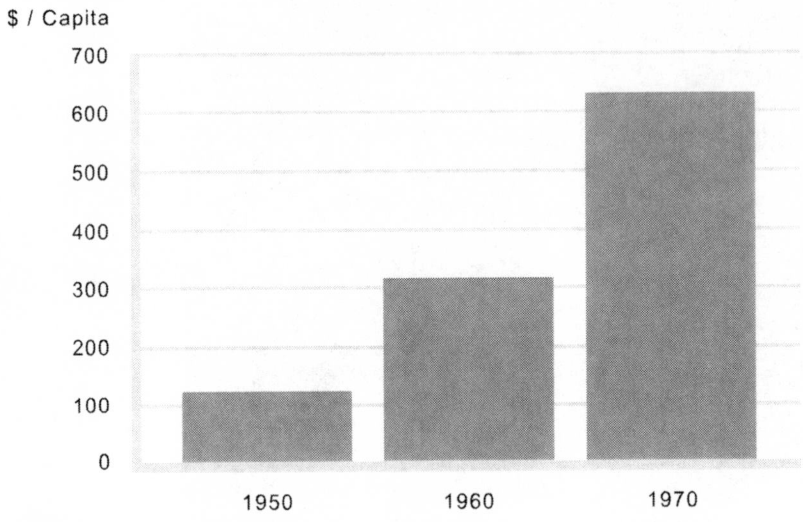

Figure 8.2. U.S. nonmortgage consumer credit (Time Series).

greater, because the new card offered access to a new set of customers. The payment card generally offered access to customers seeking the convenience of remote payment at locations where checks might be difficult or cumbersome. A merchant that declined to accept the Diners Club card feared that it would lose the potential profits from business travelers who chose to patronize establishments that honored the Diners Club card. The new credit card, however, offered the convenience of installment credit to customers' purchases.

Thus, the new credit card interacted with the existing infrastructure for consumer debt, which by that time was already a major part of the American economy.[7] As Figure 8.2 illustrates, even before the introduction of the credit card Americans were borrowing substantial amounts on an annual basis. The ability to offer installment credit has been a major competitive attribute of U.S. merchants for the greater part of this century.[8] The ability to sell on credit while outsourcing the credit functions to a general-purpose credit card issuer was a major benefit to a retailer that was not large enough profitably to operate a credit program of its own.[9] Banks, of course, by this time had much more experience with installment credit than large retailers did.[10]

For the same reasons, the card had the potential to be attractive to a new group of customers for whom the Diners Club product was not useful. Specifically, as consumer debt became a greater part of American culture, a substantial majority of Americans became potential customers for a product that offered the ease of instant credit at the point of sale, where the Diners Club and American Express products were targeted more precisely at high-salaried business travelers for whom credit was not important.

The more difficult problem was how banks could profit from this product. In theory, the banks that issued the cards could profit by charging merchants fees that would offset ordinary administrative costs and interest rates that would compensate for the cost of funds and the risk of nonpayment. In reality, even with the 18% interest rates that were typical, it was difficult for issuers to profit in the early days. It is clear, for example, that most of the issuers who started in the early 1950s left the field promptly.[11] Indeed, the most careful student of that period has concluded that even the major issuers would have left the field if they had acted rationally. Working with access to the archives of Bank of America and Chase Manhattan, Timothy Wolters provides a fascinating case study of Bank of America's decision to maintain its commitment to the product that ultimately became Visa only because of a faulty accounting process that did not make decision makers aware of the true costs of the program. At the same time, he shows, Chase Manhattan quit the field after a massive investment, based on a considered judgment that it could not become profitable quickly enough to justify continued investment.[12] Given the problems that even the largest banks faced, the substantial economies of scale in the early days made it tremendously difficult for smaller banks to maintain any presence at all.[13]

Importantly, banks had an advantage in assessing the creditworthiness of their customers during this phase, largely because of their preexisting depositary relationship with the customer. In the absence of the information or technology for any more sophisticated assessment of creditworthiness than the information readily available from the depositary relationship, nonbank entities (such as Diners Club and American Express) were not able to compete in that market.[14] Similarly,

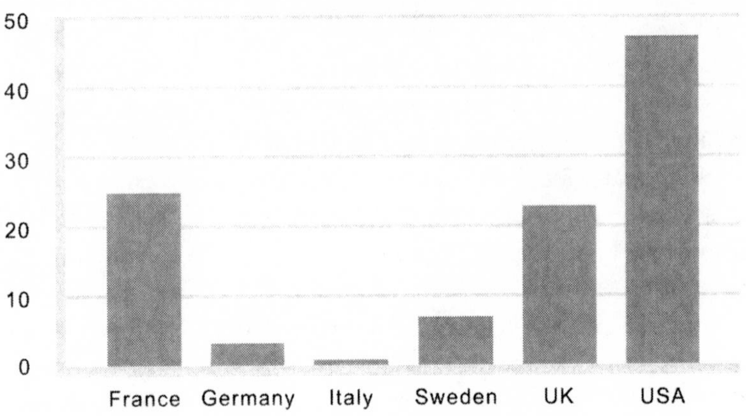

Figure 8.3. Card transactions per capita (1992).

in countries where banks were not permitted to issue cards (Japan being the obvious example), the arrival of the credit card market was delayed by decades.[15] Thus, although the Sumitomo Mitsui card was introduced in 1968 under license from the Bank of America,[16] regulatory constraints prevented the issuer of that card from extending revolving credit to its users and circumscribed the potential growth and profitability of that card for decades.[17]

During the next three decades (from about 1965 to 1995), the revolving credit product became the dominant card product in North America and began to spread into other countries. In the United Kingdom, for example, Barclays in 1966 introduced a credit card styled on the BankAmericard. Despite the early unprofitability of American credit card operations, Barclays believed that it had the infrastructure in place to profit immediately, largely because of its nationwide presence. Nevertheless, credit restrictions imposed by the Bank of England stunted the card's early growth,[18] and the Barclaycard operation was not profitable until 1972.[19] Barclays' competitors responded by introducing the check guarantee system in 1969, hoping to curtail the growing popularity of the Barclaycard as a payment device. Faced with the growing market share of the Barclaycard, however, two of its largest competitors – Lloyds Midland and National Westminster – launched the rival Access card in 1972, which was linked to MasterCard two years later.[20]

Collectively, as Figure 8.3 shows, that history suggests that a variety of credit-related regulatory obstacles slowed growth in other countries so that transaction volume on plastic cards as late as 1992 (the earliest year for which I have been able to obtain data for a substantial group of countries) remained small, even in the United Kingdom.

Another important aspect of this story is the level of concentration in the banking industry. The contrast between the market in the United States, on the one hand, and France, the United Kingdom, and Japan on the other, provides considerable support for the idea that concentration in a country's banking industry slows financial innovation and diversification. This is in part because a highly concentrated industry does not experience the high costs of settling transactions that the fragmented industry in the United States experienced. High settlement costs are a powerful motivator for some type of payment system that can be cleared and settled electronically. At the same time, highly concentrated industries are more likely to establish comfortable patterns of oligopolistic cooperation, in which the disruptive effects of innovative payment products will be delayed. This is seen most plainly in Japan, where large Japanese banks for years have exerted little effort to deploy revolving credit products, explaining that their customers do not want easy access to revolving credit. However, their explanation is belied by the success of American-style card products.[21]

A similar pattern appears throughout Europe. Consider the case of France, where the coalition of banks in the Carte Bancaire group apparently has worked hard to prevent disruptive outside entry. Indeed, their successful efforts to exclude the British avant-garde issuer Egg seem to be one of the principal motivators of the action by the European Commission charging that group with anticompetitive conduct.[22] Press reports suggest a similar dynamic in many European countries, including Belgium, Germany, Portugal, and Slovenia. In Belgium, a consortium of local banks (the Bank Card Company) that includes all card issuers other than Citibank has stifled competition in the Belgian market, with almost no promotion of revolving credit products.[23] In Germany, branch banks have stalled revolving credit card products by providing overdraft protection to their customers on generous terms.[24] In Portugal, press reports attribute the low rate of revolving credit to the fact that card strategies have been defined by wide-scale cooperation that has discouraged innovation.[25] For Slovenia, card issuance is high (more than 1.5 payment cards per capita as of 2003), but there is very little use of cards for revolving credit in a highly regulated market dominated by two local issuers with no foreign competition.[26] Even in the United Kingdom, interviews suggest that the rapid changes in the market in recent years are largely attributable to the entry of competitors from the United States, which have introduced products that UK banks easily could have introduced years ago.

9 Point-of-Sale Debit

The rapid rise of the debit card threatens to eclipse the credit card's long-standing dominance of the industry.[1] The timing of the introduction of this product in the United States and elsewhere is largely responsible for the differing usage patterns described in Chapter 6, creating varying substitution effects between debit cards on the one hand, and credit cards, cash, and checks, on the other. Differing patterns have led to payment card markets that have different levels of segmentation and, as I argue in Part IV, different policy implications.

Comparative Origins

New payment products are notoriously difficult to deploy because they depend on simultaneously building networks of issuers and users. The success of any new payment system depends on quickly achieving a critical mass of users, eclipsing the possibility of widespread acceptance of more efficient but later-developing systems. Thus, once credit card networks were established in the United States, it became difficult for alternative systems to attain a high-use equilibrium because the relative benefits of adding a new product were much smaller than the relative benefits of adding cards when they were the initial electronic payment system.

Although the debit card had to compete from the start with the credit card and also with cash and checks (the principal POS payment devices at the time), the debit card benefited from the existing credit card infrastructure, specifically the American banks and cardholders already

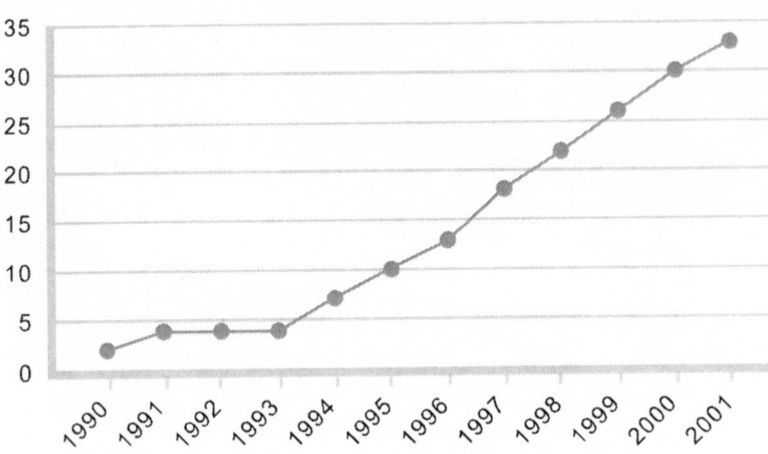

Figure 9.1. Debit card transactions/card transactions (U.S. Time Series).

accustomed to using Visa and MasterCard credit products. Thus, even in the United States – the great bastion of credit card borrowing – the share of debit cards in all card transactions has risen significantly since the early 1990s (Figure 9.1). Given the dominant position of the credit card networks, the ascendancy of the debit card might seem unfathomable.

The story is different in other countries, as the rise of the debit card reflects the first major influx of card use. The debit card provided the first major opportunity to reap the savings of a shift from paper-based to electronic payment systems. For example, in the United Kingdom, Australia, and Canada, card transactions per capita rose from about 30 in the early 1990s to much larger numbers by the end of the decade (about 80 for the United Kingdom and Australia, and 120 for Canada). Except for Australia (discussed later), debit cards drove most of that growth. In the United Kingdom, Australia, and Canada, where the revolving credit model discussed in Chapter 8 never gained the market dominance that it gained in the United States, technological advances offered a separate route to a burgeoning card industry, leapfrogging the revolving credit stage.

The continuing development of infrastructure resulted in a continuing decline in the cost of POS terminals, which made it cost-effective in many countries for all but the smallest merchants to accept debit cards at the retail counter. The business case for the card in that situation – typified by the United Kingdom – was as a replacement for the check. Because the debit card competed with the check and did not need to supplant the dominant credit card network that had developed in the United States, it was able to grow much more quickly in Canada, the United Kingdom, and Australia.

Canada is the most notable example of a country leapfrogging the revolving credit stage. Card transactions in Canada have grown even more rapidly than in the United States, so that since 1998 there actually have been more card transactions per capita in Canada than in the United States. As a latecomer to credit card transactions, however, Canada has maintained a persistently low rate of borrowing in its credit card transactions. Thus, the overall ratio of card debt to card value is now about 20%, roughly half the ratio in the United States. Similarly, in the United Kingdom, the ready technological availability of the debit card in the late 1990s came shortly after the wide deployment of the revolving credit card in the early 1990s. As a result, British credit card debt as a share of card transactions began to fall shortly after its appearance, resulting in a present-day market similar to Canada's, with a ratio of card debt to card value of about 20% at the turn of the millennium (see Figure 6.6).

Australia offers a slightly different example, because a disproportionately large share of its growth came from credit card transactions rather than debit card transactions. Australia is perhaps the only country in the world in which the relative share of credit card transactions grew during the 1990s. As such, it is not surprising that Australian regulators have been more aggressive in attacking credit card growth than regulators in any other major economy, a major topic of Part IV. Still, even in Australia, debit card transactions have grown rapidly and the rate of borrowing on credit cards has fallen steadily, so that the absolute share of debt as a portion of total card value has fallen to about the same level in Australia as in the United Kingdom and Canada.

To complete the picture, consider South Africa as an example of a less-developed country. Although South Africa has had a fully developed market for revolving credit on the cards that its consumers have, it does not have the infrastructure necessary for wide deployment of the technology necessary for a successful system of processing. Accordingly, card use in South Africa remains low, about three to four transactions per year per capita, compared to more than a hundred per year per capita in the United States and Canada. Thus, although South Africa has a substantial rate of borrowing in the card transactions that occur there (see Figure 6.5), the level of borrowing remains low in comparison to the economy as a whole.

Unraveling Substitution Issues

Seen through the lens of developments in other countries, the U.S. experience is somewhat puzzling. It is easy enough to understand that Visa and MasterCard would have a significant first-mover advantage that would make it difficult for a competitor to enter the market. But why did consumers so quickly embrace the debit card when Visa and MasterCard offered it? In the United States, for example, the debit card in many ways is inferior to the credit card. For one thing, the consumer must pay for the purchase immediately, without the flexibility and float that the revolving credit card provides. The importance of the float to American consumers cannot be overstated. Press reports contend that acceleration of the check-clearing process (generally regarded as an unalloyed improvement of the checking system) has led many consumers to shift spending from checks to credit cards (a consequence of some ambiguity).[2]

For another, the consumer that uses a debit card is much less likely to receive affinity benefits, particularly for PIN-based products. As discussed in the later parts of this book, it is plain that affinity benefits attract a significant number of consumers. The absence of affinity benefits from the debit card product should make the debit card less attractive to consumers.

Finally, the consumer receives fewer legal protections for debit transactions than it does for credit card transactions. In the United States, for example, the Truth in Lending Act and the Electronic Fund Transfer Act provide protection for cardholders against unauthorized transactions on credit or debit cards.[3] The Truth in Lending Act goes even further for credit cards, providing, among other things, a right to withhold payment that allows the cardholder, in appropriate circumstances, to present against the card issuer any defense that the cardholder had against the merchant.[4] Thus, if a cardholder purchases a book from an online bookseller and the book never arrives, the cardholder is not obligated to pay the credit card bill associated with that transaction; it is up to the issuer to recover from the bookseller.[5]

England and Canada have similar protections for credit cards. England's Consumer Credit Act imposes liability on the issuer for defects in goods and services that are acquired with a credit card. It also limits the issuer's ability to charge the customer for unauthorized transactions.[6] Canada limits liability to $50 for unauthorized transactions that occur before notification of the creditor, but does not protect telephone-order or Internet transactions.[7] Japan has a somewhat similar, though even narrower, protection that applies only if the purported cardholder announces at the point of sale an intention not to pay for the purchase in the first monthly billing cycle.[8] None, however, has substantial protections for debit cards.[9]

For several reasons, however, I doubt that the breadth of the legal protections significantly influences choice among card-based payment systems, in either the United States or elsewhere. First, the statutes can motivate consumer behavior only if consumers understand the protections they afford. It is unlikely that most American consumers understand the difference in legal protections between a debit card and a credit card. This problem has become more serious as multiple credit and debit applications have begun to reside on a single card and as terminals progressively have lost the ability to interpret those applications accurately.[10]

Second, consumers would have to weigh the risks accurately when selecting a payment system. Experimental research shows that, in many circumstances, consumers do not rationally assess the likelihood of unfortunate events that occur infrequently. If that is the case here, some consumers will not accurately predict the likelihood that the differential legal protections will matter.[11]

Third, in many cases the protections would not affect the consumer's use of the card. Stronger protections against unauthorized credit card use probably will not motivate cardholders to use a credit card in an ordinary face-to-face transaction. Most people do not walk around with such a high level of distrust. Maybe the cardholder thinks the shopkeeper might steal the card number. The handheld wireless payment terminals common in Europe apparently are designed to assuage the concerns of cardholders that a waiter might write down the cardholder's card number if the waiter took the card out of the cardholder's sight. It is difficult to believe, however, that such a concern is driving the use of cards in the United States.

The available empirical evidence about the use of cards buttresses the commonsense understandings. Card use does not seem to be influenced in any obvious way by the extent of legal protections. For example, the statutory protections for credit card transactions in the United Kingdom and Canada are relatively similar, while Australia has no similar protections. Yet the rates of credit card usage per capita are almost twice as high in Australia and Canada as they are in the United Kingdom. Similarly, rates of credit card usage have increased significantly over the last ten years in many countries, but none has recently strengthened the statutory protections for credit cards in any cognizable way. Finally, and most tellingly, the facts of debit card usage are profoundly inconsistent with the consumer-protection hypothesis. The United States has by far the most effective consumer protections for debit cards. Yet, debit cards in the United States have an unusually low share of all card transactions, lower than their share in countries like Canada and the United Kingdom, both of which have much more favorable protections for credit card transactions than they do for debit card transactions.

Still, despite the apparent attractiveness of the credit card, it is easy to see strong reasons for the rise in use of the debit card. First, even in the United States, a significant part of the population does not have credit cards. Estimates vary widely, but press reports suggest that about 25% of the adult population does not have a credit card.[12] The numbers surely are declining, as card issuers become more adept in advancing greater debt to less creditworthy customers, but even now, a substantial group of American adults does not have access to a credit card for regular purchases. Likewise, there is a greater share of people in the less active subprime lending markets of other countries (Europe, for example) without access to credit cards; thus, debit cards are the only available payment card in those contexts. Others may be facing binding credit limits or be carrying revolving credit balances and wish to minimize interest payments and fees. Again, for those people the debit card is a more attractive payment card.

One interesting crosscurrent on this point relates to the small but growing market for payments in electronic commerce. As that segment of the market grows, we can expect the use of payment cards to increase substantially. Indeed, even for the new online payment vehicles that have come into wide use in the United States (PayPal and the various mechanisms for bill payment and presentment being the most obvious), the most important policy aspect is that the vehicles and mechanisms generally piggyback to some degree on the credit card or checking accounts.[13] Within that market, debit cards have had relatively little online penetration to date, largely because of the technological difficulties of online PIN authorization (a problem that should not persist). The rise of PIN-less debit cards, however, has in the last few years made it just as easy to pay with a Visa or MasterCard debit card product in an online transaction as it traditionally has been to pay with a Visa or MasterCard credit card product. Thus, with the online market now functionally resembling the face-to-face market, we may see a substantial share of that market shift to debit cards in the immediate future.

Another interesting part of the story, by contrast, is the market for small value payments. The introduction of debit cards has had a significant impact on average transaction values for payment cards, because the average transaction values for debit cards traditionally have been significantly lower than for credit cards. That distinction reflects the debit card's roots as a product that substitutes for cash and checks. Thus, for example, as of 2003 the average credit and debit card transactions in the United States were $81 and $36, respectively.[14] As the credit card market has matured, issuers have searched for new revenue streams and ways to increase transaction volume. Issuers have encouraged existing users to use credit cards for different types of transactions, including both small value transactions and more routine transactions such as bill payment, groceries, and fast food restaurants. The newer transactions tend to be small value and thus deflate the average transaction value. Debit cards, however, traditionally have been more successful in small-value and routine contexts, largely because the product gained a foothold in that market niche at a time when credit cards were used for higher value transactions.[15]

Another explanation looks more broadly at the payment systems market. Because of the migration from paper-based payments (including

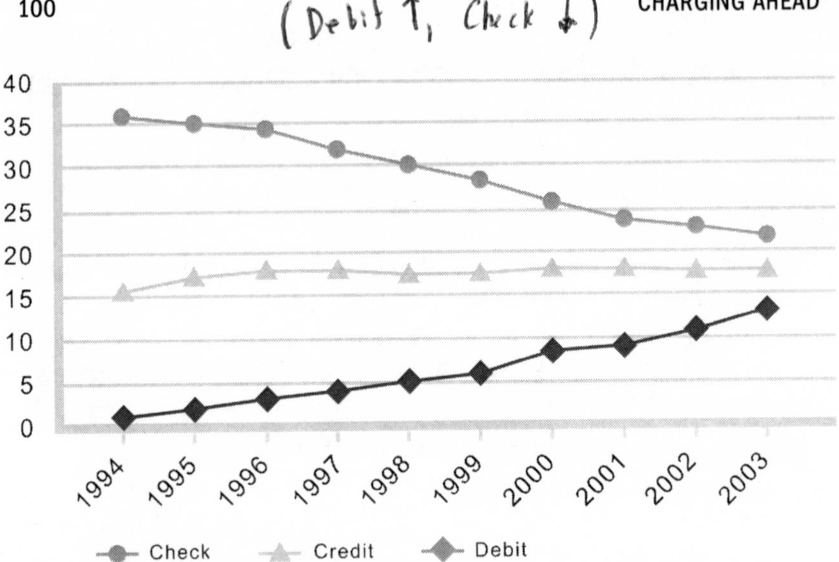

Figure 9.2. Transaction shares of noncash consumer payment systems (U.S. Time Series). *Source:* Nilson Report 799.

cash and checks) to cheaper, electronic forms of payment such as payment cards, the appropriate comparison is not between the credit card and the debit card, but between the debit card and the check. In the United States, the debit card has been introduced as a close substitute for the check, allowing the purchaser to pay for goods by authorizing the purchaser's bank to disburse funds from a deposit account directly to the merchant. The principal difference is that the customer makes the authorization electronically (with the card) rather than by paper (with a check). Thus, the growth of the debit card product in the United States could be seen not as a shift from credit cards, but as a shift from checks. That explanation is supported by statistics on retail use of payment systems. As Figure 9.2 shows, the data indicate that the use of credit cards has remained more or less constant at 16% to 18% of transactions since 1994. The growth of debit cards during that same period from about 1% to 13% has closely matched a fall of checks from 36% to 22%.

A more general explanation rests on standard types of quasi-rational behavior by cardholders.[16] Most obviously, some cardholders might prefer to use a debit card because it stops them from spending more money than they have. Of course, a rational consumer could make the same purchases with a credit card and gain the additional financial benefits that come with that product in the U.S. market. Still, anecdotal evidence suggests that a desire to avoid the temptation of borrowing – a precommitment effect – is behind a significant part of the rise of the debit card in the United States.[17]

That story resonates with the budgetism concept that Lendol Calder uses to explain the attractiveness of early consumer credit models in the United States. As Calder explains, an advantage of installment credit is that it allowed a family to commit in advance to a budgeted expenditure, with an enforcement device (the likelihood of repossession of the purchased object) sufficient to discipline the family's budgeting and spending practices. Essentially, it provided a device for families (like businesses) to match expenditures (on credit) against the consumption of the value of the product over time.[18] The modern credit card, of course, strays from that model by tolerating repayment schedules that would not repay the costs of a typical purchase within a time resembling the expected useful life of the purchased goods.

That story also mirrors the macroeconomic significance of the structure of the American card market. As Figure 9.2 suggests, the debit card first gained serious market support in the United States at a time when the credit card already had a major place in the market. Given the obstacles that network effects present to efforts to deploy a new payment system, it should be clear that the debit card would have been even more successful early on, if it had not come onto the market after the credit card had been so widely deployed.

For one thing, the precommitment effect would have had even more impact on American consumers (as it did on consumers in other countries) if American consumers and merchants did not already have credit cards. Thinking more broadly about the social costs of credit card use, if credit card use encourages prodigality, the possibility that early deployment of the credit card has stifled the debit card market suggests that the United States has become overly dependent on a unitary electronic payment system. Another consequence, exacerbated by the "honor-all-cards" rule, is that the debit card widely adopted in the United States is the signature-based ("offline") Visa and MasterCard product, which has a fraud rate more than ten times higher than the PIN-based ("online") debit product commonly used in other countries.[19]

The discussion here helps to explain the unusual failure of the debit card in Japan. Introduced with great fanfare in the spring of 2000, the product has not made any significant progress in the market. The most recent statistics indicate far less than one transaction per capita per year. Because Japan is a country in which cards are not used for borrowing, the failure of the debit card at first puzzled me. Eventually, I concluded that it had failed for two reasons. First, unlike the United Kingdom and the Commonwealth countries, there is no market impetus to promote debit cards to save the costs of checks. Japanese consumers do not use checks,[20] nor is there any need to use the product to precommit against borrowing.[21] Japan's odd credit card had already filled the market niche for the debit card. The *ikkai barai* product that is common there provides automatic payment from the account for all but the most inveterate of consumer borrowers. That arrangement gives the precommitted cardholder enough support to refrain from borrowing. Thus, if the market niche for the debit card rests on a fear of borrowing coupled with a desire to precommit to avoid excessive borrowing, the existing Japanese products already fill the niche adequately. From that perspective, the Japanese debit card has failed because there is no clear business case for the product.

Inhibitors of Payment Card Use

Most markets exhibit a clear movement from paper-based systems to payment cards. Some have suggested, however, that a country's preference for cash might slow the development of card-based payment systems. Generally, it is argued, payment card use should be less common in countries where public places are sufficiently safe to make people feel secure in carrying large amounts of cash. This "fear-of-crime" hypothesis is advanced to explain why cardholders in Japan use cards relatively little in their safe urban environments, while cards are used much more commonly in the relatively unsafe United States.[22] It is also argued that the growth of cards in Latin America can be explained by the lack of safety in some Latin American countries.[23]

Several things make it difficult to test this thesis directly.[24] First, because the thesis relies on a perception of crime that makes individuals reluctant to carry cash, hard statistical evidence about the frequency of crime cannot respond directly to the thesis. Research by Sara Sun Beale underscores that point, showing that perceptions of crime and safety are in major part constructed by the media without regard to the reality of the underlying problems.[25] That means that an ideal study would focus on data about changes over time in perception of crime. Although there has been a great deal of research about perceptions of crime, there is not enough data about how those perceptions have changed over time to permit quantitative analysis.[26]

Second, it is difficult to disentangle that thesis from related cultural norms about cash. One reason people might pay with cash in some countries and credit cards in others is the significance the payment system has as a status symbol. In the United States, credit card issuers have succeeded in creating a norm, perhaps less powerful than it was once, that payment with a credit card is a sign of status.[27] Thus, a payment of a $1,000 restaurant bill with cash in the United States surely would appear suspicious, if not incriminating evidence of money laundering. In other countries – Japan being a possible example – payments with cash carry a similar status. It may be that the existence of such a cash-status norm in Japan has links to the relatively large role in the Japanese economy of underreporting of income and the relative significance of organized crime in Japan.[28] Anecdotal evidence in some sources suggests that a similar pattern might explain the duration of the use of cash – and the related slow uptake of credit cards – in Italy,[29] India,[30] and Mexico.[31] For whatever reason, however, if that norm exists, it would be difficult to separate its effects on card usage from the effects of fear of crime.

Finally, the data available to compare crime rates in different countries are problematic in a number of ways. First, researchers typically rely on police reports and thus inevitably understate the true amount of crime. Thus, if the amount by which crime is understated differs by country, then comparisons may be inaccurate.[32] Second, because the data depend on reports of local enforcement activity, they are based on local definitions of the various crimes, which are likely to differ substantially from country to country.[33] Finally, it is difficult to measure insecurity. It is not clear which types of crimes would be most likely to support or undermine the insecurity thesis, because it is not clear what particular crimes foster the feeling of insecurity that might make the consumer reluctant to carry cash. On the one hand, property crimes would seem to relate most closely to the actual risk created by carrying cash. On the other hand, violent crimes like murder are more likely to be publicized in a way that would cause consumers to become insecure about their overall safety.

In any event, it is not clear that existing research provides substantial support for the hypothesis. David Humphrey and his coauthors developed a model with data from fourteen countries over a seven-year period (1987–1993). The model includes a variety of indicators of payment card use and institutional factors, one of which is crime. Their paper unfortunately does not identify the source of the crime data used in the regressions. Moreover, it is evident from the tables that the statistical finding on crime is not at all robust.[34]

Against that background, I tried to replicate and update that study. I collected data from Interpol about the rates of homicide and violent crime in the Group of Ten countries for which the Bank of International Settlements periodically issues its so-called Red Book of payments statistics.[35] Although violent crime probably is a better variable for purposes of testing the hypothesis in question, I collected data on homicides because of the likelihood that data on homicide rates would be more accurate and comparable across national borders. I also collected data on the use of various card and non-card-based payment systems over time from various editions of the Red Book (which appears to be the source for the payment systems data in Humphrey's paper).[36]

Notwithstanding the many problems discussed in the preceding pages – which collectively suggest that the data are quite noisy – the data indicate an intriguing connection between the two crime data points that I collected and the use of plastic cards. Specifically, regressions testing the relation between crime rates in one year against the use of credit cards one (or two) years later found in each case a statistical relation significant at the .001 level. In each case, the coefficient was positive, suggesting that an increase in crime was associated with an increase one (or two) years later in the use of cards. The models explained between 64% and 71% of the variation in credit card use. Table 9.1 summarizes that analysis.[37]

I ran a number of additional models to test the robustness of the regressions – altering the lags and including information about changes in GDP (to test the possibility that the relation was related to changes in the economic cycle). None of the models undermined the significance of that data.

The small number of years and countries makes any reliance on that data tentative. The strong time-series correlations, however, do suggest that card use remains in flux even in developed countries as local economic conditions alter the incentives for and against card use. In developed countries at least, the cards appear to have gained such a firm footing that substantial increases in use are a normal response to relatively minor macroeconomic events (such as a shift in crime rates). On the specific point, they also suggest a strongly positive aspect of card use – namely, lowering the profitability of certain kinds of violent crime, a point emphatically predicted by Hendrickson more than thirty-five years ago.[38]

Table 9.1. Credit cards and crime

	LAG1		LAG2	
	Murder	Violent Crime	Murder	Violent Crime
Crime	620** (52.5)	2.44** (.5180)	674*** (57.6)	2.68** (.555)
Unem	−92.0 (53.7)	−144** (.5180)	−93.6 (57.6)	−149** (79.7)
GDP	.0215# (.0116)	.0301** (.0060)	.0214 (.0128)	.0304** (.0065)
R^2	65%	71%	64%	71%
N	46	48	46	48
Mean VIF	1.11	1.07	1.11	1.07

#p < .10; *p < .05; **p < .01; ***p < .001

10 Convergence and Exceptionalism in the Use of Cards

In the final two parts of the book, I discuss various proposals designed to address concerns about the relations among spending, debt, and financial distress, focusing both on the risk associated with the credit card as a payment device and the risk associated with using the credit card to borrow. Before turning to the proposals, this chapter considers whether the levels of spending and debt in U.S. card markets are likely to spread to foreign markets through the credit card.

Geographic card markets fall into one of two patterns. The first is the free market global response. Exemplified by Australia, Canada, and the United Kingdom, card markets are characterized by an increasingly dominant use of payment cards, but with a substantially lower use of credit cards and credit card borrowing than the United States. The path dependence explanation discussed in earlier chapters suggests that the markets in Australia, Canada, and the United Kingdom maintain more segmentation between the credit card and other payment products than the market in the United States.

The second is the pattern evidenced by countries like Japan and the continental European Union that limit access to consumer data, making it difficult for modern credit card products to develop. The basic thesis, familiar to any reader of the literature on globalization, is that standardized products that are more effective than local variants will dominate markets absent some important obstacle to convergence on the global norm. Here, the norms of data protection in the continental European Union and elsewhere have sufficient weight to force divergence from the global norm.

The Unimpeded Global Norm

The pressures of the global economy have resulted in the convergence of products and brands in developed economies. We see this already in a number of contexts. For example, a Japanese consumer finance company introduced the first American-style revolving credit card in Japan after making a series of field visits to American monoline issuers like Providian.[1] Similarly, the rise of loyalty cards and aggressive marketing in the United Kingdom and Ireland often is attributed to the entry of American competitors like MBNA.[2] Press accounts suggest a similar pattern in Belgium and Portugal, where American issuers successfully have entered foreign markets long stunted by local cooperation.[3]

Interestingly, Citibank's marketing strategy has been to introduce revolving credit products in countries where competing card issuers focus on cards only as a payment medium.[4] In countries that have a relatively undeveloped market, this model tends to support a substantial increase in the number of cards by justifying cards as individual profit centers rather than conveniences offered only to good customers. Mainland China doubtless is the most important test for that strategy. China is a vast market in which the number of true credit cards has quintupled between 2001 and 2004. Industry experts expect continued geometric growth in the immediate future, as China enters the WTO in 2007 and hosts the Olympics in 2008.[5] Similarly, even in countries like Thailand that impose substantial limits on consumer credit, the companies that are developing the local market are American companies like GECC.[6]

Much of the apparent differentiation in products reflects a marketing strategy typified by the global McDonald's chain where American products are altered to suit local tastes. That strategy allows local consumers to reassure themselves they are using a product reflecting their unique heritage, while firms retain the underlying features that make the product profitable.[7] Consider, for example, the rise of "Sharia-compliant" credit cards in the Middle East, which are marketed as offering the benefits of American-style credit cards while maintaining a technical compliance with Islamic law.[8] The distinctions between that card and a conventional credit card doubtless are important for some purposes. Only a customer's depositary institution, for example, typically offers that product. The marketing and attractiveness of the product, however, draws on the features that have made the American product successful.

Although it is plain that the branding and concept of an American-style credit card is a prominent example of globalization, it is less clear that widespread use of the revolving credit feature first introduced in America has spread. Indeed, the most common explanation for the limited use of credit cards is that certain countries have cultural norms against borrowing, making the revolving credit feature of the credit card unattractive. I encountered this frugality hypothesis while studying the Japanese card market. It is not, however, limited to that market. Observers also attribute low rates of card use in southern Europe to similar norms.[9] Press reports tell a very similar story in the Netherlands, where the low rate of revolving credit is attributed to a "traditional Dutch aversion to credit." Yet, as in Japan, local banks did not issue a revolving credit card product until recently, and found it successful when it was issued.[10] Frugality proponents worry that the rise of credit cards can be attributed to the gradual assimilation of a global norm that includes the prodigality characteristic of American society.

To be sure, the limited use of consumer credit in some countries reflects differences in the receptivity to borrowing. For example, the Islamic rules that forbid the payment of interest presumably have stifled the development of credit in countries like Saudi Arabia and Indonesia.[11] That is not to say that there is not and never will be consumer credit in countries with dominant Muslim populations.[12] Rules prohibiting the payment of interest do suggest, however, that the relatively low level of consumer borrowing in Saudi Arabia, particularly for a country with such a high level of economic development, might be attributable to the effect that religious beliefs have in retarding the development of credit institutions. As current events in that country suggest, in a short time the obstacles are likely to dissipate and leave Saudi Arabia and similar countries[13] with a rate of consumer borrowing commensurate with their developed status.

Most countries, however, do not have such an objective obstacle as the religious tenets of Islam. Absent such an obstacle, the frugality hypothesis rests on a parochial view that resistance to consumer borrowing is an artifact of a particular culture. To take the most prominent example,

Table 10.1. Consumer debt/GDP

Country	Cons. Debt/GDP
Canada	17.8
United States	16.4
UK	15.9
Singapore	15.1
Japan	14.4
France	12.0
South Korea	11.7
Australia	11.6
Netherlands	10.4
Hong Kong	9.1
Taiwan	8.0
Germany	7.0
Belgium	4.8
Brazil	4.7
Italy	3.9
Spain	3.5
Argentina	3.3
India	2.1
Mexico	0.5

Source: Morgan Stanley

Japan commonly is regarded as a frugal country, in stark contrast to the United States. Yet Japan essentially has the same amount of consumer borrowing as the United States.[14] The large amount of consumer credit in most developed countries suggests that a substantial consumer credit market is an attribute of a fully developed economy and that only a substantial institutional obstacle like the Islamic religion will prevent that market from developing.[15]

To illustrate that point, Table 10.1 displays data from Morgan Stanley showing the ratio of consumer debt to GDP for 2000 for nineteen countries.

Several things about Table 10.1 are illuminating. First, regarding the idea that credit cards are necessary for a high level of consumer debt, consider two countries that have similar cultures but strikingly different levels of credit card usage: the United States, at the high end with more than seventy transactions per capita per year, and the United Kingdom, at the low range with around twenty transactions per year. Both the United States and the United Kingdom are near the top of Table 10.1, both with roughly 16%. Similarly, with respect to the idea that cultural differences might be driving rates of borrowing, notice how the continental EU countries (most of which have very low rates of credit card use) are scattered throughout the distribution, from Spain and Italy at the bottom, to Belgium and Germany in the midrange, to the Netherlands and France near the top.[16]

What is important in Table 10.1, however, is that lesser developed countries are likely to have a lower level of consumer debt: the three lowest countries are Mexico, India, and Argentina, doubtless the three least developed countries in that data set. To get a sense for what Table 10.1 says about more fully developed countries, consider the example of Japan, which appears near the top of the chart despite a low rate of credit card borrowing. In Japan, restrictions on credit card borrowing have resulted in a shift of the consumer debt market (at least compared to other countries) to less savory nonbank lenders such as *sarakin* and *yenya*.[17] The nonbank lenders are considerably more likely to rely on extra-legal means of enforcing their loans than the banks that have been prevented from developing a credit card market. In the end, the consumer debt market is about the same size as in other developed countries. It is just less hospitable to the borrowers that use it.

Of course, the suggestion that consumer debt is higher in countries at an advanced stage of development is consistent with the view that consumer borrowing has risen as the frugality characteristic of countries is overcome by the norm of American prodigality that accompanies globalization. If credit card use has risen generally throughout the world, perhaps the reason is that the pressures of globalization during the last decade have contributed to the development of a single homogenized culture, of which credit card usage is a significant part. Recall that the leading marketers of modern revolving credit cards are either American companies or businesses that consciously adopt the business practices of American companies.

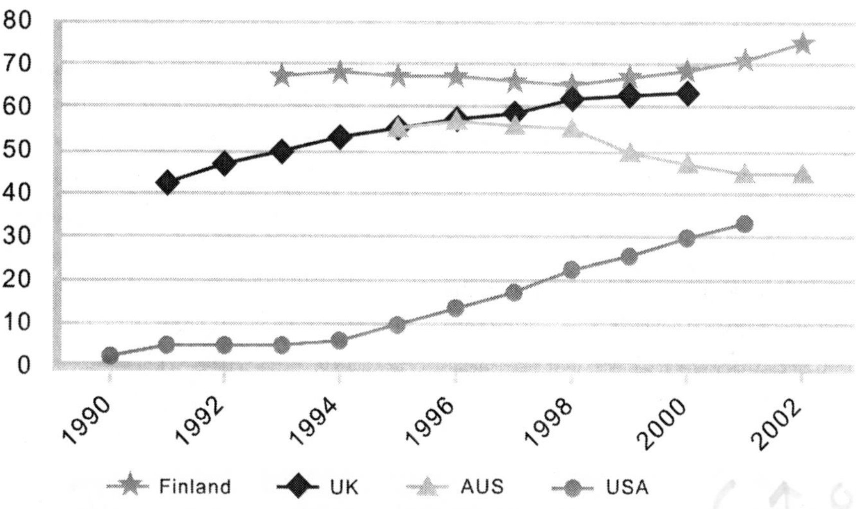

Figure 10.1. Debit card transactions/card transactions (Time Series).

One problem with the globalization hypothesis is that the data do not clearly indicate a convergence toward U.S. practices. On most of the metrics illustrated in the tables in the preceding chapters, the United States is an outlier, not a trendsetter. So, to use the example most important to my analysis, Figure 10.1 shows how the relative rate of debit and credit card usage in the United States has for the last decade been rapidly rising from an almost uniquely low rate to a rate much more in line with the practices of other developed countries. That evidence buttresses the historical explanation provided earlier, which suggests that the situation of the United States depends on attributes of its history that other countries do not share. If that explanation is correct, then there is little reason to believe that other countries will have the same patterns of usage as the United States. Thus, although the spread of American cultural norms may support the growth of the credit card to some degree, there is room for variation that speeds or retards the rate of growth, and there is indeed reason to expect an endpoint that involves less card-based borrowing in countries that do not share the unique situation of the United States.

The conflicting intuitions about the data suggested an empirical test to assess whether the factor that relates to a high level of consumer credit is a high level of economic development or assimilation of global culture. Accordingly, I ran regressions of the consumer credit data reported earlier against indicators of economic development and globalization. As an alternate measure of indebtedness, I used the ratio of household debt burden to net wealth as reported by the OECD. The OECD data set had fewer points than the data that I discuss here and did not indicate any statistically significant relationships. (That is not surprising, given the likelihood [discussed in detail in Chapter 5] that debt burden data are systematically inaccurate.) For economic development, I used the level of GDP/capita. For cultural globalization, I used the globalization index published periodically by *Foreign Policy*. That index combines normalized data on a variety of things, including trade, foreign investment, personal contact (through tourism and international travel), international telephone traffic, and cross-border remittances.[18]

When the metrics were analyzed separately, each was significantly related, at the 0.1% level, to the level of consumer credit as a share of GDP. When I combined both metrics in an OLS regression, however, only the level of economic development retained significant explanatory value. In the multiple regressions, GDP per capita was significant at the 5% level. Globalization was only marginally insignificant (a probability that the relation occurred by chance of about 14%). Given the small number of observations, a larger data set might reveal a significant relationship for that variable as well. As it is, the model (summarized in Table 10.2) explains about 61% of the variation in borrowing.

Although the evidence is rough, and limited to a small number of countries, it does support the view that the institutional infrastructure associated with economic development is at least as likely to explain the level of consumer credit as the weakening of cultural norms against borrowing.

Table 10.2. Globalization and consumer debt

GDP/Capita	.2971** (.1224)
Globalization Index	–.1078 (.0681)
N	17
Adj. R^2	61%
Mean VIF	1.95

Data Protection as a Speed Bump to Globalization

This chapter began with the assertion that the United States' uniquely credit-dependent use of payment cards rests on the "lock in" of the U.S. market. The early rise of credit cards made it harder for the more efficient debit card to obtain the market dominance it has in most countries. If there is any other factor that is likely to cause a substantial developed country to depart from the global norm, it is the institutions related to data protection. To understand that point, it is necessary to discuss the relation between information technology and the modern deployment of credit cards.

Credit bureaus were formed in the 1950s, shortly before credit cards first appeared in the American market.[19] They allowed lenders to access not only negative information about defaults and arrearages, but also positive information that helps them make sophisticated determinations about the likely performance of potential cardholders.[20] The ability of this technology to increase the accuracy of risk assessment is prodigious. Most prominently, specialized software products allow lenders to analyze credit information in increasingly sophisticated ways, culminating in the credit scoring products that dominate modern consumer credit underwriting.[21] Lenders considered the idea of scoring individual credit histories as early as the 1930s. The technique was not widely used, however, until the ready availability in the 1990s of computer and software technology capable of processing the large amounts of relevant data.[22] The results are staggering. One Federal Reserve researcher, for example, estimated that automated credit assessment through credit scoring reduced bank loan losses on consumer credit by $5 billion per year.[23]

The importance of information technology to a modern credit card program also has substantially altered the competitive landscape of the issuing process. In a system where a depositary bank is the only entity that can issue a credit card profitably, there is little competition on the terms on which the card is to be issued. Cardholders will use the card if the terms on which their banks offer the card make it valuable for them to do so. However, where a bank's ability to offer profitable card products depends on its information technology and marketing prowess more than its depositary relationships, any bank can compete for the customer's business. Thus, we see in the United States the rise of monoline banks – banks like MBNA, Capital One, and Providian – that focus primarily on the credit card market, without substantial depositary businesses. The competition that they bring to the card market is so pervasive that by the late 1990s more than 80% of active credit card accounts in the United States were with banks that do not have a depositary relationship with the customer.[24]

That understanding of the American market has profound implications for the rise of credit card markets in other countries, because many other countries have impediments that prevent their markets from developing along that path. The most common obstacle is that the customary use of such information by sophisticated globalized issuers is profoundly offensive to the privacy customs in much of the developed world, particularly mainland Europe. Thus, although the Fair Credit Reporting Act[25] might be a high point in the largely ineffectual protections U.S. law provides for personal data,[26] that statute provides much less protection than the European Data Privacy Directive, to which all countries in the European Union are obligated to conform.[27] Under that directive, the storage and transmission of identifiable credit information to third parties without the specific knowledge and consent of the customer is plainly illegal.[28] Hence, in countries adhering to such a regime, it is not possible for a lender to obtain the kind of broad-ranging positive and negative information on which American-style credit scoring depends.[29]

If the absence of such information would have the negative effects on the profitability of the American industry that observers suggest,[30] it is easy to see how the absence of such information would suppress the expansion of the credit card. Empirical work by European academics shows a strong causal connection. The inability of lenders to obtain both positive and negative information about borrowers appears to correlate with smaller consumer lending markets.[31] It is not clear which phenomenon would cause the other. Thus, greater credit card use in continental Europe might have driven legal changes that would have tolerated laxer information practices – just as increases in consumer lending appear to be leading to more accessible bankruptcy systems. Yet it is enough for my discussion to point out the connection between norms of data protection and limited use of credit cards as a borrowing device.

The most interesting part of that story is the notably higher rate of card use in the United Kingdom. To be sure, the United Kingdom formally adheres to the directive, and the directive's provisions are implemented into law in the United Kingdom in the Data Protection Act, §§ 4 (and Schedule 1), 11. Its acceptance of a modern credit card market is reflected in its tolerance for a complicated system that allows credit card issuers to work around the constraints of the directive. As explained in interviews with Experian's UK Bureau, credit bureaus permit issuers to evaluate files of individuals stripped of identifying information. After the issuers determine which files reflect suitable credit histories, the issuers can send solicitations to the individuals reflected in the files. The legal environment for a similar system apparently exists in Germany, Italy, and the Netherlands, but not elsewhere in the EU.[32] Thus, despite the similarities of formal legal rules, the United Kingdom's payment cards market diverges substantially from the continental norm, resembling much more closely the Canadian and Australian markets that seem typical of the unimpeded global norm.

The issue has come to the fore in the EU in the last few years, as proposed revisions to the European Consumer Credit Directive would make it all but impossible for monoline issuers to operate in Europe.[33] For example, Article 6.3 of the proposed directive would require lenders to provide advice to customers about the proper product for the customer's particular use. That requirement would be burdensome for credit cards because of the difficulty of predicting at the time of the application how the card ultimately will be used. It would be particularly difficult for monoline issuers that do not ordinarily maintain staff to engage in personalized discussions with each customer.[34]

The problem is not that the directive is hostile to monoline banks in particular. Rather, it reflects the continental perspective on consumer debt and data protection, in which it is difficult even to imagine the reality of sophisticated modern lenders, crunching numbers about millions of consumers to tease out the particular individuals most likely to be profitable customers.[35] Still, whatever their motivation, regulations that make it difficult for monoline issuers to operate are likely to have the inevitable effect of stifling innovation. Rules that exclude monolines will limit competition so that for most cardholders the only plausible issuer will be the bank at which the cardholder maintains the primary deposit account. The rise of monolines in the United States, for example, arguably is connected with the general decline of net interest rate

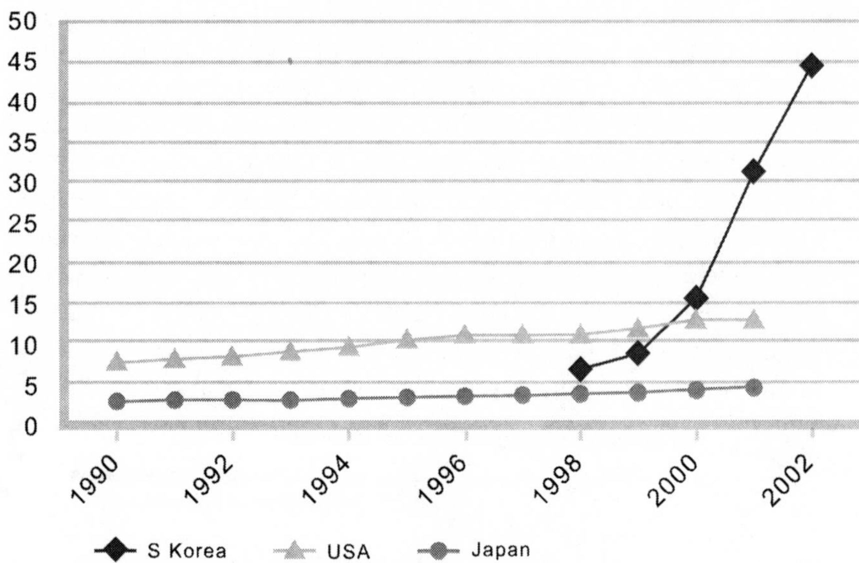

Figure 10.2. Credit card spending/GDP (South Korea Time Series).

margins in the industry in the early 1990s.[36] Similarly, in the United Kingdom, the advent of American monoline issuers in the late 1990s is connected with the growth of credit card spending and debt. Some policymakers – particularly policymakers with a continental perspective – might look with horror on the kinds of innovation that monolines provide. It is doubtful, however, that the products that monolines offer are the sole source of the problem with credit cards.

To see the risks associated with the regulation of information markets, consider the cautionary tale of South Korea. Issuers in that country have engaged in heavy marketing and issuance of revolving credit cards, despite the absence of the kind of credit-assessment system customary in the United States. Generally, the government decided that increases in consumer spending were the best way to foster economic growth and that increased consumer credit was the easiest way to foster consumer spending.[37] At first, efforts were successful, as shown by the rapid increase in credit card spending displayed in Figure 10.2.

However, the increase in credit card spending also led to an unnatural increase in the volume of credit card lending, as shown in Figure 10.3. The consequence of lending without appropriate information, as the earlier discussion argues, is an unacceptable rate of defaults. In the case of South Korea, it led in 2003 to delinquencies by 12 million cardholders

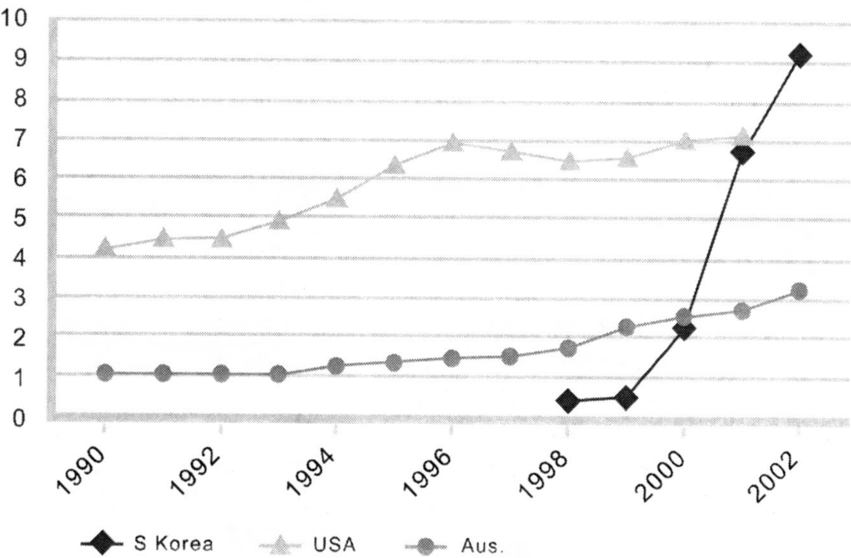

Figure 10.3. Credit card debt/GDP (South Korea Time Series).

(in a country with a population of less than 50 million), approximately 30% of all households.[38] The delinquencies eventually required a $4 billion government bailout of the major credit card issuers,[39] and resulted in a doubling of the annual individual bankruptcy rate.[40] It was not until after the crisis that issuers had access to positive ("white") data as a tool to assess the creditworthiness of potential cardholders.[41]

Divergence and Convergence

If information is central to the development of a modern card industry, then the responses various countries have to the conflicting pressures of the business model of the globalized card product and the loss of data privacy that accompanies it will shape usage patterns. Turkey, for example, has what is by European standards a strikingly successful revolving credit card market, attributable at least in part to its early development of a national credit bureau.[42] In recent years, the two largest developing countries in the world – India and China – have announced plans to support national credit bureaus that would include both positive and negative information.[43] Similarly, Hong Kong introduced such a bureau to help rein in charge-offs that increased by 600% in the wake of the SARS crisis in 2002.[44] Central banks are attending to this specific concern even in Eastern Europe, where communism once stifled financial markets,[45] and the Middle East, where Islamic law at least technically prohibits lending for profit.[46]

It is clear that culture will affect how information practices develop in ways more complex than a binary question of availability would suggest. Among other things, many countries are likely to resist private credit bureaus. In France, for example, the Banque of France provides the information. There is good reason to think that public agencies will do a much less effective job at making the information useful than the profit-oriented agencies in the West. Here, press reports suggest that France and Italy are opposing moves to facilitate EU-wide credit scoring. Of course, they also might do a much better job at protecting the privacy of the individual whose information is involved. The point for my purposes, however, is that data protection policies – whatever their policy basis – relate directly to the infrastructure on which a successful cards industry rests. Thus, if laws or norms slow the use of data in a particular country, it is likely that credit card markets will develop more slowly, if at all. Similarly, the experience in countries like South Korea and Hong Kong suggests that another likely result is poorly managed lending rather than a continued economy of limited lending.

Another potential outcome, exemplified by Japan, is the creation of silos of information held by separate groups of lenders in the economy. Thus, when I visited Japan at the turn of the millennium, consumer finance companies had developed a reasonably inclusive database of information that they shared among themselves. The database was not, however, available to bank lenders and did not include information about transactions with bank lenders. That type of insular credit bureau might be better than a state-owned bureau or no bureau at all, but it certainly will not facilitate the accurate risk assessment that is characteristic of the more inclusive systems in the United States and the leading Commonwealth nations.

Of course, one could argue that a stunted lending market is much better than the robust credit card market in the United States with all of its attendant problems. The point of this chapter, however, is that there is good reason to think that an unimpeded market will lead not to American-style card use, but to the more moderate usage patterns evident in Canada, Australia, and the United Kingdom.

PART IV

Reforming Payment Systems

The problems plainly differ from country to country, and the U.S. pattern is not likely to become the global norm. Still, policymakers around the world struggle with the effects of credit card use and debt. The data discussed in Part II suggest that their concern is well founded.

How should governments respond to the problems with credit cards without undermining the efficiency of retail payment systems? A useful framework is to distinguish two categories of risks or consumer errors as jointly contributing to the problem of excessive card usage. The first relates to the efficiency of the credit card as a lending device. I call this the convenience risk and discuss it in Part V. The concern is that it is so easy to use a credit card (i.e., the transaction costs of credit card lending are so low) that borrowers underestimate the risks associated with future revenue streams. The response is to intervene in the market for consumer lending. The second, the topic of Part IV, I call the instrument-induced risk. This risk is attributable specifically to the use of a credit card as a payment device. Because credit cards encourage consumers to spend more than they otherwise would, and perhaps more than they can repay out of monthly incomes, credit card use can lead to unanticipated debt.

The latter risk is more of a concern in the United States than elsewhere. As discussed in Part III, the share of card transactions on credit cards in the United States is unusually high, and the relative levels of credit card spending and debt are high. That credit-dominant pattern flows from the strong position that credit card networks had established in the United States by the time that debit cards were first introduced. As a result, the markets for debit and credit cards in the United States

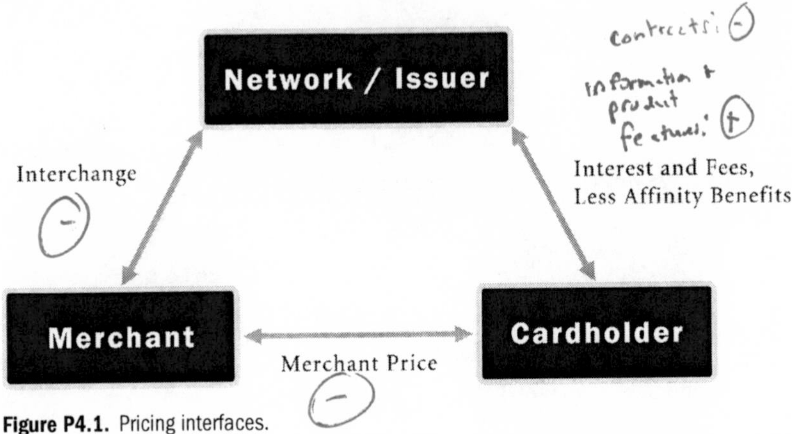

Figure P4.1. Pricing interfaces.

are not as segmented as the markets in other countries, and consumers in the United States are more likely to use a credit card than a debit card to make routine payments. Regulatory proposals designed to shift payments from credit to debit cards should have salutary effects as they shift the United States closer to the use patterns of other countries.

Part IV addresses proposals aimed at encouraging that shift. Figure P4.1 suggests three different interfaces on which regulators might focus: the relation between the issuer (or the network) and the merchant, the relation between the merchant and the cardholder, or the relation between the issuer and the cardholder. There are reasons to believe that the market fails at each interface and thus that there is a potential for intervention at each of them. On balance, however, I contend that regulators should direct their attention primarily to the interface between the issuer and the cardholder.

I present the argument in four separate chapters. Chapter 11 discusses the difficulties with relying on regulation of interchange (the merchant/network interface) or merchant surcharges and discounts (the merchant/cardholder interface). Turning to the issuer/cardholder interface, Chapter 12 discusses the problems with credit card contracts. Finally, Chapters 13 and 14 discuss proposals related to information and product features.

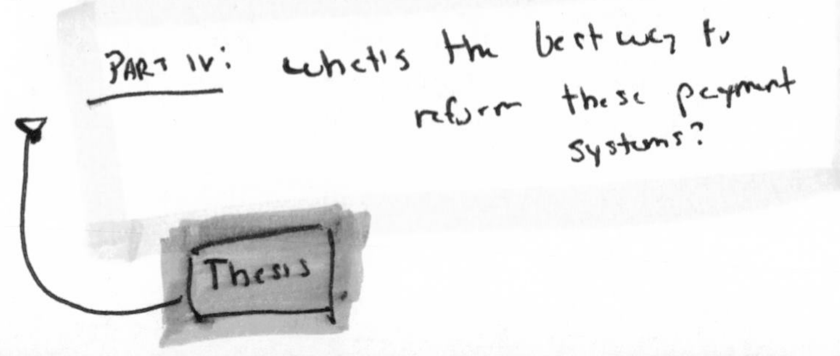

11 Indirect Approaches: Regulating Interchange and Encouraging Surcharges

The Network/Merchant Interface: Interchange

Around the world, the most popular proposal relating to credit cards in the last several years has been to regulate the price that networks charge merchants for credit card transactions.[1] The proposals – implemented by regulators in Australia, the EU, Israel, Mexico, and the United Kingdom – target a problem distinct from spending and debt. Those regulators worry that a high interchange fee for credit card transactions – one that is not passed through from merchants to credit card users – will increase the overall level of consumer pricing. That possibility is troubling if customers that use cheaper payment systems implicitly subsidize customers that use credit cards. Subsidizing credit card users creates a perverse incentive for credit card use at the point of sale.

Still, it is not clear how regulation of interchange will affect credit card use. Put differently, a reduction in interchange would not necessarily reduce credit card use. It is possible that a reduction in interchange could cause more merchants to accept credit cards, thereby increasing overall credit card spending. In the American market, for example, Discover has been lowering interchange rates in recent years to secure more merchant acceptance of its card. Conversely, an increase in interchange might reduce card use. If the market is functioning properly, we should assume that the networks are pricing interchange at levels designed to maximize the growth of their networks. If so, any departure from those levels will be less than optimal for the network and should lower the network's rate of growth. As should be clear from Chapter 3, however, this kind of blunt interference with credit card networks is a risky approach if it undercuts the acknowledged cost savings of electronic payments.

In reality, of course, the expectation of regulators is that their actions will shift users from credit cards to cheaper payment systems, consistent with the proposals that I discuss in the pages that follow. Thus, they surely expect that a reduction in interchange will bring the effective price of using the card closer in line with its actual social cost, both because cross-subsidization will be reduced and because issuers will have less revenue available to reward cardholders for use. This is clear, for example, from the public statements of Australian regulators justifying the reductions they have imposed on bank card interchange in Australia.[2]

Even if interchange regulation affects credit card use, it is less clear that consumers will benefit. For example, Visa conducted a study of retail prices following Australia's decision to regulate interchange fees charged by Visa and MasterCard. Visa found that the fees that card issuers charged cardholders rose substantially, but that retail prices did not fall noticeably.[3]

A related concern is that interchange regulation will have a differential impact on issuers that focus on transaction volume rather than revenues generated through borrowing transactions. Consistent with that concern, it is worth noting that another early effect of the Australian regulation has been that issuers have focused more directly on products that will generate borrowing.[4] In the end, if the problem with credit card pricing is the divergence of the marginal cost to the user from the marginal social cost of credit card use, it makes more sense to regulate the point-of-sale price directly.

The Merchant/Cardholder Interface: Encouraging Surcharges

A more pointed response would be to charge customers different prices based on the payment system used. That response addresses the problem of cross-subsidization directly. If credit cards are more expensive for merchants than other payment systems, merchants should charge customers fees for using credit cards. The available evidence suggests that consumers likely would respond by using a less costly payment system. In Norway, for example, when banks charged customers per-item fees for checks, but not debit card transactions, the customers generally switched payment systems to avoid the extra fees, suggesting that customers are highly sensitive to such charges.[5] In the aftermath of that program, Norway now has one of the highest rates of debit card use in the world (about 100 annual transactions per capita).[6]

To be sure, differential pricing at the point of sale does not respond directly to the problems associated with excessive levels of credit card spending and debt. Yet as long as the private costs of credit card use are higher than the private costs of competing payment options, concerns about cross-subsidization align with concerns about excessive spending.

In fact, data on merchant costs related to different payment systems are scant. The most reliable data, however, suggest that credit cards often are (at least from the merchant's perspective) the most expensive system and that debit cards are almost always less expensive than credit cards and often even cheaper than cash or checks (after taking into account the costs of labor, delays in checkout lines, and the like).[7] Although it is difficult to get reliable data for other countries, the global picture is similar. In Japan, for example, the discount rate for credit card transactions typically is 3% or more.[8] In the EU, even after regulatory initiatives directed to that charge, the discount rate for credit card transactions remains about 1%.[9] In each case, the costs are likely to be higher than the costs of competing payment systems. Knowing that merchants rarely charge more for credit card payments than they do for other payments, we must accept this as a system in which consumers have an inappropriately high incentive to use credit cards.

Credit card surcharging might have other beneficial effects as well. For example, if merchants could price differentially, based on the amount each issuer or network charged, there might be greater competition in the market for the rates merchants pay. Here, the problem is not just that a single price for all payment systems involves a subsidy running from consumers that do not use credit cards to consumers that do. Increasingly, there is a differentiation of surcharge rates even within the class of credit card holders. For years, American Express has charged substantially higher interchange rates than other card networks, which it has justified by reference to evidence that the typical American Express cardholder spends more per transaction than the typical cardholder.[10] The evidence does not show that cardholders lack other options at merchants that do not accept American Express, and thus it is not directly responsive to the concerns of merchants. Thus, the higher rates from time to time have led to boycotts of American Express by resistant merchants.[11] Similarly, Visa and MasterCard increasingly have offered substantially higher interchange rates for their premium cards.[12] The use of those rates creates a new mechanism for cross-subsidization, from low-income individuals carrying a standard Visa or MasterCard product to high-income individuals who use the super-premium cards with high interchange rates. If merchants are bound by network rules that prevent them from rejecting premium cards selectively, surcharging might induce an element of greater competition into the rates charged.

The bottom line is that we must ask why merchants in competitive retail markets decline to charge their customers differentially based on the customers' selected payment system. The most obvious answer is the legal system. For some time, federal law barred any price discrimination between cash and credit card transactions.[13] Current law has reversed that policy in part. TILA § 167 bars card issuers from imposing any rule that would prevent merchants from granting discounts for payments by methods other than a credit card. Thus, discounts for noncredit card payments are now lawful. That change has had a limited practical effect, however, because the card networks continue to have rules that prevent merchants from imposing surcharges on credit card use.[14] Moreover, about a dozen states continue to bar (or limit) surcharges for the use of credit cards.[15]

At first glance, the distinction between a discount and a surcharge seems trivial. Why would a knowledgeable consumer make a different choice at the point-of-sale depending on the fee structure? Previous writers have argued, however, that this distinction is important in practice. Alan Frankel, for example, suggests that it may be more acceptable in the retail marketplace for a merchant to charge for credit card use than to discount for cash.[16] A surcharge arguably would be seen as a service offered the customer for which the merchant must pay, while a discount might suggest to the customer that the merchant's price has an unduly high margin of profit. Adam Levitin, in his paper on the subject, argues that framing effects make consumers react differently to surcharges than to discounts and that surcharges would be more effective than the discounts permitted under current law.[17] Others suggest that the problem is that a discount-only system requires merchants to price all credit card transactions in the same way. It does not permit, for example, distinctions between different types of credit cards based on distinctions in their merchant-discount rates.[18]

Whatever the reason, the legislative history of TILA suggests that credit card issuers fought hard for the right to bar surcharges.[19] The politics of enactment were complex, with the Reagan administration opposing the bar, wanting to let merchants in a free market set the appropriate price. Many senators supporting the bar argued that surcharges would harm the lower- and middle-class consumers who use credit cards. Others, reacting to the heavy lobbying of credit card issuers, argued that the bar would obscure the cost of credit and thus lead to increased borrowing.[20]

Assuming that credit card issuers acted in their own interest when they lobbied for the right to bar surcharges, it is reasonable to think that the discount-only system is a substantial restraint on the practical ability of merchants to discriminate in pricing. If there is any truth to that point, then the existing statutory policy does not really go far enough to foster full competition at the point-of-sale in merchant-discount rates. Thus, absent some reason to think that a rule permitting surcharges would be harmful, a revision of TILA to permit surcharges would be a step in the right direction.

There is surprisingly little in the existing literature to support the status quo. Given the obvious market power of the credit card networks as against merchants, and the existing history of antitrust litigation indicating a willingness to exercise that power, it should be easy to accept the idea that regulators might bar a specific contract term in the network/merchant contract if that term had external social costs, as this one does. The only substantial argument in the existing literature to support the surcharge ban is the idea that surcharges currently appear in circumstances where merchants have substantial bargaining power, so that the fees are used to extract a greater share of the surplus from the underlying transaction. That is thought to be the case, for example, in Australia, where firms with near monopoly power (Telstra, the major phone company, and airlines like Qantas and Virgin Blue) appear to be the only major merchants that have assessed surcharges in response to initiatives by the Australian central bank.[21] Similarly, when Visa executives justify surcharge limitations publicly, they offer anecdotes like the operator of a wrecker on a rural road in the middle of the night imposing a surcharge for credit card use only in circumstances in which a cardholder cannot readily obtain access to an alternate payment system. Yet rare indeed is the retail environment without some ready payment substitute, particularly since the rise of the debit card. The risks of price gouging should not be allowed to drive a systemic issue such as pricing payment system options in competitive markets.

In conclusion, there is some reason to believe that we would see more merchant price discrimination if legislatures invalidated network rules that prohibited surcharges. Other countries – the United Kingdom, Netherlands, and Sweden – have taken similar steps.[22] I do not want to overstate the effects of such a change. It is unlikely that all or even most merchants will change. On the other hand, intense price competition among American retailers has brought an increased focus by leading retailers (most notably Wal-Mart) on the amounts that they pay for payment services. It is certainly plausible to believe that Wal-Mart and competing retailers might lead a trend in the coming years to charge extra for customers that want to use payment products that are more expensive for Wal-Mart to process.

The Limits of Indirect Approaches

Returning to the theme with which this chapter began, I believe that surcharges by definition cannot be a complete solution. As Chapter 4 explains, a substantial part of the problem with the credit card is that its union of a lending and payment vehicle leads to spending transactions that result, in turn, in financial distress and associated social costs. If we harness the incentives of merchants to set prices, we can expect them to set prices that will maximize their profits.

Therefore, if the costs associated with the credit card are higher than the costs of competing payment systems, and if a shift to the competing payment systems would not affect spending levels, we could believe that merchants might impose surcharges on their credit card customers. One of the major points of this book, however, is that some of the people using credit cards in fact are going to spend more if they use a credit card than if they use some other payment system. If that is the case, it is not reasonable to expect merchants to charge more for using a credit card at the point-of-sale.

Thus, I explain the limited use of surcharging by merchants differently than other writers. What I discern is a pattern of surcharges by merchants that sell products that are not good vehicles for discretionary consumption. Qantas is not going to drive consumption of its services by accepting credit cards in addition to debit cards, so why would it wish to pay more to accept credit cards? Indeed, airlines in the United States increasingly press their customers to use services like Bill Me Later, rather than credit cards, to avoid the interchange fees associated with credit cards.[23] The same is true of merchants like the U.S. Post Office or wrecker and taxi drivers. They might want to take credit cards to make it easier for their customers to pay, but their customers are not really going to spend more with credit cards than they would with some other payment system.

By contrast, most retailers will have a different view. Most retailers use every obvious tactic to encourage their customers to spend more, and if they believe that customers using credit cards will spend more they hardly can be expected to discourage them from doing so. Do we really expect Bloomingdale's to impose a surcharge on credit card customers?

Once we recognize that point, we are brought back to the problem that attention to the network/merchant and the merchant/customer interfaces is at best an indirect, incomplete response. It might be a beneficial response, but it cannot solve the problem in any comprehensive way. I turn now to responses directed to the heart of the problem: the cardholder/issuer interface.

12 Contract Design

Over the last several years, I have presented this research to various groups: American law faculties, undergraduate students, bar associations, and economists at central banks in different countries. I make the argument that the problem with credit cards lies in the cardholder-issuer interface, and then propose ways to redress the imbalance between the product-design capabilities of the card issuers and the typical cardholder's limited capacity to resist skillful marketing. The most common response is that it is simple for any well-educated person to avoid becoming a revenue-generating cardholder. All that is required, one would think, is careful attention to the terms of the contract between the cardholder and the issuer.

Thus, someone usually claims to have found a simple way to avoid the risks of card usage. Some will say, for example, that the trick is to find a card with no annual fee and be sure to pay your bill on time every month. More recently, with increased attention to shortened grace periods, I have heard colleagues explain with pride their careful efforts to pay their bills multiple times a month to avoid interest payments (sometimes doing so even before the purchases are made). Still others claim to have successfully mastered the practice of shopping teaser rates or making the most of rewards programs without paying interest or fees. I have not yet engaged any of those respondents in a conversation without concluding (usually silently) that the person in fact is probably a profitable customer for their card issuer. It surely is true that some cardholders are less profitable than others are, but it is equally the case that most of the people that believe they have outsmarted their issuers are mistaken.

As this discussion makes clear, and as the great variety of "simple" resolutions suggests, I believe that the problems are intricate. The difficulty with proposing sensible solutions stems from three central points. The first is the blending of payment and credit features, which has been the source of the credit card's success and is at the same time at the root cause of the problems. The second is the difficulty of designing policies to alter ingrained market networks without abandoning the efficiencies those networks create. The third is the intractable problem of responding to the cognitive failures that plague consumers in financial transactions. This is particularly true in diverse markets like the credit card market, where at least some cardholders believe they are taking advantage of card issuers and benefiting from the less rational tendencies of other cardholders. As I work through potential policy responses targeted at the cardholder-issuer interface, I attempt to keep those three points at the forefront of my analysis.

The relationship between the cardholder and the issuer is based almost entirely on the "boilerplate" form contracts drafted by lawyers for credit card issuers. Cardholders have no opportunity to negotiate the terms of the contracts. The boilerplate forms suffer from many of the problems associated with other standardized consumer lending contracts. They are lengthy, detailed, and written in fine print. It is often hard to locate the contract documents from among the other correspondence and advertising materials that the lender provides, and the contract itself might include multiple documents. Reading the contract documents requires a level of literacy and reading comprehension that is far beyond the grasp of the normal person.[1] More fundamentally, the substantive issues that the agreements raise play into several common behavioral biases that unite to desensitize consumers to the risks of spending and borrowing.

Credit card contracts also raise distinct issues that make them even more complex than other consumer lending contracts. The structure of credit card transactions (with separate points of agreement, purchase, and borrowing) deemphasizes the significance of the contract itself. Consumers make the important decisions when they decide to spend and then later to borrow.

Those decisions seem trivial because of the small amounts involved. To illustrate, on the day when I first wrote this passage, I made eight purchases with my cards, paid two credit card bills, and discarded (without opening) three solicitations offering new cards, balance transfer programs, and similar offers to extend credit. Although each of those actions was routine, even trivial, the collective impact can be significant.

Time is also a factor. Because credit card transactions occur over an extended period, issuers generally retain the right to change the terms on which they extend credit. They do so with some regularity. The changes typically apply to outstanding balances, which means that consumers are required to weigh the risk at the sales counter that the credit terms for that purchase will change later. A related concern is that issuers typically provide little or no advance notice when making changes. This means that consumers often are not able to find other credit arrangements in time to avoid retroactive adjustment of the contract terms.

A final point that distinguishes credit cards from other consumer credit transactions is the number of account agreements. Many consumers have not one but several different accounts, with terms that differ in important respects. Indeed, in 2004 the average American household held a stunning thirteen credit cards.[2] Consumers that read their card agreements must be able to associate the correct agreement with the particular card they choose to use at the point of sale.

Considering the unique problems with credit card contracting, the lack of regulation of credit card contracts compared to other consumer financial contracts is hard to justify. Other important consumer financial transactions – purchases of insurance, borrowing money for a home – display a common pattern, in which regulators or intermediaries have standardized terms in a way that focuses competition on the attributes of products that are most readily comprehensible to consumers. Is there a justification for the disparate regulatory approaches? Are consumers immune to the credit card contracting problems? Do issuers have market incentives to internalize the risks? Do courts protect the interests of those consumers by policing credit card contracts?

The remainder of this chapter discusses those questions. In the two subsequent chapters, I broaden the discussion to consider ways to respond to other problematic features of the credit card transaction: information deficits and marketing strategies.

Credit Card Account Agreements

CONTEXT

The issuer-cardholder relationship begins when a card issuer sends a solicitation to a group of prescreened consumers, usually through direct mail. Issuers sent more than five billion direct mail solicitations in 2004, for an average of more than five offers per month to more than 70% of U.S. households.[3] Although the response rate typically is quite low,[4] tens of millions responded last year by submitting a credit card application. Upon approval of the application, the issuer sends the card and a cardholder agreement to the applicant. After receiving the card and the contract, the consumer must validate the card over the telephone – the telephone validation occurs after the cardholder has received the agreement and before the card is used. Thus, to generalize, the contracting process is still primarily paper-based, and satisfies traditional contracting doctrine that looks for mutual assent through offer and acceptance of identifiable and disclosed terms.

Still, the robustness of assent is undermined by the cardholder's investment of time in the relationship before receiving the cardholder agreement. A typical cardholder probably will not read the agreement. The account is open by the time the cardholder receives it. And the agreement is likely to be hard to read and impossible to revise.[5] If the cardholder does attempt to read the agreement, it is far from clear that a cardholder of reasonable care and intellectual capability will understand it.

A typical credit card agreement, for example, might have about eight single-space pages of small (seven-point) type, including about eighty separately numbered provisions. Many of the terms in the agreement are comprehensible only for cardholders with specialized knowledge. Financial terms such as "annual percentage rate" or "APR" assume proficiency with interest calculations, and legal terms such as "arbitration," "forum," and "default" assume an advanced understanding of the legal process. Furthermore, a single account may have multiple APRs that apply to different types of credit extensions or different periods.

The likelihood that the cardholder will have cards from multiple issuers only exacerbates the complexity of the relationships. The agreements for the thirteen cards that the typical household will have are likely to contain choice-of-law provisions that select the laws of different states. Moreover, unlike the issuers of home mortgages[6] or insurance policies,[7] to take the closest parallels, each credit card issuer is likely to use a standardized agreement that is in form (if not substance) almost entirely different from the forms of other major issuers. Thus, the cardholder that wants to maintain a comprehensive understanding of the status of cardholder agreements will need to understand the relevant legal rules in the applicable states, will need to study a different agreement for each card, and will need to remember as cards are pulled from the wallet which agreement corresponds to each card. This in a world in which few consumers are likely to notice, much less retain, the relevant agreements as they arrive in their stack of daily junk mail.

Another point is that it is not always easy for a layperson to determine which papers constitute the agreement for each card. The current Bank of America agreement, for example, consists of a separately printed eight-page standardized form, together with a set of "Additional Disclosures" that appear in the billing statement at the bottom of a sheet labeled "Important Summary of Changes to Your Account." The cardholder that skips the summary after reading the agreement would fail to notice such additional terms as a default provision that permits Bank of America to impose a penalty APR of about 10% per annum more than the standard APR.

Finally, a cardholder also would need to keep track of the frequent amendments of each of the agreements. It is typical for major issuers to amend their agreements in important respects with remarkable frequency. Amendments are not the typical bargained-for modifications of contract theory. Rather, the typical agreement reserves to the issuer the right to amend the agreement at any time, with the issuer promising at best that it will provide notice of the amendments. When it does provide notice, the notice typically is in the form of a new agreement included in a billing statement together with a variety of other promotional materials. The cardholder who discards all marketing information that comes with bills is likely to fail to notice such amendments. As a matter of traditional contract doctrine, it is not clear that such amendments are enforceable; however, several key states explicitly permit amendments based on notices enclosed with billing statements followed by subsequent card use.[8]

To be sure, issuers obtain consent before applying some new financial terms, but consent is inferred from such actions as continuing to use the card after notice of the amendment, or failure to close the account and send a prompt written objection to the amendment. Issuers often require a consumer seeking to avoid modified terms to opt out of the modified terms in ways that might not be feasible or desirable for all accountholders.[9] Importantly, amendments often apply to funds already borrowed. For example, a change in the terms of default might substantially increase the interest rate the cardholder will pay on balances outstanding at the time of the amendment.[10]

In evaluating the contracting problems that the card presents, it is important to remember the unusual nature of the reciprocal obligations on which the relationship rests. On the cardholder's side, there is no commitment to use the card. Moreover, even if the card is used, timely payments often obviate any obligation to pay interest or fees. Nor is the lack of a commitment illusory. In many (perhaps most) cases, the cardholder can switch credit sources easily. Viewed on a purchase-by-purchase basis, the typical cardholder makes a different decision for each transaction at the moment when a card is presented at the checkout counter.

On the issuer's side, the business of card issuance involves a similar evanescence of obligation. As with most lending transactions, the lender is not in any practical sense obligated to lend until the moment at which the lender actually extends funds to the borrower. Rather, the parties proceed on the useful rule of thumb that absent an unforeseen change of circumstances it normally will be profitable for the lender to extend the credit for which the lender has expended time and energy to structure a transaction. Issuers deal with the possibility of such changes by reserving the right to refuse to extend credit on a transaction-by-transaction basis.[11] If this were not permitted, issuers would be deprived of the ability to terminate accounts based on deterioration of the borrower's credit over time. It would also make it difficult to respond to concerns about unauthorized use.

More broadly, because interest rates and the competitive landscape change rapidly, credit card issuers require a great deal of flexibility to operate. Forcing an issuing bank to adhere to credit terms in a dynamic economic environment would not promote an efficient credit relationship. That is not to say that lenders cannot commit at one time to provide credit at some specified future date. It is to say, however, that lenders typically charge for such a commitment and that the absence of a commitment (and related fee) from the credit card market should surprise nobody. In sum, market conditions require that issuers retain some ability to modify the terms of their agreements.[12]

As suggested earlier, the difficulty of obtaining individual consents from large numbers of cardholders has led issuers generally to reserve the right to change the terms of their agreements when cardholders use their cards after receiving notice of the change.[13] In the context of the business model, however, that provision is much less onerous than it might seem at first glance. Given the lack of obligation – on either side – it makes more sense to view each separate purchase transaction as a separate agreement between the cardholder and card issuer that is completed when the card issuer agrees to extend credit for a particular transaction that the cardholder wishes to enter.[14] When the cardholder decides to borrow funds from the borrower, it borrows them on the terms available from the issuer at that point, just as we purchase a CD from a bank at the interest rate available on the day we contact the bank to purchase it.

RAMIFICATIONS

The key question is whether consumers are making choices with sufficient care and rationality to drive the market to a competitive and optimal set of products and prices. These are complex relationships. It is unlikely that the typical consumer will be able to evaluate all of the attributes of the transaction that have economic significance.

■ **Decision Making.** I draw here on a long-standing body of experimental literature indicating that the ability of a typical consumer to evaluate separate attributes declines rapidly after the number of relevant attributes exceeds three.[15] Applied to this particular context, Jeffrey Davis has conducted an empirical study of consumer comprehension of consumer finance agreements,[16] using an agreement much less complicated than a modern credit card agreement.[17] Davis found that most consumers that read the agreement could not understand most of its terms. Davis's findings emphasize the difficulty that consumers face in understanding terms that involve complex concepts that are not common in daily experience.[18] Although the study is relatively informal, its findings dovetail with the reality of the modern credit card agreement. In particular, a consumer must account for costs and fees that differ from card to card and shift over time (often after the purchase in question), as well as complex concepts of default and a litany of fees payable as a consequence of specified actions.[19] In reality, we cannot think it likely that consumers understand most of the terms even when they do review the agreements.

Rather, theory suggests that the typical cardholder will select a product based on a small number of price and service attributes that are of obvious relevance, recognizing that the remaining terms of the agreement are nonnegotiable. For example, a consumer might select a bank based solely on the cost of writing checks, the minimum balance required to avoid a monthly fee, and the location and fees for using automated teller machines to withdraw cash. In the case of a credit card contract, empirical research suggests a typical consumer selects a card based on the brand, annual fee, grace period, affinity or rewards benefits, and the stated interest rate if the consumer expects to pay interest in the immediate future.[20] Because those terms are contained in the advertising materials, consumers in most cases are unlikely even to look at the contract. Thus, a consumer of typical decision-making capacity would not rationally consider the terms defining or explaining the consequences of late payment or excessive borrowing, even though they generate a substantial share of issuer revenue (in the form of fees and default APRs). If consumers do not consider those terms, it is fair to wonder if issuers will draft them in a competitive way.[21]

A second concern, one to which legal academics have paid considerably more attention, is the likelihood that consumers would not price the risks of card agreements accurately even if they did invest the time and attention necessary to understand and evaluate the relevant financial terms. Tom Jackson has suggested that systematic failures in the cognitive process cause individuals to underestimate the risks that their current consumption imposes on their future well-being.[22] Building on that point, behavioral economics literature suggests that consumers give excessive weight to the conspicuous "up-front" aspects of a relationship and inadequate weight to less conspicuous "back-end" terms.[23]

The pricing problem is associated with several related cognitive tendencies. One is a so-called "optimistic" bias, which leads people to underestimate the likelihood of adverse events – in this case, to underestimate both the likelihood that they would suffer financial distress and the costs that the distress would impose on them.[24] Another is an "availability" bias, which leads people to overweigh the probability of common occurrences (which are readily available to their decision-making faculties) and underweigh the probability of uncommon occurrences. If financial distress is an uncommon event, that bias might cause consumers to underweigh the likelihood and consequences of financial distress.[25] Another concern is hyperbolic discounting. Generally, this causes consumers to make intertemporal comparisons that are unstable over time – so that future behavior will be systematically inconsistent with present predictions of that behavior.[26] In this context, it can lead to excessive borrowing.[27]

Shrouding and Debiasing. Those cognitive tendencies justify concerns that are exacerbated if card issuers are in a position to exploit them.[28] David Laibson and his coauthors discuss a strategy that they call "shrouding," in which merchants identify a myopic class of customers and exploit the lack of rationality by systematically backloading the less attractive terms into a less prominent time and place in the relationship.[29] Stewart Macaulay's work on credit cards before TILA suggests that card issuers used similar techniques to make cardholders responsible for the losses from stolen cards.[30] At that time, the strategy was to omit any language about lost cards from the application and then include a fine-print clause on the back of the card indicating that the cardholder was responsible for all transactions in which the card was presented (even if the transaction was conducted by a thief with a stolen card). Similarly, Oren Bar-Gill's article on credit card contracting argues that credit card companies use pricing features such as teaser rates to take advantage of a concern for near-term costs by marketing products that depend on systematic underestimation of long-term borrowing costs.[31]

Those strategies are less successful where competition can "debias" markets. Consider, for example, how the entry of Netflix has trumped the earlier shrouding strategy on which Blockbuster relied. Generally, Blockbuster's profit model in the early years of this decade coupled low rental fees with high late fees. If consumers underestimated the amount of late fees or the probability that they would pay them, they would underestimate the costs of renting from Blockbuster. By designing a product that exploited that error, Blockbuster increased its short-term profits. Netflix responded with a two-pronged approach: a pricing model that does not involve late fees and an education strategy designed to create an aversion to late fees. It is too soon to tell whether the Netflix approach will result in a long-term market position for Netflix,[32] but it did disrupt Blockbuster's profit model.

As the Blockbuster/Netflix example suggests, educating consumers of both front-end and back-end costs can disrupt a profit model that relies on back-end costs. In the credit card context, issuers at one time might have been vulnerable to sophisticated cardholders who avoid the payment of interest and fees by using a card with no annual fee and making timely monthly payments.[33] Thus, as the number of sophisticated users grew, it became increasingly difficult for card issuers to profit by hiding expensive back-end interest payments.

Similarly, there is some reason to think that the ability of card issuers to derive high profits from shrouded late and overlimit fees may be subject to debiasing. Federal Reserve data suggests that the revenues from those fees doubled during the 1990's, from about 0.7% of outstandings in 1990 to a plateau of 1.4% or 1.5% of outstandings, from 2000 through 2004. But 2005 witnessed both the rise of major issuers competing for business by promising *not* to collect those fees, and a more than 10% drop in the revenues collected from those fees.[34]

The complexity of the modern credit card transactional structure minimizes the likelihood that issuers will be forced to use transparent pricing models without regulatory intervention. The Blockbuster/Netflix example describes a single market segment with a shrouding technique that was destabilized when consumers were encouraged to develop accurate perceptions of their future behavior. Modern credit card issuers, however, have used at least two tactics to prevent increased customer sophistication from destabilizing their profit models.[35]

Segmentation and Multiplicity. The first tactic has been to develop product features that segment the market into smaller niches. The earlier discussion describes a single credit card product offered to all customers. That product was attractive to the sophisticated because it was free to them and to the unsophisticated because they failed to understand either the costs of the product or their likely use of it. Responding to the growth of card users that do not borrow, issuers have developed a number of different products that make it harder for sophisticated users to free ride. For example, the sophisticated cardholder that wishes not to pay interest and fees is likely to be attracted to an affinity or rewards card issued by MBNA or one of its competitors. For that product, the cardholder is likely to pay an annual fee,[36] which the sophisticated user will rationalize as costing less than the value of the rewards (frequent flyer miles or the like). There is every reason to expect that the cardholder's calculation often will be incorrect.[37] Moreover, those calculations accord no weight to the value of the information MBNA obtains from the relationship.[38] Even if that calculation is correct, the new product certainly has made the relationship more profitable on a cardholder-by-cardholder basis than it was in years past, when there might have been a direct cross-subsidization between convenience users and borrowers.

The concept of segmentation is not a new one. As Lizabeth Cohen explains in *A Consumer's Republic*, the strategy of segmenting consumers into ever more finely delineated classes has been a dominant strategy for a half century. It was identified in the 1950s in academic writings by people like Wendell Smith and Pierre Martineau, and swiftly transformed the business models of all American businesses aimed at consumers.[39]

The second tactic is to take advantage of the fact that consumers are likely to have multiple account agreements, all of which are likely subject to frequent unilateral modifications, both of which work together to hinder consumer understanding. If each issuer has a different set of rules, and if the pitfalls hidden in the rules differ for each issuer and from time to time, only the most careful cardholder will avoid any level of interest or fees. The point of this tactic is that within each of the market segments described earlier, even for the cardholders who attempt to position themselves as nonborrowing convenience users, it will require an increasing level of attention of detail to successfully avoid paying fees to the issuer.

Those strategies make the card industry more resistant to debiasing than parallel industries. That leaves us with a policy question: how to regulate a contracting market in which a seller faces a heterogeneous set of purchasers, some but not all of whom are sufficiently careful and sophisticated to respond rationally to the terms offered by the seller. If purchasers are homogeneous in their preferences, a relatively small number of sophisticated customers can produce competition in the market that will drive the seller to offer an efficient product.[40] Alternatively, if purchasers are heterogeneous in their preferences but are always sophisticated, then each purchaser will respond rationally to the terms offered by the seller. We would expect this to be the case, for example, in relatively high-dollar markets. We are left here, however, with the case that falls between those simple cases: a market in which only some customers understand the offered terms, and in which the choices of those customers do not produce competition that alters the terms available to the other customers.[41]

Solutions to the Contracting Problem

If the allocation of risks in existing cardholder agreements is not the result of effective competition or rational choice by cardholders, the natural question is whether and, if so, how the law should respond. Lawrence Friedman describes a common pattern of consumer contract regulation. After an industry develops to a point where a stable set of products and transactions have developed, the typical response is for the legislature to step in and transfer those areas "from the realm of abstract contract law" to the realm of economic regulation.[42] As Stewart Macaulay explains, we can view this as a process by which commercial areas "spin off" for special treatment.[43]

For example, as the mail order industry grew in size, the Federal Trade Commission (FTC) adopted a set of standardized contract terms, eliminating competition on terms that consumers are unlikely to notice. The FTC Mail Order Rule establishes a set of procedures that retailers must follow if they are unable to ship goods within the time they estimate at the time they take the order. If the delay is moderate, they must give the customer an opportunity to cancel the order. If the delay is extreme, they must cancel the order unless the customer explicitly consents to the extension.[44] We can imagine that in the absence of such a rule, retailers might have different terms in their contracts to deal with the possibility of delayed shipments. We also can be sure that few consumers would examine and analyze those terms. Therefore, even if the FTC delay term is not optimal, it does serve to focus competition in that industry on the price, selection, and quality of delivered products, terms customers are most likely to notice.

Viewing the regulatory framework within that paradigm, it is striking how little the existing law does to regulate the credit card agreement. Most of the rules that govern credit card transactions are found in TILA and Regulation Z.[45] The legal regime defined by those rules is primarily a disclosure-based system,[46] with only a few substantive constraints on the practices of card issuers. For example, TILA does prohibit banks from issuing unsolicited credit cards to consumers.[47] TILA also has several provisions relating to unauthorized use and merchant disputes that give consumers a right to cancel payment that is much broader than the consumers' rights in any of the competing payment systems.[48] Still, the existing framework assumes, at least if the card issuer makes the required disclosures, that cardholders are best situated to decide with which entities and on which terms to enter card agreements.[49] That framework reflects an almost complete acceptance of the concern that terms established by government fiat will be less flexible, less innovative, and less likely to allocate risks sensibly than the terms selected by parties to a freely negotiated commercial arrangement.[50]

The question is whether there is some reason to think that credit card contracts are sufficiently afflicted by contracting inefficiencies or externalities to warrant spinning them off from the general hands-off realm of contract enforcement to the realm of interventionist social planning. On the question of whether or not market obstacles prevent efficient contracting, the preceding section summarizes a number of reasons to think that the process by which cardholders enter into card agreements does not function well. With regard to externalities, I show in Part II that increased credit card borrowing is uniquely associated with an increase in personal bankruptcy filings – even when we hold constant the total level of borrowing and account for general conditions in the economy. Following up on that point, the increased financial distress associated with rising card use can cause harms that the borrower might not adequately consider when the borrower makes contracting decisions.

Assuming that some form of economic regulation is called for, it is less clear what type of intervention makes the most sense. If the existing literature makes anything clear, it is that a sensible intervention must pay attention to the situation on the ground, lest it end up doing more harm than good.[51] The biggest concern is that a regulatory intervention viewed as minor and benign by regulators or scholars might in fact undermine the business models prevalent in the industry in ways that harm competition. That is a major problem in this context, because the credit card is an especially efficient payment and borrowing device. Working from that perspective, the rest of this chapter considers a series of possible responses.

RUNNING IN PLACE

To understand the feasibility and effectiveness of interventions in the credit card market, it is important to understand not only the contracting problems discussed earlier, but also some more general difficulties with consumer behavior in those markets. To that end, one of the themes running through this book is that the excessive borrowing associated with credit cards results from both a convenience risk (the subject of Part V) and an instrument-induced risk (Part IV). The instrument-induced risk occurs when consumers use a credit card as a payment device and do not intend to borrow. Because some evidence suggests that the credit card encourages consumers to spend more than they otherwise would, and perhaps more than they can repay out of monthly incomes, credit card use can lead to unanticipated debt. The convenience risk arises from the low transaction costs of credit card lending: borrowers are more likely to underestimate the risks associated with future revenue streams than they would be in another type of consumer credit transaction. Both of those risks arise against a transaction structure that makes the contracting decision less important to most consumers than the spending and borrowing decisions. Thus, both types of mistakes occur after the contracting decision has been made. Because policy analysis has failed to understand that trifurcated framework and its effect on consumer decision making, neither the current regulatory framework nor the leading proposals in the existing literature respond adequately.

For example, the simplest possibility is the response of the common law: ex post judicial invalidation of terms as unconscionable. There is nothing new about this idea, which dates (at least) to work by Friedrich Kessler in the early 1940s.[52] A similar idea appears in Section 211 of the *Restatement (Second) of Contracts*. But several considerations limit the effectiveness of that doctrine as a general tool to police contracting problems. For example, judicial decision making under a vague rubric of unconscionability often leads to the disparate readjustment of terms in ways that the parties did not contemplate in their pricing decisions. Moreover, courts that apply such an approach with sufficient vigor to have a substantial effect on contracting practices are likely to do a poor job of sorting provisions that make economic sense from those that reflect overreaching.[53]

This is not to say that the unconscionability doctrine can serve no useful purpose. For example, the unconscionability doctrine might encourage businesses to think more carefully about the enforceability of the clauses that they write, leading them to use larger print, simpler language, and the like. However, it seems more likely the doctrine does not substantially constrain the major industry actors, who easily can obtain legislative redress in areas where questionable practices are important to their business models.[54]

In the credit card context, the use of unconscionability as a tool to police contracting excesses also must overcome the widespread use of arbitration clauses in cardholder agreements.[55] When courts enforce arbitration provisions, they have no serious opportunity to assess the substantive provisions of credit card agreements or to consider whether issuers have complied with those provisions.[56] Still, I doubt that judicial or regulatory invalidation of arbitration provisions will have any substantial impact. For one thing, arbitration clauses might not contribute to the business models that permit excessive cardholder borrowing. Arbitration clauses are, at most, a detail in the history of the credit card industry. It is clear that most issuers did not use arbitration clauses in the United States until the late 1990s, and they are used rarely overseas.[57] Yet the rise in borrowing and attendant rise in consumer bankruptcy that troubles policymakers was well on its way even before those clauses came into common use. Nor would removal of arbitration clauses respond substantially to the contracting problems at the heart of this chapter. To be sure, arbitration clauses probably deter at least some class actions. However, the class actions that would be available if the clauses were not enforced would only buttress the weak TILA disclosure regime and increase the ability of cardholders to hold issuers to the terms of the agreements the issuers have drafted.[58] Thus, they would have little effect on the substance of the relationship.

This is not to say that there are not serious problems with arbitration clauses in credit card contracting. For example, there is at least some evidence to support the view that issuers have colluded to adopt the clauses broadly because of concerns that customers care enough to shop for issuers that do not force arbitration.[59] There also is some reason to think that the problems of bias have a serious effect in this industry, where the major issuers have gravitated to a single provider (the National Arbitration Forum) that seems to be competing for business (at least in part) on a reputation for providing results that are satisfying to card issuers.[60]

All in all, there is good reason to believe that arbitration clauses are not the result of competitive contracting. It is at least possible, however, that the cost savings of arbitration are sufficiently valuable that inclusion of the clauses is efficient.[61] Moreover, arbitration proceedings probably could be constructed in a cost-effective and neutral way if the card networks were inclined to intervene. Regardless of the outcome of that debate, it does not seem likely that prohibiting the use of arbitration provisions or regulating their content will solve the problem of excessive borrowing.

MOVING FORWARD

I turn now to the possibilities of direct regulation of the terms of credit card agreements. Here, I consider two approaches: prohibiting unpriceable terms, and promulgating agreements that provide a standard contractual template for the relationship.

Prohibit Specific Terms Ex Ante. The first solution would be to prohibit specific terms. That approach is common in other jurisdictions. Consider, for example, the European Union's Unfair Terms Directive,[62] which generally prohibits the inclusion of certain types of unfair terms in consumer contracts unless they are the result of individual negotiation.[63] By American standards, the list is intrusive, prohibiting, among other things, unilateral modification and arbitration clauses.[64]

Such a broad regime might seem almost unthinkable to American businesses. Yet it is not significantly different from the regulatory approach taken in other consumer financial transactions where a small number of important issues dominate the forms. For example, consider the residential lease contract, in which the most important term for consumer protection purposes is likely to be a warranty of habitability. After a period during which courts struggled with property owner efforts to disclaim such a warranty, it is in many jurisdictions now settled by statute or regulation that the owner of a residence provides such a warranty.[65] Similarly, in the home mortgage context, it is now uncommon to see a provision providing for mandatory arbitration.[66]

In this context, there are price terms that consumers might assess more rationally if the contracting process did not obscure them. Provisions that permit retroactive price adjustments interfere with the ability of consumers to assess the risks of default and nonpayment, because they allow price adjustments that come into effect after the time of the purchasing decision to which they apply.[67] For lack of a better term, I call those "unpriceable" terms, not because consumers can never evaluate them, but because few consumers can be expected to evaluate their significance accurately.[68] That impulse would follow naturally from the idea that it is appropriate to ban terms whenever it is likely that all or almost all consumers will fail to respond accurately to the terms.[69]

Thus, regulators could concentrate on the notice and opt-out provisions that accompany retroactive price adjustments. The fifteen-day notice requirement mandated by federal law gives consumers little time to find alternate credit sources.[70] Depending on the requirements of the particular opt-out provision,[71] the absence of another credit source might make compliance with opt-out requirements impractical. For example, a provision stating that the consumer must repay the entire balance immediately will not provide a realistic option to a liquidity-constrained customer. Regulators thus could enhance consumer decision making by lengthening notice requirements so that consumers would have additional time to find alternate credit sources. Regulators could also explore ways to improve the readability and presentation of change-in-terms notices, broaden consumer opt-out rights, or even ban post-hoc application of unilateral amendments entirely.

A similar example is the universal default provisions that are the focus of current regulatory initiatives. Essentially, universal default terms in credit card agreements permit an issuer to raise the rate it charges one of its borrowers substantially if that borrower commits a default on an unrelated debt to a different lender, even if the borrower has not missed a payment to the credit card issuer in question. It is one thing for an issuer to stop (or raise the rate on) new extensions of credit based on adverse credit information – we expect (and hope) that issuers will do that routinely. It is quite another, however, for creditors to increase the interest rate on debts already incurred, solely because of a late payment to a different creditor. Regulators, upset by the application of universal default provisions, have responded by insisting that credit card issuers provide better disclosure of the provisions in their agreements with customers.[72]

My analysis shows why a disclosure regime is not the appropriate response. For one thing, it rests on the premise that consumers who receive the disclosures will alter their behavior, which is improbable. An emphasis on disclosure misses the point. The underlying complaint is that the provisions are fundamentally unfair: "We shouldn't have to pay more to Bank One simply because we were late on a payment to Providian." Policymakers for the most part have retreated to a disclosure-based response because of their unwillingness to press that fairness argument.[73]

The fairness argument conceals an economic argument for barring universal default provisions. Universal default rules are one of the attributes consumers are least likely to price in their contracting and product-selection decisions. This is true because they are a boilerplate attribute that will not be of great significance for most consumers selecting products. It also is true because the cost of the provision is difficult to assess up front. It is difficult when I make a purchase today to factor in the likelihood that the interest rate on that purchase at some distant time in the future will increase by some unspecified amount because of a default I make in a payment to some other creditor. If an omnicompetent consumer could not take account of the rate differentiation, then the differentiation is not effectively altering borrowing behavior. Because consumers are not pricing this term, there is no reason to rely on its existence in contracts as evidence of its optimality.

The absence of contracting competition does not prove, however, that the term is less than optimal. It is possible that the provisions operate to shift the net burden of charges by credit card issuers to some extent toward the most distressed borrowers, the ones most likely to default, and away from those least likely to default. The increased collections from those customers might support lower charges for convenience users that do not borrow or default. Thus, a rational and fully informed cardholder might think the benefits of such a clause exceed its costs.[74]

More broadly, universal default provisions are part of the developments in the credit card market that have fostered segmentation, which has led in turn to a marked differentiation of rates among cardholders with different risk profiles.[75] Generally, that trend is positive because it permits more accurate pricing. The role of universal default terms in that market segmentation depends on the odd ramifications of default in the credit card market. In conventional commercial markets, an act of default by a borrower is a data point that indicates to the lender that the transaction has become riskier than previously anticipated and thus more likely to produce a loss. Typically, lenders respond proactively by managing the transaction in a way that responds to the increased risk of loss.[76] In the credit card context, however, an event of default (such as a late payment to another creditor or even a late payment to the card issuer) is a signal that the cardholder is financially constrained. To the issuer, such an occurrence is a signal of two cardholder attributes that collectively make the cardholder a likely profit center for the issuer. First, the cardholder is likely to borrow more in the immediately ensuing months. Second, the cardholder's switching costs have increased because of the difficulty the cardholder will face in repaying the entire outstanding balance in a time of financial distress. Thus, the issuer can respond by substantially increasing the fees charged to the cardholder with a diminished concern that the cardholder will shift the borrowing to a different lender. Indeed, one might imagine that a cardholder's anticipated value as a customer rises almost to the point of a bankruptcy filing.

The issue, then, is whether it matters that cardholders in fact do not understand the clauses (or their consequences) when they enter the agreements. Should we prevent this choice on that basis? If we think of this as tantamount to a unilateral alteration of terms after the fact, we might be inclined to ban it. On the other hand, if we want to protect the ability of convenience users to choose a card that might be cheaper for them because of the increased revenues issuers receive when they exercise universal default provisions, we might want to allow them.

An intermediate approach, parallel to the analysis of opt-out clauses discussed earlier, would focus on providing cardholders with a practical opportunity to respond before adverse action. For example, regulators might forbid issuers to raise interest rates based on application of a universal default clause without providing cardholders a substantial notice, coupled with an opportunity to challenge the relevant information and to shift their outstanding debt to a different issuer.

In the end, the most sensible approach is to ban the clauses entirely. I am driven primarily by the notion that convenience users as a class should be shifted to debit cards and newer payment systems. I recognize that one likely effect of such a ban would be more extensive and detailed default clauses, focusing on events internal to the cardholder-issuer relationship. That seems positive, at least in part because of the likelihood that it would lessen reliance on external sources of information (with questionable reliability) such as credit reports. Moreover, it might be that cardholders eventually could come to understand and react to those terms.

Another likely effect would be a contraction of credit (or increase in price) to the affected borrowers. Again, that response would be beneficial if financial distress by cardholders imposes costs on society and if current business models encourage borrowers to wait too long before filing for bankruptcy. A system that induces issuers to terminate lending earlier might lower the social costs of financial distress by pressing risky borrowers into an earlier resolution of their financial affairs.

Presumably, the most sensible way to implement such an approach would be for a relatively well-informed regulator (such as the Federal Reserve or the Office of the Comptroller of the Currency [the OCC]),[77] or, less plausibly in the current environment, the FTC) to engage in a cooperative examination, with participation by the affected parties, of the relevant terms. The point here is that a regulator that bans a particular term that commonly is part of the product is likely to affect the market for the product in some cognizable way – by either increasing the cost or lowering the amount or quality of the product in some way.[78] The justification for regulation is the idea that contracting is inherently lawmaking,[79] and that standardized adhesion contracts in practice operate as "unilateral codes," by which the parties that promulgate them "usurp the law-making function," effectively providing "government by private law."[80] The idea is not a new one. Indeed, it is at least as old as the work of Arthur Leff, who viewed defective contracts as analogous to defective automobiles.[81] The decision confronting a regulator, he explains, is whether consumers are better off with the higher price (or lower quantity or quality) of the product that comes in a market without the choice to accept the prohibited term. The FTC has applied such a perspective for many years.[82] Thus, the earlier discussion suggests banning universal default terms based on the idea that the most likely effect would be a contraction of credit in a market that is both functioning poorly and generating substantial externalities. The analysis is comparable to the decision of the Department of Transportation to require all cars to have airbags – some of us would buy cars without airbags, but the government has determined that we all are better off if none of us can make that choice.

We cannot ban all contract terms that consumers misunderstand solely because they are designed to produce profits for the merchants that draft them. It is natural for merchants to view customers as assets, and to work to acquire customers on the hope that the customers will generate a predictable stream of profits after they have been acquired. If we are not to ban all such tactics, we have to identify something special about the credit card market to make these tactics different. The most obvious possibility is the problem with the credit card as a product. If retailers used the tactics discussed here to increase the use of hotels, few would complain, thinking that there is little social cost from excess consumption of that product. When we see a burgeoning social problem from excessive credit card use, we have a basis for concern about contracting practices that increase that problem.

There are obvious problems with intervention.[83] Among other things, it is not clear that regulators will do a better job than courts in identifying terms to be invalidated. Still, there is at least some reason to believe that an ex ante approach – that can be applied evenly across contracts and incorporated into the price – is preferable, because of the likelihood that the opportunity for input from affected businesses will lead regulators to avoid (or quickly repair) truly egregious errors.

Standardized Terms. Term invalidation is probably an incomplete response. Another response would be to develop standard terms for credit card agreements.[84] At first glance, that approach seems more intrusive because it abandons reliance on the market to develop the optimal terms. The use of preapproved terms, however, is the conventional approach for remedying contracting problems in other consumer finance markets.

Credit card agreements stand out as one of the rare types of consumer financial transactions that do not proceed on some set of preapproved terms.[85] Home mortgages, of course, are executed almost entirely on the standard Federal National Mortgage Assocation (Fannie Mae or FNMA) form. A glance at the form would convince most of us that – although it suffers from many of the readability problems discussed earlier – it is not a form drafted to exploit consumer myopia or cognitive weakness. Similarly, state regulators largely determine the major terms of insurance policies.[86] Major real estate transactions – such as the sale of a home – typically proceed on forms that in major part are standardized by a government agency[87] or some intermediary that at least in part represents the interests of consumers.[88]

A standard account agreement would include mandatory provisions for the legal aspects of the relationship, with specific options on issues where there are substantial business reasons for product differentiation. Thus, we might expect several variations on the method for calculating the outstanding interest-bearing balance – one without any grace period, one with a full grace period, and a moderate provision in between. There also would be options for the financial terms on which issuers compete, including the interest rate and the amount of annual, late, and overlimit fees.

Such a proposal would respond directly to the problem of multiplicity of terms and agreements summarized earlier. Thus, like the FTC Mail-Order Rule, it would funnel competition among card issuers directly into the attributes for which variation is permitted, predominantly price-related attributes as to which consumer understanding is heightened and for which competition is easier to imagine.

To be sure, this solution would do little to respond to the problem of complexity. Yet the relationship necessarily is a complex one. Even if standardization substantially lowered the number of terms that a typical cardholder would need to understand, it is doubtful that it would simplify the relationship sufficiently to make a fully competitive cardholder reaction a realistic possibility. The number of attributes of relevance to a fair assessment of a modern credit card product, even putting the agreement aside, is sufficiently large as to make it implausible to think that most cardholders can aggregate and assess the attributes rationally.[89]

Still, standardization should advance cardholder understanding considerably over time. Take, for example, the typical apartment lease, a document of comparable complexity, read directly by few consumers. However, most of us have a reasonable understanding of the typical aspects of that business relationship, predominantly because the terms are relatively standardized and stable over time. If the terms of credit cardholder agreements were uniform, we would expect that through experience many cardholders would come to understand the basic terms that define the events that lead to late payments, over-the-limit fees, events of default, and the like. Given the ways in which multiplicity of terms and term cycling exacerbate the role of complexity in the existing market, there is good reason to think that standardization would be helpful.

Furthermore, the oft-cited objections to using mandatory terms are less troubling in this context. The first is that standardization will narrow the range of product attributes that issuers can use to attract and satisfy customers. As suggested earlier, standardization decreases consumer welfare to the extent that it drives attractive products out of the market.[90] In this context, however, firms do not currently compete to attract customers based on the nonprice terms of these agreements. Indeed, the root of the problem is that there are terms that have a substantial economic effect that consumers nonetheless ignore. A regime that eliminates differentiation on those terms would not make the products less attractive to most customers. The dominant effect would be a long-term one, in which customers eventually might come to understand the boilerplate terms sufficiently to consider them in assessing the risks and appropriate pricing of their purchasing and borrowing behavior. To the extent that opportunities for delivering products to odd, insular classes of cardholders are limited, I expect that the benefits to the cardholders in the mainstream would far exceed the harms.[91]

A more difficult problem is the likelihood that regulators will draft the terms less capably than card issuers will. The terms will be more obscure, will not improve over time, will include more unintentional ambiguities, or will not produce the optimal allocations of risks among the parties. In many contexts, such concerns would be serious, and the record of obscure drafting of disclosures by the Federal Reserve suggests that it is not immune to bad drafting. In this case, however, against the background of existing contract practices, the problems are less troubling. For one thing, the discussion here suggests little reason to think that existing terms are drafted with care to be clear and unambiguous or to create an optimal allocation of risks. Rather, the market currently seems to drive competitive issuers to obscure their terms to escape the notice of their customers. Moreover, as long as the terms are standardized and within some broad range of reasonableness, differences in their impact can be treated by alterations in the price terms that would be left to card issuer discretion (grace periods, interest rates, amounts of the various fees, and the like).

The problems of government drafting suggest an alternate approach that might be useful: pressure from federal regulators on the networks to promulgate uniform terms. Many of the examples to which I refer do not involve direct government regulation. Rather, they involve drafting by intermediaries in a framework that motivates the intermediaries to consider the interests of consumers. In this context, the obvious candidates for standardized drafting would be Visa and MasterCard. If Visa and MasterCard believed that the issuance of uniform and stable terms on a network-by-network basis was a prudent course to avoid federal intervention and government standardization, we might reach the best of all possible outcomes: a well-drafted and sophisticated allocation of risks, with sufficient stability that customers could adapt to it.

For example, if networks were motivated to allocate risks efficiently, they might include a low-cost dispute resolution process like the one used for consumer-merchant disputes governed by TILA. Andy Morriss and Jason Korosec persuasively demonstrate that TILA's shift of the costs of dispute resolution to card issuers has led to an efficient and technology-driven system for resolving claims of inappropriate charges.[92] A system in which an individual network committed that its issuers could be held to the terms of their agreements at least theoretically could be a powerful marketplace tool. Imagine, for example, if MasterCard advertised that consumers who are troubled by "unfair late fees" and "unresponsive card issuers" should use their MasterCard, knowing that they could rely on MasterCard's consumer protection guarantee.

Finally, a still narrower solution might avoid the risks of centralized drafting, but still force the production of terms in a way that makes them amenable to evaluation by intermediaries. There is some reason to think that public scrutiny of the terms of cardholder agreements is more effective than person-by-person negotiation with cardholders. For example, a review of cardholder agreements used by major issuers indicates that the flurry of public attention to universal default terms has led several major issuers to remove those terms from their agreements.[93]

Late fees also have generated a great deal of public scrutiny, both because the fees themselves have become so high and such a sizeable part of issuer revenues, and because of complaints that several of the large card issuers have failed to timely post customer payments. The most prominent allegations are associated with Providian, which was accused of destroying or hiding payments and then charging late fees to the affected cardholders. Those allegations were part of an OCC enforcement action that led to a $300 million consent decree against Providian in 2000.[94]

Whether due to careful manipulation of grace periods or actual misconduct in connection with customer payments, the increasingly substantial late fees associated with regularly-paying cardholders are a cause for concern. British regulators have responded to those concerns by proposing a fixed cap on late fees at an amount equal to the administrative costs associated with a late payment (presumably something much less than the fees now typical in the United States).[95] Less aggressively, it would be easy to support a rule standardizing the time by which consumers must send payments to avoid late fees – a bright-line rule, for example, that lenders must treat payments received by mail at 3:00 P.M. or 5:00 P.M. as made on that day.[96] Another simpler possibility is reflected in a recent bill that would require issuers to indicate a "postmark date" in their bills – coupled with a requirement that all payments postmarked by that date would count as on time.[97] Those solutions would be naive if the problem truly involves outright destruction, but they would respond to the difficulties consumers face in managing grace periods. Issuers uniformly have denied any misconduct, and it is hard to see that a bright-line rule would impose any burden on legitimate business models.

The Internet makes broad dissemination of standard terms much easier than it would have been when TILA was enacted. Thus, credit card issuers could be required to post the major nonprice terms of their agreements in a uniform format on either their own sites or publicly available Internet sites (such as a site hosted by the FTC, the Federal Reserve, or the OCC). The simplest approach probably would be to post them on the FTC's user-friendly Web site, so that intermediaries reliably could find all of the terms in a single place. Issuers that wished to do so also of course could post their terms on their own sites. Indeed, if the FTC required issuers to provide a URL for an address at which the issuer had posted the terms, it would not matter where the terms technically were posted, because the FTC site could provide a catalog of links to the individual postings. The benefit of requiring the terms to be posted directly at the FTC, however, is that it would facilitate downloading all of the terms in a readily analyzable format such as a spreadsheet.

The business models of credit card issuers do not require them to withhold the terms of agreements until prospective cardholders have submitted applications and received the cards. In the United Kingdom, for example, cardholders typically receive the terms twice before they receive the card itself.[98] I am not suggesting that the United States implement such a reform. Individual cardholders are unlikely to read the terms if they are sent to them. Thus, it would be no more useful to print and send the agreements repeatedly than it was for banks to print and send privacy policies shortly after the enactment of the Gramm-Leach-Bliley Act in 2002. Rather, if the only benefit from disclosure of the terms is that intermediaries would examine them, the most effective course is to require that the terms be posted publicly.

Regulators also could require that any set of terms remain in effect for a certain minimum period (such as ninety days) to facilitate the activity of intermediaries that might examine the postings and provide public assessments of the various terms. In the current environment, terms are not publicly available, so consumers do not see them until they have responded positively to a solicitation and received a card, at which point their credit rating already reflects the extension of credit. Initiatives to educate consumers about the meaning of unpriceable terms or to persuade responsible issuers to avoid unpriceable terms can have a positive effect only if it is possible for consumers to pick among issuers based on the terms. Public disclosure of the terms is perhaps the simplest way to jump-start such a regime.

13 Regulating Information

The most intriguing response to the problems with credit card borrowing is to alter the information available to the borrower. After all, the problem is not one of coercion, but rather that consumers make decisions that in hindsight seem to give inadequate weight to later adverse consequences. Furthermore, because many card transactions are beneficial, it is difficult to identify particular transactions that should be prohibited. Restrictions that bar transactions based on cognitive problems that afflict portions of the population may have a negative impact on those not similarly afflicted.[1]

Would it improve the quality of consumer decisions if relevant information were more readily accessible at the point of decision? Although it sounds easy enough, disclosure regulation sometimes is ineffective, costly, and even counterproductive. Thus, it is much easier to say that consumers are making bad decisions than it is to determine how to alter decision making through provision of information.[2]

This chapter proposes two limited interventions in the market that provides information to potential card users. First, I suggest a ban on marketing directed at minors and college-age persons. Second, I recommend disclosures at the time of purchase and the time of borrowing in addition to or instead of the existing disclosures at the time of contracting. This chapter closes with some thoughts about more radical ways to increase the segmentation between payment and credit functionality.

Information Campaigns and Advertising

If the existing disclosure regime is inadequate, as suggested in Chapter 12, the natural question is whether some broader information-based initiative could work – one that bypasses the challenges of the trifurcated decision structure. The goal would be to solve the borrowing problem that afflicts card markets without limiting the ability of market participants to design and select products, through the provision of information that might "debias" consumers and thus overcome the cognitive defects emphasized in Chapter 12. Xavier Gabaix and David Laibson, for example, talk of required "warning labels" like those used on cigarettes.[3] As applied to this context, the basic idea is that warnings of some sort might limit improvident and impulsive spending.

One way to warn consumers is through public information campaigns responding to the availability heuristic – making consumers more cognizant of the problems of excessive borrowing by telling consumers about those problems.[4] Yet the parallel to smoking campaigns illustrates how difficult such a campaign would be. It has taken decades of concerted effort at all levels of the government to bring the growth of smoking among young people to something of a standstill – this for a product that is without redeeming social value, plainly addictive, and associated with catastrophic health consequences.

Consumer expenditure and credit, on the other hand, have much more ambiguous effects on the economy. We can hardly expect governments to urge consumers not to spend. An information campaign designed to limit consumer borrowing would face a natural obstacle in the longstanding government policy in the United States to foster a culture of consumer spending. Thus, as Lizabeth Cohen cogently explains, the federal government in concert with the private sector has waged an intensive campaign since World War II to encourage consumers to spend as part of their patriotic duty. It is not a coincidence, for example, that Walt Disney introduced the miserly Scrooge McDuck in 1947.[5]

Although it is possible to imagine a campaign that urges consumers to "spend, but don't borrow," it would be very different from the existing campaign. The history has been one of government initiatives to broaden the availability of credit specifically to enhance spending. Since the 1950s, our tradition has been one in which "thrift is now un-American."[6]

In addition, we certainly cannot expect a government to ban advertisements urging consumers to spend as we have banned most cigarette advertising. Juliet Schor persuasively argues that discretionary consumer spending is such an integral part of American culture that it would be even harder to eradicate it than it has been to slow the growth of smoking.[7] Collectively, those concerns make reliance on information campaigns an incomplete choice at best, and probably a politically impossible choice.

However, information campaigns that target discrete segments of the population – those for whom the risks of excessive borrowing are particularly acute – would make sense. The obvious possibilities are the young and the retired who have not entered or are no longer a part of the workforce and for whom discretionary spending is more clearly harmful. Yet, anyone who has walked through the main campus of a large university would wonder whether such a campaign would succeed, because of the countermessage existing on-campus advertising conveys so pervasively.

If the concern about credit cards is that consumers use them without fully appreciating the costs and risks associated with incurring substantial amounts of debt, then we should be particularly troubled about transactions by minors. The law often relies on the possible susceptibility of minors and articulates special paternalistic rules designed to protect minors from their own mistakes. Consider, for example, rules invalidating certain contracts made by minors and rules validating spendthrift trusts.[8] More notably, Section 50 of Britain's Consumer Credit Act prohibits direct marketing of credit cards to persons under the age of eighteen.[9]

The problem is not unique to persons under age eighteen, but to the younger population broadly defined.[10] Specifically, it is plain that credit card issuers have seized on college campuses as an important venue for marketing efforts.[11] Empirical research by psychologists suggests that credit cards play an important role in fostering compulsive buying by college students in particular.[12] Several states have adopted rules restricting the marketing of credit cards on campuses.[13] It seems most improbable, however, that the rules could be enforced against the national banks that dominate the credit card market.[14]

It is important to understand the depth of the problem, which Robert Manning has chronicled in some detail.[15] Credit card institutions devote great effort to marketing targeted at college students. Thus, a survey of the college-student card market in 2004 concluded that 76% of undergraduate students have credit cards and that the average outstanding balance is more than $2,000. Most tellingly, the survey reports that the first year in college was the modal time for obtaining a card (56% of the students having obtained their first credit card at the age of eighteen). Card usage swells steadily through the college years, so that 91% of all seniors have cards, with more than half of them carrying four or more cards. With respect to borrowing patterns, only 21% pay off their balances each month, 44% make more than the minimum payment but carry a balance, and 11% make less than the minimum payment each month.[16]

A separate study on the penetration of the graduate student market is even more distressing. That study finds that 96% of graduate students carry cards, that the students carry an average of six cards each, that the average debt is more than $7,500 per student, and that 15% have balances exceeding $15,000. Only 8% of graduate students paid their bills in full each month.[17]

Several things about the rise of university marketing are troubling. For one thing, it is plain that in many cases the marketing proceeds with the approval of university administrators, who voluntarily permit issuers to implement card-issuance programs directly on university campuses.[18] Empirical evidence suggests that students that accept cards from on-campus marketers are likely to be more indebted than those that obtain cards through other channels. At the same time, they are likely to believe that the issuers are more reputable because of screening by the college that has permitted the activity.[19]

In addition, a growing number of America's top universities encourage credit card use by accepting credit cards in payment of tuition. A survey of the Web sites of leading universities – including Vanderbilt University, New York University, University of California at Los Angeles, the University of Texas, Columbia University, and Johns Hopkins University – indicates that many universities accept credit card payments for tuition, and some impose substantial surcharges on the use of credit cards. Thus, even among students that receive student loans, more than a quarter now use credit cards to fund a portion of their tuition.[20] Second, it is plain that the heavy use of cards is having adverse effects on students shortly after they leave college. News reports explain, for example, that high credit card debt by recent graduates often inhibits their ability to obtain credit (for car loans or the like) and in some instances even impairs their employability.[21]

The broader concern, of course, is that card issuers are trying to gain a foothold with young consumers who will establish long-term borrowing patterns. Consider, for example, a Citibank product that offers 3% cash-back to minors based on their purchases – but only if they do not repay their bills in full each month.[22]

A simple and direct response to this problem is obvious. Congress readily could add a provision to TILA based on Section 50 of the British Consumer Credit Act, which prohibits the direct marketing of credit cards to consumers under the age of eighteen. Given the particularities of American marketing, it would make sense to extend the provision to include college students. It is difficult to imagine broad-ranging opposition to such a provision.

It is easy to imagine broader reforms, such as banning minor cards altogether, treating debt incurred by minors differently in bankruptcy, or requiring special repayment rules. However, each of those ideas has special problems that make them less attractive than the narrower reform proposed here. For example, the efficacy of the card as a payment system makes me reluctant to deprive families of the ability to permit use of cards by their children, particularly when their children are in a semi-independent situation like college. Of course, if many of the benefits of credit cards could be reaped with a conventional debit card, then the costs of banning credit cards in that context might be relatively slight. This is particularly true if a ban led to development of a contrary habit: the budgeting skills associated with managing a debit card.

Another possibility would be to subordinate in bankruptcy the right to recover debts incurred by minors on credit cards. My concern about that proposal is that it does raise a considerable possibility of countervailing abuse by minors taking advantage of the rules. I am also ambivalent about special repayment rules, although a baseline idea might be to have issuers require minors to make minimum payments that would repay all debts within twelve months.[23] That rule would have the virtue of quickly bringing home to minors the real cost of purchases and borrowing. I suggest in Chapter 16 a similar (though less onerous) proposal for cards in general. It is not clear to me, however, that it is useful to consider that presumably more controversial proposal in this context where a narrower marketing proposal might be more palatable and have important beneficial effects.

Disclosures

Of course, reforms directed at the youth market address only the tip of the iceberg. Any serious response to problems with credit card use must address the market in general. This brings me to the topic of individualized disclosures. This is the response of the Truth in Lending Act, which – rather than prohibiting any substantial class of transactions as imprudent – takes the less paternalistic approach of requiring the issuer to provide more information to the cardholder.

That approach is, of course, a common compromise solution in the American regulatory regime. In some contexts, disclosure makes sense. For example, disclosure can be useful in contexts like securities markets, where sophisticated intermediaries can receive and process information that would be of little value to most individual investors.[24] As Chapter 12 emphasizes, however, the disclosures required by TILA are made at a point when a consumer is less likely to process the information with adequate rationality. Thus, the existing disclosure system is ineffective and arguably a waste of money. Similarly, the legislation promoting so-called Schumer boxes is merely an aggravation of the existing problem, not an improvement.[25] And England's pending decision to adopt a similar disclosure requirement is equally unfortunate.[26]

Collectively, the system produces complicated paper disclosures that are not comprehensible to the typical consumer. The information contained in the disclosures – for example, the total amount of interest that will be paid over time – is not particularly useful. Consumers are unlikely even to read the disclosures and most unlikely to act more intelligently if they do. A related problem is that the existence of the disclosure scheme undermines political pressure to provide an effective response. For example, card issuers have relied on the existence of Schumer boxes to justify the fact that cardholders in the United States do not see the terms of their agreements until the card has been issued.[27]

It is not clear, however, that all disclosures would be ineffective. The existing disclosure regime (under TILA) focuses on the point of contracting.[28] Disclosures at that point require a forward-looking assessment of future transactions, as Chapter 12 emphasizes. TILA requires no disclosures at the point of purchase or borrowing.[29] If consumers currently fail to appreciate the significance of their actions at the moments when they purchase or borrow, then disclosures at those points might be effective.

DISCLOSURE AT THE POINT OF BORROWING

If the problem with credit cards relates to borrowing, the most obvious point to focus a disclosure would be at the point of borrowing. In the American system, this is the point at which cardholders select the amount of their monthly payments. Supporting a regulatory response is the possibility that consumers will fail to appreciate the consequences of making low monthly payments. Under the current system, low minimum payments join with the increased reliance of card issuers on fees as part of a system that can lead to aggregate outstanding balances far in excess of the original borrowed amount. Chapter 16 suggests several reasons why we ought to require larger minimum payments.

Still, at this point in the discussion, there is reason to consider a purely informational reform that might attempt to influence the cardholder's payment decision. Because the relevant information is tailored to each particular bill, it seems implausible that sophisticated intermediaries could filter and assess information on behalf of cardholders.[30] Hence, a judicious response would settle for the disclosure of information that is sufficiently simple to be understood by a typical cardholder and to be implemented by an issuer relatively cheaply.

Presently, disclosures need not go beyond the mechanical information necessary for explanation of the status of the account.[31] The point of a more robust disclosure would be to enhance the rationality of the bill-payment decision a customer makes in response to that bill. I suggest a requirement that each account statement also include the date by which a cardholder would pay its balance in full if it made no further purchases and continued to make equal monthly payments in an amount equal to the last monthly payment. Thus, a March 1, 2005, statement to a cardholder that paid half of the bill in February 2005 might indicate that the balance would be paid in full with two further payments. A similar statement to a cardholder that paid only 3% of a balance accruing interest at 18% (far beyond a typical minimum payment) should indicate that a stream of similar payments would repay the balance in full in December 2008.

By comparison, the new disclosure requirements adopted in Section 1301 of the Bankruptcy Abuse Prevention and Consumer Protection Act of 2005 seem more likely to confuse than to illuminate. Specifically, the new disclosures must provide a hypothetical example of the time that it would take to repay a stated balance at a stated interest rate. There is little reason to think that any particular example would match the balance, interest rate, or payment habits of any particular cardholder. Accordingly, it would be difficult for any cardholder to obtain any useful information from such an example. Thus, many cardholders are likely to assume that their account would be paid in roughly the same number of months as the hypothetical account if they made payments of a similar share of the outstanding balance. Given the state of information technology today, the marginal costs of providing a tailored example to each bill could not amount to more than the cost of monthly postage. The ease of providing such information is evident from the automated calculators readily available on the Internet.[32] Further evidence is available from a recent GAO study. That study reports information obtained from issuers indicating that customized disclosures would be relatively inexpensive. It also reports the results of a survey in which cardholders report that customized disclosures would be quite useful, especially to cardholders that revolve balances.[33] If the reasoning here is correct – that those disclosures would be even more useful than customers understand – then the case for requiring them seems clear.

DISCLOSURE AT THE POINT-OF-SALE

The final possibility is to regulate the information provided to customers at the point-of-sale. Presently, federal law does not require disclosures at the point-of-sale for credit transactions governed by TILA, although it does require a tangible acknowledgment of the transaction (typically a printed receipt) for transactions governed by the EFTA.

Point-of-sale disclosures would remedy the confusion problem highlighted in Chapter 2. If consumers do not understand whether they are using a debit or credit feature when they use a payment card, they cannot be expected to understand that they are financing the purchase if the credit feature is used. Nor can they be expected to understand the finality consequences for the underlying sales transaction if the debit feature is used.

The need for point-of-sale disclosure is further underscored by the importance to credit card issuers of fees incurred at the point-of-sale (in particular overlimit fees). Although the fees once were small, they have risen rapidly in recent years, now typically exceeding $30 at the largest and most prominent issuers.[34] Disclosures would help to the extent those fees reflect an imperfect ability to manage the credit card account. In other words, if the transaction does not exceed the limit because of a crisis-driven need to borrow, but because of a lack of information as to the amount of the balance on any particular card at any particular time, a point-of-sale reminder of the account balance might cause a consumer to respond differently. The consumer could switch to another payment device or discontinue the sales transaction entirely.

My analysis assumes that fees often are incurred because of mistakes. To test that assumption, it would be useful to have information on the relation between late fees and penalty fees on the one hand, and financial distress on the other.[35] Specifically, it would be useful to know what share of accounts that pay late charges or overlimit fees become delinquent by thirty days within twelve months after payment of such a fee and the extent to which that share differs significantly from the share in the overall pool of cardholders. My hypothesis is that there would be little significant risk of delinquency presented by cardholders that incur an overlimit fee or a late charge for a payment less than five days late, and have not incurred a similar charge during the preceding twelve months. I am influenced by the occasional willingness of commercial lenders to agree that late fees are due only if a borrower misses a due date multiple times in a single year. A more aggressive response would cap late fees. British regulators have proposed such a cap, arguing that "fair" charges should not exceed a reasonable estimate of administrative costs that the issuer expects to incur as a result of default.[36] This might make sense to the extent that the fees result from mismanagement of information, as opposed to increased risk of default.

As to the substance of the disclosures, cardholders should be told at the time of each transaction the amount of their credit line, the amount of credit available at the time of the transaction, and the amount of any overlimit or other fees that would be charged for engaging in the transaction. In transactions that are authorized online with a contemporaneous electronic communication from the issuer, the relevant information could be transmitted to the merchant along with the authorization; the merchant's payment terminal could display the information to the cardholder before the cardholder finally approves the transaction. As mentioned earlier, EFTA already requires a paper receipt in electronic point-of-sale payments.[37] Essentially, this would be similar to the common screen requiring the cardholder to approve a fee charged by an out-of-system ATM machine before the transaction proceeds.

My proposal is influenced by the borrowing patterns in Japan. It is likely that the low use of borrowing on credit cards in Japan rests largely on the *ikkai barai* system under which a cardholder must make an affirmative decision to borrow at the point-of-sale. The system I contemplate differs in that it would simply bring the extent of existing borrowing to the cardholder's attention. It would not require a cardholder to verbalize the intention to borrow and communicate it to the merchant at the counter. Thus, the disclosure probably would have a considerably smaller effect on borrowing than the Japanese system. Still, the parallel suggests that this type of reform could have important positive effects.

I also am influenced by the psychological literature discussed in Chapter 4. That literature suggests that, for reasons not yet fully understood, the card itself triggers spending activity without careful consideration by the customer. Thus, Feinberg suggests that cardholders become conditioned to associate the logo with the pleasure of spending activity.[38] Joydeep Srivastava and Priya Praghubir suggest that the difficulty is that the point of expenditure is insufficiently painful to give the spending decision sufficient prominence in the mind of the spender.[39] In either case, there is a possibility that a small amount of prominent information – the total amount owed on the card at the moment of purchase – could break the link.

The biggest concern with the point-of-sale disclosure system I propose relates to the costs of executing it. The Federal Reserve recently estimated that the costs of disclosing fees in debit transactions would be in the range of $5 to $10 billion.[40] I am skeptical that point-of-sale disclosures are as expensive as the Federal Reserve suggests, in part because the Federal Reserve appears to have accepted industry estimates of high costs for such things as reprogramming network accessible databases to provide the relevant information, without recognizing the increasingly routine nature of changes to the technology of such databases.

In any event, a process that included industry consultation to facilitate an adequate transition period and standardization of format could minimize the costs of implementation. Moreover, whatever the costs of such a system might be today, they certainly will continue to decline rapidly with advances in information technology and the accompanying advances in the sophistication of typical merchant terminals and payment-processing networks. Even if the costs were of approximately the magnitude that the Federal Reserve estimates, the proposal seems easily worthwhile. The costs would amount to about one-half of 1% of annual credit card volume in the United States. Viewed in comparison to the outstanding debt, a simple back-of-the-envelope calculation suggests that issuers could recoup the costs over a three-year period by an increase in what would amount to an interest-rate premium of about three-tenths of 1% per annum.[41]

Disclosure at the point-of-sale would require considerable delineation before it could be enacted, and it would not be practical for Congress to articulate the details of the proposal. Among other things, the proposal would depend on alterations in the method by which terminals process transactions, and details about such things could be ironed out only after consultation with affected industry groups: terminal manufacturers, issuers, acquirers, and merchants. Moreover, it might be impractical to extend the proposal to the small share of transactions that are cleared without contemporaneous electronic authorization.[42]

Federal data protection laws provide a good model. Responding to heightened concerns about identity theft, Congress in 2003 enacted the Fair and Accurate Credit Transactions Act (the FACT Act).[43] The FACT Act adds several new provisions to the Fair Credit Reporting Act. Among other things, the FACT Act requires entities that accept credit cards to truncate card account numbers on electronically printed receipts. To limit transition costs, the truncation requirement is phased in for older terminals over a three-year period.[44] A similar phase-in here would lower implementation costs considerably.

Segmenting Payment/Credit Functions

Throughout the book, I have emphasized the lack of segmentation in the U.S. payment card market and have suggested that strategies to push the U.S. card market toward the global norm would be constructive. Recently, a number of American academics have made broader proposals aimed at addressing the fuzziness of the payment and borrowing functions. In my view, proposals of that sort warrant careful scrutiny, primarily because of the risk that an ill-considered proposal will undercut the efficiencies of the existing systems unnecessarily.

As Chapter 3 emphasizes, perhaps the most important feature of the credit card is that it is a uniquely effective and inexpensive mechanism for consumer lending. Therefore, any policy initiative that targets the credit card must start from the premise that the credit card as a retail-borrowing vehicle must be preserved. The evidence from other countries discussed in Chapters 8 and 9 makes this point. For example, Japan, until recently, did not permit banks to issue revolving credit cards. The effect of that policy has been a somewhat diminished level of consumer borrowing and much higher interest rates for the borrowing that occurs. In a country that has struggled for more than a decade to find ways to stimulate economic growth, this cannot be salutary. Similarly, Germany has developed a consumer credit alternative that relies on checking-account overdrafts as a substitute for the credit card, but that product is much less desirable than the card. For one thing, it almost by definition can be issued only by the consumer's depositary bank. That vitiates competition among credit providers for the business of any particular consumer. More broadly, the product is not well suited to the risk-based underwriting and pricing that have facilitated efficient lending in the United States. It would not be impossible to design an overdraft product with close tailoring to individual customers, but it certainly has not occurred in Germany or other EU countries in which the overdraft vehicle is dominant.

Thus, I think it would be a bad idea to limit the use of credit cards – either directly or through some default rule requiring transactions to be treated as debit transactions unless the cardholder objects.[45] For one thing, although I obviously support the general point that regulators should focus on the credit/debit decision at the point-of-sale, this particular idea tips the scales toward dual-use cards that can be used for either debit or credit. As I show in Part III, the widespread use of those cards is a unique feature of the American market that arguably is responsible for the high level of borrowing. My argument is that we would accomplish a great deal more if we could separate the functions onto different cards – one debit card and one (or more) credit cards – and create incentives under which customers would choose to make their routine daily purchases with debit cards, not credit cards.

It also is relevant that the adverse consequences of mistakes, fraud, and identity theft related to debit card accounts are considerably more severe than with credit cards.[46] In that context – where debit card use is considerably more risky than credit card use – a default rule shifting payment transactions into riskier legal schemes has its own costs. To be sure, those problems could be mitigated by changes to the legal rules that govern debit cards, but those changes would interfere significantly with the ability of merchants to obtain finality in sales transactions.[47]

Finally, any proposal that relies on deposit accounts necessarily will impose some competitive disadvantage on monoline card lenders – issuers like MBNA, Providian, and Capital One that do not have any substantial base of depositary customers. Those lenders are central to the modern market in the United States – they issue the overwhelming majority of credit cards used by U.S. cardholders. Competition from those issuers is largely responsible for the relatively low rates in the United States – at least by comparison with places like Germany, Japan, and the United Kingdom. UK regulators, for example, have held hearings challenging their small group of issuers to explain why UK card prices are so much higher than U.S. prices.[48] Unless policymakers want to usher in an era of designedly uncompetitive pricing for consumer borrowers, it would not make sense to enact proposals that will disadvantage those issuers.

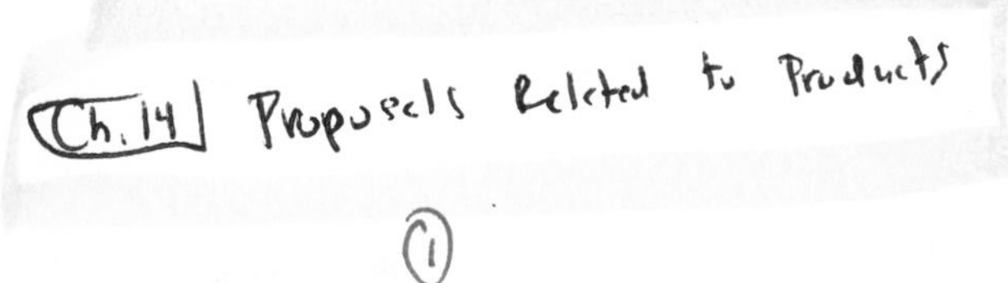

14 Product Design: Affinity and Rewards Programs and Teaser Rates

If issuers conceal contract terms related to default, fees, and penalty rates, and avoid meaningful disclosures of account information, on what product features do they compete? The two product features I have chosen to highlight are affinity and rewards programs and teaser rates. Both of those features lower the marginal cost of using a credit card. Both are features on which issuers compete, which clearly attract consumers. Both are terms that consumers probably overestimate in value. Both encourage consumers to spend or borrow more than they otherwise would.

Affinity and Rewards Programs

In the case of an affinity program, the incentive to spend is indirect: the cardholder is motivated by the fact that some portion of the profits or receipts from use of the card will be paid to the affinity sponsor. If the cardholder derives utility from such a payment – a Democrat, for example, might benefit from payments to the Democratic Party from Providian, the issuer of a Democratic Party affinity card[1] – then the gratification gives the cardholder a positive reason for using the card. Rewards programs do the same thing more directly by providing some tangible benefit that is tied to use of the card, such as a cash rebate[2] or airline miles.[3]

Affinity and rewards programs are a major part of the competition by which different issuers retain customers and encourage them to spend.[4] In Australia, for example, policymakers believe that the singular rise of credit card spending in that country[5] is attributable to aggressive and effective implementation of such programs by Australian issuers.[6] It is difficult to overestimate their importance to the industry's growth. The share of loyalty cards in the United States has grown from 10% to 25% since 2000, while the market share of standard cards has fallen from 57% to 36% (with cobranded cards making up the third category).[7] As card use grows in other countries, the loyalty program is a major factor.[8] The reason that affinity cardholders are attractive is the industry's perception that they are better customers. Recent data suggest that the average monthly expenditure on a rewards card is $943, compared to $360 on a card that does not offer a reward.[9]

The variety and sophistication of the programs increase rapidly as technological advances permit greater differentiation of benefits.[10] For example, MBNA attributes much of its growth and profitability over the last decade to its position as the market leader in the development of affinity and rewards programs. To give my favorite specific example, Citibank has had great success in recent years with a program (its Upromise Card) in which a percentage of purchases is invested as a college savings plan for children of the cardholder.

As a matter of payments policy, prohibition of rewards programs would directly increase the cost to the consumer of using a credit card and thus would do much to mitigate the cross-subsidization problem that has troubled overseas regulators focused on interchange fees. In addition, in contrast to the surcharge rules discussed in Chapter 11, there is good reason to think that this kind of reform would have a substantial impact. First, the fact that debit card usage is rising so rapidly even in the United States – where affinity programs are pervasive for credit cards and uncommon for debit cards – suggests that consumers in fact perceive some of the risks associated with using a credit card. Second, the limited available evidence suggests that consumers are highly sensitive even to small per-item transaction charges. In this context, for example, one recent story declared the market advantages of a program that provides affinity benefits as a device to help persuade tenants in Manhattan to use credit cards to pay their rent.[11] Thus, a shift in the relative advantages of different payment systems – lowering the attractiveness of the credit card by approximately 1% of the transaction value[12] – might shift consumers away from credit cards and toward debit cards in a significant way. Given the data discussed in Chapter 4 about the relation between credit card usage and total borrowing, that shift alone could be valuable.

It is less clear that a ban on affinity programs – which benefit cardholders only indirectly through the possible transfer of funds to the affinity sponsor (the Democratic Party in the example discussed earlier) – would be beneficial. Absent data to the contrary, I doubt that affinity programs alone are likely to affect overall credit card spending patterns, although they may drive purchases toward affinity cards. MBNA's annual reports, for example, show that its affinity cardholders spend more than typical cardholders do. However, it is just as likely that the affinity programs are attractive to cardholders that spend more, as it is that the programs cause them to spend more. It seems much more credible to think that conventional rewards programs – Discover's 1% cashback program, for example – elevate spending because of the direct and tangible reward.

I also doubt that retailer cards are afflicted. In the context of retailer cards, an affinity program is simply a discount for volume purchasing. Because the seller receives all of the revenue from the covered sales transaction, the retailer cards do not raise the same price-discrimination problems as third-party cards. It presumably would not be difficult to draft regulations that specify how the provision would apply to cards issued by entities that are distinct from the retailer, but under common control with the retailer.

It is, to be sure, less clear that a ban on rewards programs would match a reduction in imprudent credit card borrowing. Press reports suggest that the 2001 repeal of a similar law in Germany has been followed by rapid increases in credit card usage.[13] It is not clear yet, however, whether that increase in usage will lead to a substantial increase in credit card debt.[14]

However, there is one narrow group of rewards programs, conditioning benefits on a cardholder's bill-payment practices, that directly affects borrowing. Specifically, the programs provide affinity benefits only to cardholders that do not repay their bills completely each month.[15] Another variant (offered by American Express) increases the amount of the normal rewards benefit for cardholders that carry a monthly balance.[16] In a sense, the programs provide rewards benefits as a rebate out of the interest revenues earned by the issuers. Because they are tied

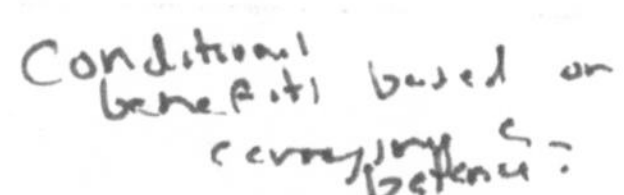

directly to borrowing, a ban of conditional benefits programs would respond directly to both the cross-subsidization problem and the prodigality problem.

At first glance, of course, a ban on affinity and rewards programs seems politically insane – a statute designed to protect consumers that takes away something consumers value. In a way, the question is whether it is feasible politically to characterize the charges as kickbacks paid to encourage inappropriate behavior. To be sure, the basis for regulatory intervention is largely paternalistic: Consumers do not accurately understand the costs of credit, and they are particularly vulnerable to prodigality when the credit is extended through the convenience of a credit card. Of course, as emphasized in the preceding chapters, there is good reason to think that this particular type of prodigality imposes costs on the rest of society when it leads to financial distress. A cardholder's willingness to accept a kickback to impose external risks on the rest of us is not a salutary exercise of free will.

Another likely concern is that eliminating affinity and rewards programs would simply make credit card issuing even more profitable than it is now. To understand that point, consider data from Australia, where affinity and rewards programs are much less pervasive than they are in the United States. There, affinity programs cost about forty-six cents per transaction, about 20% of all of the expenses of issuers on their card programs.[17] Removing the costs of affinity programs would raise the profits of card issuers substantially. However, that assumes that all of the pricing is entirely independent and that removal of affinity and reward expenses would have no effect on the prices set at the other exchange points in the network. That is a naïve view of the economics of credit card networks. It is much more likely that credit card markets – at least in the competition among issuers for active cardholders – are relatively competitive, despite the highly oligopolistic structure.[18] Data from Australia, for example, suggest that the amount by which issuer revenues exceed the costs of their operations and a reasonable profit is almost exactly the amount by which they subsidize their cardholders with affinity and rewards programs.[19]

This suggests at least the possibility that in the relative near-term, a ban on affinity and reward programs would result in a drop in interchange rates through the simple press of competition, as outlined in the economic models about the rational operation of a card network. If that occurs, then the cross-subsidization problem would be mitigated from a second side, reducing the cost differential that merchants face (as well as the negative cost that attracts consumers). If we could be sure that would be the outcome, then we might expect merchants (as well as customers too impecunious to have rewards-based cards) to support the reforms as well.

In the end, the political viability of a ban on rewards programs depends on the perspective of the regulator in question. Any regulator that takes the prodigality problem seriously should want to prohibit programs that reward carrying a monthly balance. Given the empirical evidence of a link between debt and financial distress, together with the intuitive plausibility of the relationship, rewards programs offer a good place to start any such reform.

Moving forward, other regulators might wish to act more broadly. For example, a regulator highly motivated to solve the cross-subsidization problem might view a broader ban on all rewards as an important option. Conversely, a regulator less interested in that problem and less persuaded by the evidence I present about the adverse effects of credit card spending might be concerned that the proposal interferes with market transactions that are not tied with sufficient directness to the problem. Still, a regulator that takes seriously the concerns discussed in Part II and the empirical evidence presented about the costs associated with credit card spending should take seriously the broader ban on all rewards programs.

Teaser Rates

My initial reaction was that a ban on teaser rates would intrude too far into the market. The interest rate seems to be one of the product attributes on which the contracting market is most likely to be effective. As discussed in Chapter 12, the psychological and economic literature on consumer decision making suggests that consumers identify a small number of product attributes (not more than about five) and compare products based on those attributes. Consumer reactions to teaser rates are likely to fall into two classes. Consumers who are confident that they will not borrow in the immediate future will not care about the rate at all, so there is no reason to ban the rate based on its appeal to them. Consumers that expect to borrow, by contrast, are likely to notice the teaser rate and react to it.

However, I have come to view teaser rates as a form of reward program that is tied specifically to borrowing. The concern from that vantage point is that consumers that are attracted to the rate will assess it inappropriately. Specifically, consumers might fail to appreciate the consequences of the introductory period. They might overestimate their chances of switching to another teaser card at the conclusion of the teaser period. They might overestimate their chances of paying off all of their balances by the end of the teaser period. Alternatively, they might simply misunderstand the consequences of the rate increase at the end of the teaser period. The costs of permitting teaser rates are the costs of those errors. The size of those errors is an empirical question as to which reasonable minds can differ – certainly some substantial group of consumers makes those errors some of the time.

There is, of course, a counterbalancing benefit, which is that consumers in fact benefit directly from the teaser rates. Consumers that read teaser card solicitations, understand them accurately, acquire the cards, and repay balances before the conclusion of the teaser period benefit from those offers. Again, it seems clear that some group of consumers obtains those benefits. Of course, a similar group of cardholders closely tracks the airline miles issued on their cards and redeems them annually in values that exceed the annual fees charged on their cards. Probably, in each case, a small group.

The policy question, then, is whether it is appropriate to ban this particular choice – to protect the consumers who will misunderstand these offers and harm themselves by accepting them, at the cost of depriving the consumers that benefit from the offers through accepting them. To phrase it differently, the question is whether we see positive social value in an offer that is profitable to the issuer only if customers that accept it ultimately borrow funds from the issuer after the conclusion of the teaser period.

Again, a straightforward value choice is presented. We cannot practically ban all marketing efforts that offer discounts to new customers. To justify a ban in this particular context, policymakers must believe that the product to which customers are attracted – borrowing on a credit card – is a product that the customer does not adequately evaluate or that imposes external social harm. If the credit card presented as easy a choice as the cigarette, most would agree that these kinds of restrictions would be appropriate. Because of the countervailing benefits of card usage, the policy choice is harder. For me, the key consideration is a desire to push cardholders whenever possible from credit cards to debit cards and newer forms of payment. To the extent that bans on these programs have that effect, the salutary consequences are important.

PART V

Optimizing Consumer Credit Markets and Bankruptcy Policy

Sir Walter Scott was a dominating literary figure at the dawn of the nineteenth century. From poems like "The Lay of the Last Minstrel" and "The Lady of the Lake" to novels like *Old Mortality, The Heart of Midlothian,* and *The Bride of Lammermoor,* his works display not only an endearing and perceptive infatuation with the troubled history of his Scottish homeland, but a genius of "extraordinary range" and "the greatest diversity of realistic human characters outside Shakespeare."[1] Still, though his work has provided an addictive fascination to generations of readers and served as a fount of inspiration to later writers and composers, critical opinions of his work vary widely. It is fair to say that the received wisdom is that his early brilliance was compromised by the less imaginative work that occupied the last years of his life.

For present purposes, however, Scott is more useful as an example of financial distress. The story is well known. After a dispute with the publisher of his early (and financially successful) poems, Scott founded a new publishing house in 1809 with the Ballantyne Brothers, which quickly became seriously indebted to one Archibald Constable. Over the next few years, Scott's various activities, many of them backed or financed by Ballantyne and Constable, left Scott with debts of about £120,000, quite a large sum, even for the most successful writer of his age. Like many modern individuals, Scott's debts were a tangled mixture of consumer spending (mostly to improve his estate at Abbotsford) and entrepreneurial activity (mostly risk-taking either in borrowing money on the strength of works he had not yet written or in expending money to publish the works of lesser-known favorites of his).

In the end, Constable became insolvent because of speculative investments that failed in connection with an 1825 panic in London. Because Scott's borrowings had left him with secondary liability on many of Constable's obligations, Scott was unable to satisfy his own obligations. One option available to Scott was to file bankruptcy, which would have provided considerable relief, although he would have lost his estate at Abbotsford and several public offices that he held dear. Instead, Scott chose to enter into a voluntary arrangement with his creditors, under which they would receive all revenues from subsequent literary works until Scott's debts were repaid. The remaining six years of Scott's life were consumed by a grinding productivity that produced a torrent of novels and other works. The earnings from Scott's works ultimately did pay off his debts, but not until fifteen years after his death, which surely was hastened by the pace of work and emotional strain of those last years.

Some regard Scott as a signal example of the good old days, when a combination of stigma, shame, and the rigors of bankruptcy prevented an easy flight from obligation. So, for example, Judge Edith Jones and Todd Zywicki describe this and the story of Mark Twain as "the tales of honest and noble individuals . . . who worked for years to repay their debts . . . "[2] More generally, they valorize the choice to avoid bankruptcy:

> Bankruptcy represents a repudiation of one's promises, a decision not to bestow a reciprocal benefit on someone who has given you something of value. As a result, filing bankruptcy traditionally has been treated as a socially shameful act. Promise-keeping and an instinct for fairness and reciprocity are deeply embedded in our natures and underlie our social structure. It is not surprising that most people feel great personal shame from a failure to keep their promises. It is also not surprising that society punishes and stigmatizes an individual's failure to keep his promises. Personal shame and social stigma go hand-in-hand. Shame is the internal, psychological compass that forces one to keep his word; stigma is the external, social constraint that reinforces this.[3]

There is, of course, some truth in that perspective, however much it brings to mind the style of Gradgrind in Dickens' *Hard Times*. Still, it is not unreasonable to look with disappointment on the poor work – "trashy" in Scott's own words[4] – that occupied the last years of his life. Would society as a whole have been better off if Scott's entrepreneurial debts had been wiped away and he had written three great literary works during those last six years? What if he had not literally worked himself to death and instead had an additional five years within which to produce a masterpiece to crown his oeuvre? Would it matter if spillovers from those works had led to important follow-on creations – perhaps another series of major operas like those founded on earlier novels? More prosaically, is society better off if the perils of entrepreneurial failure deter people like Scott from taking the risks involved in starting the business ventures that were largely responsible for Scott's insolvency?

* * *

A prominent theme of this book is that credit cards are the main instrument for discretionary and entrepreneurial spending in modern economies. They have a pervasive influence over many consumer lending and payment transactions. They introduce substantial cost savings by shifting consumers from paper-based payments and closed-end bank loans to card-based (and mostly electronic) payment and borrowing transactions. In addition, they are available to entrepreneurs even when conventional bank lending is not. Yet credit cards do not just speed up checkout lines and reduce the waiting times in bank lobbies. They blur the lines between conventional payment and borrowing decisions, and, in doing so, they are associated with substantial increases in consumer spending and borrowing levels. Moreover, those trends are occurring against a backdrop of increased demands on social welfare programs and rising bankruptcy rates.

Part IV addressed the instrument-induced risk of the credit card and made several proposals that respond to the problems associated with credit card spending. Those problems are particularly serious in markets like the United States where the same cards are used as payment and lending devices. Yet those policies are not a complete fix; they will not solve a problem that arises directly out of the use of credit cards to borrow money. Because of the misalignment of incentives between participants in card markets and cognitive defects that cause consumers to misestimate risks, it seems likely that the excessive borrowing problem will persist. To respond to that concern, Part V looks more closely at bankruptcy policy and credit market regulation in the modern age of the credit card.

In Chapter 15, I begin by sorting out some of the realities of consumer lending markets, focusing on the ways that the leniency of the bankruptcy system might affect the size of those markets and the ways in which the openness of the credit markets might drive the need for a lenient bankruptcy system. In Chapter 16, I turn to consumer credit regulation. Generally, I argue that usury reforms have only a limited prospect for success, largely because of their inability to distinguish between value-increasing and value-decreasing transactions. Thus, I propose two alternate approaches. The first would be to impose mandatory minimum payments on credit card contracts. Although that might be useful, a better approach, I argue, would be a tax on distressed debt, particularly defaulted credit card debt. Finally, in Chapter 17, I return to bankruptcy policy, challenging the assumption of existing work that the purpose of bankruptcy policy should be to alter the incentives of borrowers to avoid financial distress and bankruptcy. Rather, I contend, the task is to allocate the losses between borrowers and lenders in a way that minimizes the net costs of financial distress. Generally, I argue that this calls for rules placing more risks on lenders, so that they will have an incentive to use information technology to limit the costs of distress.

15 Causation, Consumer Credit, and Bankruptcy

The ambiguity of the link between consumer credit and bankruptcy creates real challenges for policymakers. For example, academics have explored the likelihood that expansion of the bankruptcy discharge can both increase the demand for credit and decrease the supply.[1] Similar work has considered the effect of bankruptcy exemptions on the supply and demand for credit.[2] An important problem for either analysis, underscored by Tom Jackson, has been the likelihood that quasi-rational behavioral biases of consumers undermine the policy prescriptions one might draw from models focused on fully rational actors.[3]

Historical and political economy perspectives, in contrast, focus on the possibility that the expansion of the supply of credit necessitates a broader discharge. Several writers, for example, have pointed out the progression from relaxation of consumer credit regulations in much of western Europe in the 1980s, to increased financial distress by consumers, and finally to the adoption of bankruptcy systems that offer an increasingly more accessible discharge.[4] Political economists argue that globalizing economies must provide some form of relief (here, the bankruptcy discharge) for consumers who bear the adverse effects of the unforgiving competitive markets that globalization induces (here, those who borrow to the point of financial distress).[5] Indeed, the United States appears to be unique in responding to rising levels of credit-induced financial distress by making the bankruptcy process less friendly to debtors. I should not make too much of this point, because in many respects the American system still could be viewed as one of the most, if not the most, lenient. From that perspective, some (though certainly not I) might argue that the comparative trends reflect convergence on an ideal system.[6]

In truth, however, the link is considerably more complex than those perspectives suggest. For example, data and policy about consumer credit blend two markets with distinct macroeconomic implications and justifications. Thus, a dominating motivation for opening consumer credit markets is the hope that an increase in consumer credit will jump-start consumer spending and thus lead to overall growth of the economy. Although the academic literature supports the idea that loosening credit constraints can increase personal consumption, it is much more ambiguous on the relation between personal consumption and real economic growth.[7] However, the policy intuition is widely followed in the United States and elsewhere.[8] The most noted example is South Korea, discussed in Chapter 10. At the same time, there seems to be a link between entrepreneurship and economic growth. Because entrepreneurs often use personal loans to fund their businesses,[9] the robustness of the bankruptcy system is thought to be an incentive to entrepreneurialism.[10] A telling example is the Enterprise Act of 2002, which lowered the discharge period in the United Kingdom from three years to one year.[11] Part of the justification was the intuition that a broader discharge would encourage entrepreneurial risk taking.

Academics have tried to test that intuition quantitatively. John Armour, for example, suggests that the leniency of the bankruptcy discharge is associated with measures of the level of entrepreneurial risk taking – venture-capital investment activity and self-employment, in particular.[12] Michelle White has presented data suggesting that increases in property-exemption levels help to foster small business formation by providing a form of implicit wealth insurance.[13] In a related paper, using plausible values for the level of opportunistic activity in existing debt markets, her models indicate that the optimal bankruptcy system would have a substantial and nonwaivable postbankruptcy income exemption – something much like Chapter 7 of the Bankruptcy Code as it existed before 2005.[14] More recently, a study by Robert Lawless and Elizabeth Warren shows that many personal bankruptcy filings are due to small business failures,[15] suggesting that entrepreneurs do use the bankruptcy system as a safety net.

Previous academic analyses of credit policy have not focused on the difficulties of untangling the separate effects that entrepreneurial and consumer lending have on credit and bankruptcy policy. A complete analysis, however, must account for the separate effects of both types of activity.

Understanding the Link

It is easier to recognize that there is a link between consumer credit and bankruptcy than to understand what that link is. To say anything informative about the policy implications of the interaction, it is necessary to develop some factual premises about how one affects the other. Thus, it requires some understanding of the causative effects that run from borrowing to bankruptcy and from bankruptcy to borrowing.

FROM BORROWING TO BANKRUPTCY

At first glance, it seems odd to ask whether borrowing causes bankruptcy. Of course it does. How easy is it to become bankrupt without debt? The point here, however, is to understand the policy ramifications of the link between borrowing and bankruptcy. For example, assuming that there is an optimal level of bankruptcy and that current levels are hyperoptimal (at least in the United States), why is it that the parties to lending transactions do such a poor job of estimating the risks of those transactions? It should be no surprise that I think the credit card is at least one of the major culprits,[16] and that the answer is found in the separate points of agreement, purchase, and borrowing that characterize credit card transactions.

The separation of the three points in the credit card lending transaction hinders a borrower's assessment of the risks and returns of card transactions. The first point is the time of account opening – when the contract that will govern the borrowing is made. This point has little significance to the overall transaction, because the borrower has not made a decision to use the card. The second point is the time of the purchase – when the decision to spend is made. The third point is the time of the monthly bill – when the decision to borrow is made. The crucial decision point is deferred at least until the time of the purchase. In that context, it is difficult to countenance the assumption that contracting decisions rationally assess the risks and rewards of a particular borrowing transaction – the general foundation of the economic literature on consumer credit. That assumption does not map in any plausible way to the transactional structure of the dominant retail payment system in the American economy.

Structural considerations aside, the data in Chapters 4 and 5 bear out the idea that credit cards are unique contributors to the overindebtedness problem, an idea that is inconsistent with the view that credit cards merely substitute for other less efficient forms of consumer lending. The data indicate that credit card debt correlates with subsequent increases in consumer bankruptcy, even when overall borrowing is held constant. Therefore, in a country in which annual credit card debt increases by about $100 per capita, there is an increase in bankruptcy filings one year later of about 200 per million people.

That problem might raise no substantial concern if borrowers and lenders were the only ones affected by excessive borrowing. It might reflect a value transfer from consumer borrowers to lenders, or a diversion of consumer resources toward the repayment of loans and away from investment or spending – indirect effects that would not justify broad policy responses. In fact, however, as Chapter 4 explains, consumer credit contracts generate substantial externalities, at least when they lead to financial distress. Thus, those designing regulatory policies for consumer credit markets and bankruptcy systems would be well advised to account for the causative link between borrowing and bankruptcy.

FROM BANKRUPTCY TO BORROWING

The converse question is the extent to which the existence of the bankruptcy system influences borrowing in the economy. On that point, for example, the dominant models of consumer credit markets examine a world populated by omnicompetent and wholly rational actors. In that world, a loosening of bankruptcy standards – to make bankruptcy less rigorous or more readily available – would lead to an increased demand for borrowing. The central concern of those models is the resolution of the moral hazard problem. ("Moral hazard" is the term economists use to describe the fact that insurance can change the behavior of the person being insured.) Thus, most scholars reason, rules that permit borrowers to display their repayment proclivities by accepting such remedies as arm-breaking are important to allow signaling that can prevent markets from unraveling as more borrowers succumb to the moral hazard.[17] That concern is the subject of Chapter 17.

More pointedly for present purposes, writers in the populist vein emphasize the possibility that a loosening of the rigors of bankruptcy might lead to opportunistic borrowing. Thus, they contend that consumers often borrow because they know that bankruptcy will forgive their obligation to repay the loan.[18] Yet what we know about the reality of bankruptcy filers makes it difficult to credit the opportunistic-borrowing theory. First, the existing literature includes a rich series of research projects designed to collect evidence about the nature of the people that file for consumer bankruptcy in the United States. Although that literature is nuanced and does not always provide firm conclusions,[19] it does suggest that the overwhelming majority of people that file for consumer bankruptcy in the United States are in deep financial distress.[20] Thus, that evidence suggests that the abusive and highly compensated filer, seeking to discharge luxurious consumer spending, is largely a myth.[21] Surely, there are abusive cases, but there is little reason to think that they are sufficiently frequent to undermine the need for a broad discharge.

We also now have the empirical evidence presented in Chapters 4 and 5 from a comparative study of nation-level data about consumer credit, credit card debt, and consumer bankruptcy in about two-thirds of the world credit card market. If the opportunistic-borrowing theory was correct, we would expect to see a steep rise in credit card debt shortly before bankruptcy (i.e., in the six months immediately preceding the bankruptcy). As bankruptcy grew closer, the causal connection between increases in credit card borrowing would grow more significant and display a substantially higher coefficient. As it happens, however, the evidence is contrary to that understanding. Rather, the evidence suggests that the relation between increases in borrowing and consumer bankruptcy plays out over a long period. This suggests a slow pattern in which consumers borrow ever farther beyond their means, leaving their financial position so fragile that they are unable to withstand the typical misfortunes so common in a global economy. Furthermore, statistical tests of household-level data have not provided a great deal of support for the opportunistic borrowing hypothesis.[22]

There is a distinct but related question about the relation between bankruptcy laws and bankruptcy filing rates. Although a bankruptcy system that provides more relief should lead to more filings than one that provides less relief, we know little empirically about the fine details of that point. For example, although the Japanese are thought by some to be the most culturally averse to bankruptcy,[23] the Japanese bankruptcy filing rates are now higher than bankruptcy filing rates in Australia and about the same as bankruptcy filing rates in the United Kingdom, apparently in response to the recently adopted Westernized consumer bankruptcy system.

The extent to which the higher filings rest on the new system, as opposed to cultural or institutional factors, is an important one, but one that cannot be resolved without detailed statistical analysis that has not yet been undertaken in any country. For example, evidence from Canada tends to suggest that debt levels have been much more important in the level of filings than anything else. Diane Ellis points out that bankruptcy filing rates in Canada rose quite rapidly after Visa entered the market. She compares that link to the similar rise in filings in the United States shortly after the deregulation of credit card interest rates. Her argument is that the increased filing rates in the United States are more likely attributable to higher credit card debt than to the major changes in U.S. bankruptcy law at about the same time.[24]

One of the hardest problems is that it is difficult to define leniency in this context. The American consumer bankruptcy system is often characterized as the most lenient, because of the immediate discharge and the automatic stay that it offers, with no requirement that debtors make payments out of future income. In Canada, by contrast, a discharge generally is not available for nine months, and a bankrupt debtor in any event is obligated to make payments of a large share (often 50% to 75%) of the income above the poverty level.[25] And in the United Kingdom, a discharge is available after a year as a result of a recent change that has just shortened that time from three years.[26] In Japan, to offer another example, there is no automatic stay and a discharge is available only upon a favorable determination with respect to the character of the bankrupt.[27]

But when you add means testing, broaden the categories of debts that are not dischargeable, and increase the period between permitted filings (all recent developments in U.S. consumer bankruptcy practice), it becomes less clear that the practical effect is more hospitable than a free and complete discharge to all after a short waiting period. It is even harder to assess the new administrative hurdles to filing (credit counseling, increased documentation, and lawyer certifications), which might limit filings by depriving potential filers of qualified advisers. Thus, any analysis that purports to predict the effects of any particular bankruptcy reform on filing rates must be met with at least some degree of skepticism.[28]

* * *

In sum, the existing evidence casts doubt on the gravity of the concern that lax bankruptcy policy will lead to opportunistic borrowing and a subsequent unraveling or deterioration of the consumer credit markets. If anything, the data suggest, particularly with respect to entrepreneurial borrowing, a loosened discharge could have positive spillover effects by increasing the demand for activity most likely to have positive external effects.

On Stigma

Views on the relation between the bankruptcy discharge and consumer economic activity are related to the problem of stigma, which has dominated academic and political debates about bankruptcy in the United States and elsewhere. Critics of the status quo claim that rising bankruptcy rates reflect a decline in moral fiber, evidenced by an undue readiness to accept relief in bankruptcy. Thus, the argument goes, there is a direct causal link between the improved public perception of bankruptcy in the last few decades and the large-scale increase in the number of people who file for bankruptcy.

It is unfortunate that this point is treated as a serious subject for policy debate. First, as noted earlier, the empirical data on this question point in one direction. Most filers in the United States are in situations of such extreme distress that it is not plausible to view bankruptcy as a planning tool for them. Indeed, it is unlikely that any particular feature of the legal system (beyond the availability of an automatic stay) would have a notable effect on their decision to file. In other words, it is just as likely that such individuals would file even under a much more onerous system. Efforts to make the system less accessible only increase the costs to both the filers and to the taxpayers that fund the system.

In addition, only a small portion of the individuals who could file actually does so.[29] Because it is difficult to collect data sets of people who have not filed for bankruptcy but are in financial circumstances comparable to people who do file, we know little or nothing about precisely what motivates the particular individuals who file. Without such data, it is difficult to credit the simplistic notion that the lack of stigma from bankruptcy is generally motivating them. If the decline in stigma is a general societal problem, why doesn't stigma motivate the millions of other similarly situated nonfilers?

Third, the studies suggesting that a decline in stigma has accounted for much of the filing surge since the enactment of the 1978 legislation are methodologically unsound. The general technique of the existing studies is to proceed by the circuitous route of identifying various other institutional reasons for filing changes, treating stigma as the cause of all remaining unexplained variation in filing rates.[30] Others use crude proxies for strength of social norms (measured, for example, by urban residency, Catholicism, and age).[31] For example, the most widely discussed paper is a 2002 study by David Gross and Nicholas Souleles.[32] Their study uses a proprietary data set of account information obtained from credit card issuers to track the propensity to default of particular cardholders. Their model explains about 13% of the variation in default rates, but suggests relationships on the basis of which they conclude that there was a significant increase in the propensity to default – a decline in stigma – between 1995 and 1997. My skepticism arises first from the oddity of the empirical conclusion – why should that particular biennium be the locus of a change in social perception we would expect to play out over decades? Turning to the analysis, the problem with that methodology is that, even taken on its own terms, it cannot possibly identify any share of filings attributable to a decline in the sense of the filers that their conduct is shameful, because that methodology cannot disentangle that effect from other closely related effects.

Moreover, the studies do not even do a credible job of including the plausible variables that might explain bankruptcy filings. Thus, the most obvious point about the Gross and Souleles study is that their lengthy list of variables does not directly account for the outstanding amount of credit card debt.[33] As I explain in Chapter 5, a relatively simple model has a better fit to a much more varied data set. My model explains more than 95% of the variation in bankruptcy filing rates in a data set from five different countries – even though it has many fewer data points. The same problem afflicts much of the other literature on the subject.[34]

More broadly, it is difficult to see how any such study, however carefully designed, could separate the effect of stigma from a learning-curve effect associated with increased awareness of the bankruptcy process. It is plain that consumer bankruptcy filings increase with increases in consumer debt. As filings increase, the average person might be more aware of the bankruptcy process and view it more charitably. Some of the change might simply be attributable to an accurate understanding of the process. Yet at the same time, increased awareness might cause some to fear bankruptcy filing even more than they did before. More importantly, it is difficult to connect the effects of increased awareness with actual filing patterns. The increased awareness is likely to affect a large number of people, of whom only a small number choose to file.

Finally, and most fundamentally, the acceptance of a stigma lever as a policy tool has unpleasant consequences, which seem perverse in light of the sociological literature and commonsense understandings of the negative effects of stigma. If we accept the possibility that even a substantial number of the current bankruptcy filers are forced into filing by exogenous circumstances that few could surmount, what is accomplished by increasing the sense of shame and blameworthiness we wish them to attach to their actions? Would we deal with the fallout of one-parent households by increasing the stigma of divorce? Judge Jones and Todd Zywicki apparently would.[35] To the contrary, most scholars who have studied the question from a family-law perspective have concluded that the decline of stigma has the positive effect of lessening the trauma of divorce.[36] As Mark West shows in his discussion of Japanese who use suicide to avoid the shame of financial insolvency, there are ways of responding to financial distress that have greater social cost than a bankruptcy filing.[37] In the end, we don't really want to live in a society where people, like Sir Walter Scott, elevate their repayment obligations into a life-or-death question.

16 Regulating Consumer Credit Markets

Most credit transactions are value-increasing for all parties. Notwithstanding the relation between an increase in borrowing and an increase in financial distress, the overwhelming majority of borrowers successfully repay their debts. Lenders in free markets presumably profit from most of those transactions, and borrowers presumably profit from almost all of them. Borrowers would profit from all of them if it were not for the likelihood that some borrowing transactions reflect poor judgment even if the borrower ultimately obtains the funds to repay the loan.

Moreover, many transactions will be valuable not only for the parties that participate in them, but for third parties as well. They will generate positive externalities, because the expenditures indirectly support the manufacturing and service sectors of the economy. Thus, as discussed in Chapter 15, there is some reason to expect a positive relation between increases in household indebtedness at one point in time and consumer expenditures and gross domestic product some years later. The goal, then, is to identify policies that burden the transactions most likely to impose costs on the rest of society, without imposing hurdles on the value-increasing transactions that reflect the bulk of consumer expenditures and borrowing.

As Part IV explains, some of the instrument-induced risk associated with the credit card could be managed by shifting payment transactions away from credit cards to other electronic payment systems (primarily debit cards). It might seem odd to think that a shift from credit cards to debit cards would have a substantial effect on prodigal expenditure and borrowing. The discussion above, however, suggests that a quasi-rational precommitment to enforced budgeting is the most plausible explanation for rising debit card use in the United States. If the debit card is associated with a practice of budgeting, then a shift from the credit card to the debit card could limit prodigality. If the shift is voluntary, it should not hinder the great mass of useful borrowing that occurs on credit cards.

Still, what we see from the United Kingdom – where credit card use as a share of plastic card use has remained small – is that a fully developed economy can develop a consumer debt load of troubling proportions even where debit cards are used to a much greater extent than they are in the United States.[1] The United Kingdom is not alone. Many of the countries with the most serious problems with burgeoning consumer credit are not countries in which the credit card has yet taken hold. Thus, although payment systems reform might do a great deal, especially in countries in which credit cards are dominant, further steps to control the social costs of excessive borrowing often will be appropriate.

Usury Regulations

A common response to the problems that afflict consumer credit markets has been to recommend formal price controls: a usury statute that would bar transactions above specific prices. For example, recent years have seen one version or another of that approach from academics of such widely varying perspectives as Elizabeth Warren and Eric Posner.[2]

Structurally, the usury proposals confront two foundational difficulties. The first is the acknowledged bluntness of usury as a tool to respond to social problems.[3] Consider the social problems that motivate the proponents of price controls. Posner worries about the external effects on the welfare system of risky credit transactions. Warren is concerned about high-priced borrowing that reflects poor judgment on the part of those that engage in it. In neither case, however, is the concern simply that the rate is too high. The idea in each case is that high interest rates are a useful proxy for the types of transactions that would justify market intervention.

There is little reason, however, to think that high interest rates are a particularly good proxy for the underlying concerns. Thus, any usury law necessarily will be both overinclusive and underinclusive. Posner recognizes this problem specifically. His model recognizes that a price limitation would ban some transactions that are value-increasing – risky but not prodigal transactions for which a high rate of interest is appropriate – and permit some transactions that impose externalities – prodigal borrowing that occurs at rates below the usury cap.

Because borrowers are heterogeneous and use borrowed funds in many different ways, the bluntness of the tool is a serious problem. If an omniscient regulator could not easily define a usury limit that would produce optimal benefits, we should be reluctant to expect that the conflicting interests that motivate legislative action will lead to anything that approximates a plausible usury limit.

The bluntness problem is aggravated by the rapid segmentation of the consumer borrowing market. Even fifteen years ago, credit card issuers charged borrowers in their portfolio one of a small number of rates, with few distinctions based on the relative creditworthiness of different customers in the portfolio. The lesson of the last ten years, however, is that information technology makes it much easier to loan larger amounts of money more reliably to individuals with worse credit histories. This has resulted in an increasingly sophisticated differentiation among borrowers, in which borrowers of different risks pay cognizably different rates of interest.[4] When it matches rates more accurately to the underlying risks, this kind of segmentation is beneficial. In the United States, for example, segmentation generally has been accompanied by a sharp decline in the effective interest rate charged on outstanding credit card debt.

To be sure, the rate of default on high interest loans is likely to be higher than the rate of defaults on a set of loans to persons of uniformly higher creditworthiness. Yet that says little about whether the transactions are so risky as to justify prohibiting them. What remains clear is that a usury regulation is not well designed to sort the undesirable transactions from the desirable ones.

Another major problem that any usury regulation must confront is the distortion it will impose on the credit market. The earlier discussion explains why a usury regulation will impose costs even if borrowers and lenders take no actions to avoid the application of the regulation. In fact, however, a usury regulation is likely to lead not only to the suppression of some transactions that impose externalities, but to the shifting of a substantial portion of the proscribed transactions either to markets that are beyond the scope of the regulation or to extralegal markets beyond the scope of any regulation.

For one thing, what little evidence we have suggests that the demand for credit is remarkably stable even across national, cultural, and regulatory boundaries. Therefore, low- and middle-income consumers have similar needs for credit everywhere, and regulatory constraints will not change that.[5] Because in practice usury regulations apply differentially and haphazardly to the highly segmented menu of consumer credit products, the potential for shifting among products – which might at first glance seem a trivial detail – is in fact a serious problem.[6]

The evidence is surprisingly varied. In Japan, for example, restrictions that have prevented banks from issuing revolving credit have led to a marginal decline in the amount of credit because of market shifts to lenders that are not as well situated as banks.[7] Nevertheless, it is also fair to think that the regulations have led to a much larger shift in lending to relatively unregulated nonbank consumer lenders (the *sarakin* and *yenya* of Japanese news media). Thus, the most notable effect of the prohibition has been to shift borrowers from the most heavily regulated and responsible lenders to the least regulated and responsible.[8] To be sure, if one believed that existing insolvency procedures are systematically too lenient, then a system that permitted people to opt into harsher procedures that involved corporal abuse or imprisonment could be optimal.[9] Although I am convinced of the value of harsh sanctions in the commercial context, I am willing to assume that in all of the important commercial nations (even the United States), the rigors of consumer bankruptcy as it currently exists are sufficient to make recourse to extralegal enforcement mechanisms suboptimal.

Similarly, American historians suggest that one of the main reasons regulators pushed for banks to enter the consumer credit market in the 1920s was to shift consumer lending from smaller and less reputable lenders to banks, which were thought to be kinder, gentler, and more reliable conduits for this activity.[10] More recently, empirical evidence about market shifts at the time of credit card rate deregulation in the United States in the early 1980s shows significantly different rates of shifts from finance companies to credit card lenders based on the nature of rate regulation.[11] Finally, the history of consumer mortgage lending in both

Canada and the United Kingdom shows a massive shift of the market to – and from – banks based on regulations that permit – or prohibit – banks from issuing consumer mortgages at market rates.[12]

The link between credit card borrowing and financial distress discussed in Part II might suggest that a shift from credit cards to other loan products would be beneficial. I think, however, that a shift induced by a low interest rate limit (in the range of 18%) in fact would be detrimental. Such a shift would drive the consumer loan market to less efficient products (bank lines, factors, and the like). Accordingly, I find the shifting problem a serious obstacle to aggressive usury regulation.

One possible response would be to solve the problem by adopting a much broader usury regulation. In Japan, for example, if regulators wished to restrict credit entirely rather than simply allocate the profitable lending to finance companies, they could apply usury limits without exceptions, so that all kinds of lending transactions would be covered. It is not clear, however, that such a rule would close off the markets for lending that depends explicitly on extralegal methods of enforcement. The experience summarized above suggests that those markets will be significant wherever usury laws are important.

More practically, the heterogeneity of consumer credit products and markets makes it likely that any broad-brush response would run headlong into the bluntness problem discussed earlier. For example, market interest rates on payday loans in the United States commonly are in the range of 400%–500%.[13] We might accept the fact that a risk premium would justify doubling or tripling the rate that a creditworthy borrower would pay, but rates like these – dozens of multiples of market rates – at first glance suggest a wholly abusive market. The difficulty, however, is that an obvious reason for some elevation of rates is the relatively small size of the transactions in question. If we suppose that there are fixed costs in administering any lending transaction,[14] then as the size of the transaction approaches zero, the rate that would cover the cost of funds, risk of loss, and transaction costs would become asymptotically high. The available data do not suggest that payday lending at those rates is markedly more profitable than credit card lending at considerably lower rates.

I do not intend to suggest that the markets for payday lending are functioning well or that the rates are low. I do think, however, that the rise of publicly traded payday lenders suggests that the market is becoming much more competitive, at least in jurisdictions that have usury ceilings sufficiently high to permit the firms to operate profitably.[15] What little comparative evidence we have – government reports issued in the United Kingdom in the last few years – suggests that consumers respond rationally to the differences in major lending products available to them.[16] Predictably enough, the evidence shows that consumers see a spectrum from relatively disadvantageous products (like rent-to-own suppliers and pawnbrokers, where consumers risk losing their tangible property) to relatively benevolent products (like payday loans, where the risks are "only" financial). A comparative study of current markets suggests, as you might expect, that consumers use the relatively disadvantageous products only in areas in which regulatory authorities have foreclosed opportunities for the relatively benevolent ones.[17] Thus, we might think, for example, that rules sufficiently relaxing restrictions in order to permit a competitive market for payday lenders ultimately would benefit consumers by giving them a sufficient supply in that market to forestall their use of more onerous rent-to-own products.[18]

The point of this discussion is to suggest that regulators will need to have a sophisticated sense of the on-the-ground value and cost structure of the various products that they are regulating to design usury regulations that will not be counterproductive. The difficulty of that problem convinces me that the bluntness implications of any sensible set of ceilings are serious.[19] This is not to say that a high ceiling (perhaps 50% per annum) might not be appropriate. Such a ceiling would have the salutary effect of prohibiting transactions at rates sufficiently high to suggest a lack of engaged consent by the borrower. Thus, they might have a targeted effect on various classes of subprime lending markets. They would not, however, provide a substantial response to the overindebtedness problem.

Minimum Payments

A less intrusive approach would require lenders to collect minimum payments on a monthly basis. For example, Britain formerly had a rule requiring cardholders to repay 15% of their credit card debt each month.[20] Even American regulators, acting through the Federal

Financial Institutions Examination Council (an interagency group that oversees standards for federal examination of financial institutions), have issued a "guidance" suggesting that lenders not permit negative amortization and require repayment in a reasonable time.[21] Although targeted primarily to the subprime lending market, the annual reports of major American card issuers suggest that the guidance has had an important effect even on mainstream lending practices.[22]

One systematic advantage of this approach is that it does not directly prohibit any value-increasing transaction. Borrowers who believe they can use funds in ways that justify payment of the market interest rates are free to borrow the funds from lenders that believe the borrowers are sufficiently creditworthy. Of course, the likelihood that the proposals would not be catastrophic does not say much about whether they would be beneficial. Although I am not convinced the proposals would make a major change, they are a step in the right direction.

First, there is some likelihood that people in financial distress will not be able to make the payments and thus will default and fall into bankruptcy sooner rather than later. This would be beneficial if (as knowledgeable writers generally assume) consumer borrowers often defer bankruptcy filings too long. If we can cause lenders to cut the borrowers off sooner, the externalities of financial distress will diminish. Although the lender does lose something in each case in which the borrower does not repay, we cannot rely on the lender to make the appropriate judgment, because the lender does not bear all of the losses of the customer's financial distress. Third parties bear a substantial portion of the losses, giving the lender an inadequate incentive to set payment plans that will minimize the total costs of financial distress.

Second, a minimum payment requirement responds to the psychological effects (discussed in Chapter 4) that seem to relate cards to increased spending and borrowing. If part of the problems with card-generated spending is the lack of pain tied sufficiently to the spending decision, then an increased minimum payment might help to break the cycle of increasingly excessive spending.

The third effect is less objective and certainly is related to the first two, but focuses more on the nature of the loan that is being extended. When lenders extend closed-end installment loans to fund the purchase of specific commodities, they generally set repayment schedules that mirror the useful life of the subject property. The lending and purchase go hand in hand in disciplining the borrower's adherence to a budget that matches expenditures (on loan repayments) with the borrower's enjoyment of the useful life of the object.[23] When the loan is extended for daily purchases, the enjoyment of which is completed in days or weeks, with repayment deferred for months or decades, we have created a loan that bears no relation to the useful life of the purchases.

This is not the place, and I am not the writer, to examine all of the implications of that shift. Yet one relevant implication certainly is the possibility that such loans will have a systematically higher likelihood of default. If that is so, the loans may be more likely to produce social costs than more conventional loans. A natural minimalist response, then, might be to adopt a rule that open-ended lending must have repayment schedules that, at the outside, would amortize a loan within sixty months (the long end of the typical range of fully amortizing loans for personal property).

It is difficult to predict whether such a rule would have important effects, but the early evidence suggests that even the weak guidance issued by American regulators has had cognizable market effects parallel to the ones discussed here.[24] In sum, this reform would not solve the problem. However, if existing business models involve substantial lending to borrowers in distress, such a reform could have a substantial positive effect.

Taxing Distressed Debt

This discussion leads naturally to a more targeted solution: a tax on distressed debt, and in particular a tax on defaulted credit card obligations.[25] Working through the details here, the idea is that the federal government would collect an annual tax from credit card issuers, calculated as a percentage of all credit card obligations that became delinquent during the preceding year. A tax that is imposed on debt that has gone into default is more carefully tailored to the transactions that are likely to impose externalities than a usury regulation. It will not cover any transaction in which the benefits that the borrower receives from the lending transaction turn out to be adequate to facilitate timely repayment.[26] And it responds to the problem more directly than an alteration in minimum payment requirements, because it directly places upon one of the parties to the transaction some of the costs that the transaction currently shifts to nonparties.

As with any tax, the most important policy question is what the effects of the tax will be. Here, the goal is to internalize some of the costs of risky credit card lending, with the hope that the lenders will respond by shifting their portfolios to less risky borrowers. Just as Australia's interchange regulation has encouraged card issuers to emphasize products that target borrowers, this regulation would encourage card issuers to move away from the riskier end of the cards market. Providian's conscious shift during the early years of this decade to a less risky group of cardholders – driven by competitive considerations rather than regulatory emphasis – suggests that card issuers could respond effectively to such a tax. If so, the tax should reduce risky lending without undue distortion of the market.

Here, the two most likely effects would be an increase in the price charged to risky borrowers and a contraction in the amounts loaned to them. From my perspective, either of those would be positive. The most serious problem with such a regulation is that it might increase the ex ante price of credit in the relevant markets. Given the rapidly developing segmentation of risk pools, we would expect a tax to lead to a surcharge of varying sizes based on the anticipated riskiness of the borrower. High-quality (high FICO score) borrowers would pay little or no surcharge; low-quality (low FICO score) borrowers would pay a much higher surcharge.[27] From a broader perspective, a surcharge is simply a shift between the parties to the transaction of the costs that they are presently jointly externalizing.

To be sure, the tax is likely to cause a contraction of lending to distressed borrowers, as credit card issuers attempt to avoid growth in their portfolio of distressed debt, or an acceleration of the time when distressed borrowers file for bankruptcy. For reasons discussed earlier, I find both of those outcomes appealing. For one thing, it is easy to see transactions foregone under a tax as transactions that go forward now only because a portion of their risks are shifted to third parties; there is no point to internalizing the risk if the tax is not going to limit some of the externality-generating transactions. More broadly, the contraction of lending would cause borrowers to file for bankruptcy earlier in their downward spiral. The dominant consensus within the body of literature that has examined empirical data about the condition of consumer borrowers by the time they file for bankruptcy is that the existing system generally causes consumer borrowers to file for bankruptcy too late, when an earlier filing might have solved problems with lower total costs. A tax on defaulted credit card debt would alter business models that rely so heavily on borrowing by distressed debtors.

17 Consumer Bankruptcy Reform

From one perspective, it makes no sense to view consumer bankruptcy policy as a separate topic at all. If the bankruptcy system is part of the social safety net, then we should think about bankruptcy policy alongside health care policy, insurance policy, entrepreneurial policy, and the like.[1] Still, bankruptcy policy is in fact largely made against the backdrop of its relation to the consumer finance markets. Thus, this chapter considers bankruptcy policy in relative isolation, as it relates to the finance markets.

As the following discussion suggests, my view is that much work remains to be done in analyzing policy issues even in that relatively confined milieu. If we could produce a sound understanding of bankruptcy policy as it relates to the finance markets, then that understanding should form a basis for considering the extent to which other major policy imperatives (like health care and social security) should influence (or be influenced by) the reality of bankruptcy and financial distress.

When we think of bankruptcy rules as a policy lever for minimizing the social costs of excessive borrowing, we confront a substantial economics literature about what type of discharge would have the optimal effect on credit markets. The general problem is that bankruptcy law must balance the protection of creditors, which promotes the availability and inexpensive provision of credit, against the protection of debtors, which prevents overindebtedness and underscreening by banks. Thus, strong legal protection of creditors may be efficient ex ante, but create inefficiencies ex post. For example, Tom Jackson argued two decades ago that economic principles called for a relatively unhindered fresh start to prevent the losses society bears when individuals become irretrievably enmeshed in financial distress.[2]

The literature has focused on various ways in which a less generous bankruptcy system might improve the incentives of consumer borrowers. The Adler-Polak-Schwartz (APS) model, for example, suggests that an optimal market would solve moral hazard problems by permitting consumer borrowers to waive their bankruptcy remedies by contract.[3] Similarly, much of Michelle White's research has at least implicitly suggested that exemptions that preserve any substantial asset base for consumer bankrupts will give consumers incentives to file for bankruptcy without adequate financial distress to justify the discharge that they will receive.[4]

Read with care, that work provides little support for increasing the rigor of the bankruptcy system. Most obviously, the APS model specifically assumes that the parties to a borrowing transaction internalize all costs of financial distress. Essentially, their paper suggests that we should permit contracting out of bankruptcy because in a world where bankruptcy is partly endogenous – within the borrower's control – contracting will allow borrowers to sort themselves and precommit to avoid moral hazard. Obviously, if bankruptcy is largely exogenous or attributable in part to quasi-rational behavior, as I argue earlier, then the significance of this effect fades. Again, what we know about the reality of bankruptcy in the United States[5] and in the United Kingdom[6] suggests that a great deal, if not the overwhelming majority, of bankruptcy is exogenous. Similarly, Michelle White's work suggests a variety of empirical scenarios in which it would be counterproductive to lower the ability of bankrupts to protect post-bankruptcy earnings.[7]

To be sure, the extent to which bankruptcy is exogenous is somewhat in the eye of the beholder. Some might think that shock-induced financial distress could be avoided entirely by appropriate levels of saving and insurance. That perspective, however, is far too simplistic. For one thing, it is not possible to insure entirely against many of the catastrophic events that lead to financial distress. More broadly, it seems most unlikely that it would be optimal to have all risks borne by private insurers. As David Moss shows, the trend in recent decades is to adopt policies that shift more risk to the government, reflecting its capabilities in managing and reducing losses from certain types of risks.[8] The rise of the bankruptcy system, properly regarded, is part of that shift.

Moreover, for reasons discussed in Part IV, we can hardly expect any government to encourage people to stop all but the most necessary consumption. On the contrary, as Lizabeth Cohen illustrates, the U.S. government has taken a firm stand in favor of consumption for decades as a way to drive economic growth.[9] In the end, we must accept that in a market-driven economy, it is inevitable that a certain number of people will fall into financial distress for reasons that we do not expect them to control.

It is important, therefore, to think about the problem more broadly. Explicitly or implicitly, all of the existing literature rests on the assumption that borrowers are better situated than lenders to avoid financial distress and bankruptcy.[10] That view might have made sense in a traditional bank lending model, where a borrower comes to a bank, sits in the banker's office, executes loan documents, receives funds, and is then free to go – unconstrained in any realistic way from later activities that might reduce the likelihood that the borrower will be able to repay the loan. In the traditional bank-lending model, for example, the bank is unable to effectively prevent the borrower from engaging in reckless future borrowing or wasting the borrowed funds on frivolous luxuries.

In the modern information-based lending world, however, it makes less sense to view the borrowers as operating in full control, to the detriment of hapless and incapable lenders. Most obviously, the modern lender (at least in the United States) has access to pervasive and frequently updated information about the credit behavior of its customers.[11] For example, the modern credit card lender has the ability to terminate the borrower's use of funds at any time by the simple expedient of refusing to permit additional uses of the card once the information available to the lender indicates that the borrower is insufficiently creditworthy. On that point, the rise of credit bureaus largely has solved the problem of multiple nonadjusting lenders harming each other's prospects without any single one being aware of the others.

In sum, in the modern world illustrated in Figure 17.1, particularly in the context of credit card lending, the rate of default in a lender's portfolio is largely in the control of the lender. If a lender wishes to lower the rate of default in its portfolio, it can simply tighten the criteria

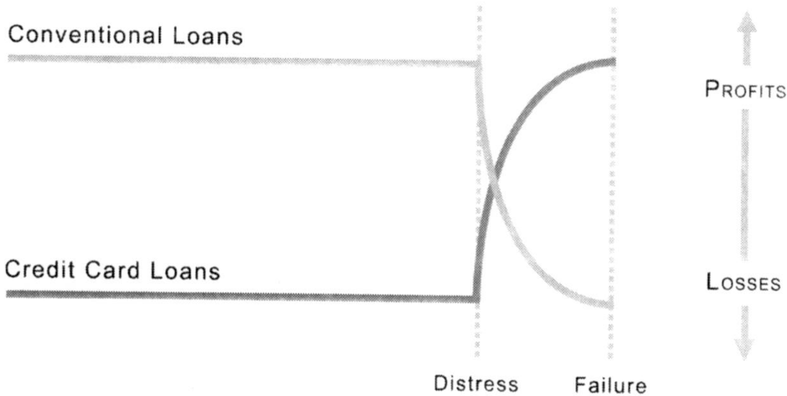

Figure 17.1. The dynamics of profitability.

it uses for determining when to cease advancing credit.[12] Tightening, of course, might not be profitable if it lowers the revenue the lender gains from loans to risky borrowers. Yet all that means is that modern lenders are optimizing their default rates in their own portfolios – balancing default losses against profits from loans to the less creditworthy potential consumers.[13]

Once we recognize that lenders are optimizing the risk of default from a private perspective that takes no account of the externalities financial distress displaces to third parties, we have a problem that warrants the attention of policymakers. A glance at some illustrative statistics about the credit card industry is useful. Under the conventional model, increasing delinquency rates by cardholders translates directly into a loss for the card issuers, which translates directly into increased charges borne by the cardholders who repay.[14]

In a world in which lenders are optimizing default rates and externalizing losses to other parties, increased delinquency rates do not necessarily suggest that lenders should raise prices and lower output. On the contrary, to the modern credit card lender, increased delinquency rates suggest a greater number of borrowers likely to have an appetite for carrying balances at a level that is profitable for the lenders.[15]

Moreover, as those borrowers spiral deeper into financial distress, their switching costs increase, which makes it easier for the card issuer to charge them higher rates and fees. This might occur because it will be difficult for the cardholder to find a new lender who will make an attractive

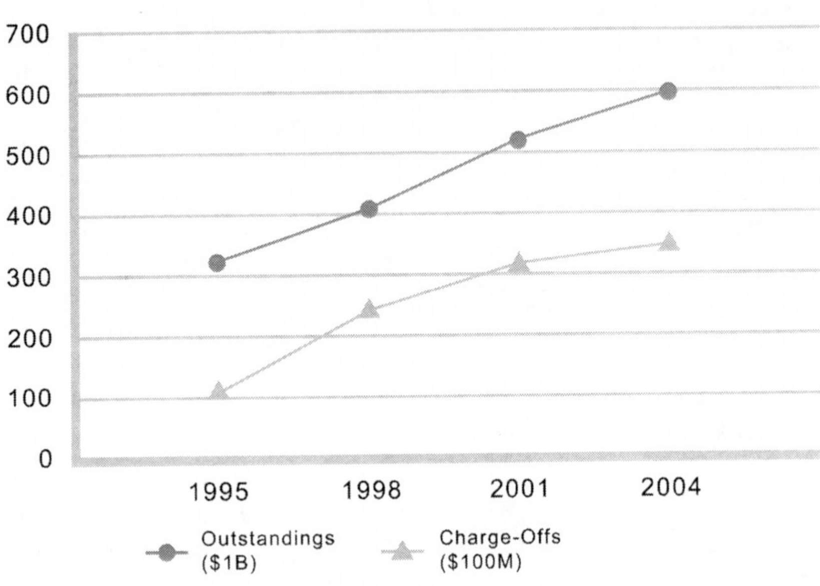

Figure 17.2. Losses and lending. *Source:* Nilson Report 829.

offer to take over the entire account. To profit from a relationship with a financially distressed consumer, an issuer will need to charge a relatively high rate of interest. The traditional teaser rates used to attract customers would not make economic sense in this context. However, if cardholders do not understand the rates on their existing accounts, the offer of a "great low rate of 18%" is likely to be ineffective.

A related problem is that new lenders may find it difficult to obtain sufficient information to price the account as well as the existing lender. Empirical researchers at the Federal Reserve suggest that the problem is one of adverse selection: An issuer who attempts to attract risky customers from their existing issuers is most likely to succeed in outbidding the existing issuer for the customers about which the existing issuer has private information suggesting that the customers are less creditworthy than they appear.[16] It is not an accident, I think, that large card lenders have resisted sending complete information about their delinquent cardholders to the major credit bureaus. To get a sense for the reality of the relations, consider Figure 17.2, which sets out charge-offs and outstandings for the ten largest credit card banks over the last decade. As that figure shows, charge-offs have been rising steadily throughout the

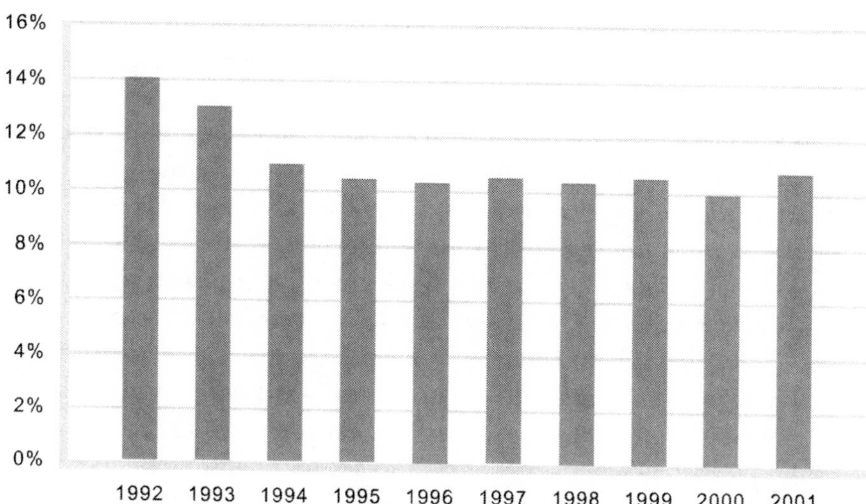

Figure 17.3. Average credit card markup. *Source:* Federal Reserve Statistical Release G-19. Payment Cards Center, Federal Reserve Bank of Philadelphia.

last decade, but there is no discernible evidence that the leading lenders have cut back their lending. Rather, their portfolios seem to have grown even more rapidly than the growth in charge-offs.

Nor should we think that lenders have reacted to the increasing charge-offs by substantially increasing their interest rates. On the contrary, as shown in Figure 17.3, interest rates over the same period of time have fallen steadily (slightly, but steadily).

Saying that lenders are optimizing the risk of default is not to suggest that borrowers have no control over default. Of course they do. The appropriate policy question, however, is whether borrowers are the *only* group that can limit the social losses of financial distress. If both borrowers and lenders can limit losses, then we should be asking how to allocate incentives between those parties to minimize the net externalized costs of financial distress. We might be able to trust the parties to minimize the costs they bear between themselves, but we cannot trust them to consider the losses others suffer.

Thus, to consider an analogy to payments policy, this is much like allocating losses from fraudulent use of credit cards. If all of the losses are placed on banks, they will have an incentive to use information technology to prevent those losses, but we might fear that cardholders will have inadequate incentives to take commonsense precautions to avoid theft of their card or card number. Currently, the U.S. legal system operates on the implicit assumption that the hassle and inconvenience of card loss gives adequate incentive to cardholders, so the out-of-pocket losses from fraud are placed almost entirely on the card issuers.[17]

In this context, a perspective that views the experience of consumer bankruptcy as a time for celebration and reveling by the released borrowers would worry that only a truly unforgiving bankruptcy system – or perhaps penal confinement – would be adequate to prevent widespread fraud.[18] In contrast, a perspective that views consumer bankruptcy – even in the United States in the twenty-first century – as a deeply humiliating and scarring personal experience would think that bankruptcy alone gives a substantial protection against moral hazard and that judges could be relied on to identify cases of overt misconduct. This perspective would shift as much of the monetary losses as possible to lenders and in particular to adjusting lenders who can control financial distress through the ability to terminate the borrower's ability to obtain future funds.

It is not my purpose here to make detailed policy prescriptions. Generally, the analysis suggests that subordination of the debt of controlling, adjusting creditors would be an appropriate response. With their practical ability to control borrowing by distressed consumers, credit card lenders are the most likely candidates, at least in the United States. My general impression, however, is that such a rule would have a relatively minor impact, because of the large number of no-asset cases in which even general unsecured creditors would receive nothing. Thus, I am inclined to think that such a rule would make sense only as an adjunct to a tax on distressed debt of the kind that I discuss in Chapter 16.

Against that backdrop, it seems worthwhile to consider the likely effects of the Bankruptcy Abuse Prevention and Consumer Protection Act of 2005.[19] Recognizing that it is too early to know how the reforms will play out in practice, it is fair, however, to examine the policy motivations that are apparent on the face of the statute to see how they compare to the policy recommendations and theoretical frameworks that I summarized earlier. Generally, the revisions reflect acceptance of the premise that the primary empirical link of policy significance is that generous bankruptcy relief tends to increase the demand for credit but lower the incentive to repay, so that more rigorous bankruptcy relief would lead to higher repayment rates and thus lower interest rates.

Even that rationale can do little to justify the statute as written. Taken seriously, that premise would suggest that the reforms should apply only to newly incurred obligations, for which interest rates presumably would be lower. From an incentive perspective, permitting lenders to use the relatively rigorous collection incentives of the new act to collect on debts already incurred under preexisting contracts can only be a windfall.

Turning to the substance of the reforms, the consumer bankruptcy reforms seem likely to have effects directly opposed to the effects suggested by the earlier analysis. I focus on two separate points: the practical limitations on the use of Chapter 7, the likelihood that the reforms as a whole will lead to later filings by distressed consumers, and the practical elevation of the priority of credit card lenders.[20]

The first problem is the portion of the reforms designed specifically to force consumers out of Chapter 7 and into Chapter 13, with a view to limiting the ability of bankrupts to discharge debts while earning a substantial postdischarge income. Quite apart from any concerns about the administrative practicality or utility of the provisions, the reforms seem incongruous in light of the theoretical discussion presented earlier. My analysis suggests that the system should increase the incentive of lenders to take steps to minimize the costs of financial distress that card transactions externalize. Yet the revisions are designed explicitly to shift the costs of financial distress to the borrower with consumer debts.[21]

Second, if the general effect of the reforms is to reduce the benefits of bankruptcy, they may cause some distressed borrowers to defer their bankruptcy filings.[22] What we know about consumer bankruptcy as it currently exists is that consumer borrowers probably file too late, not too early. The reforms are likely only to exacerbate that problem. The proposals that I discuss, by contrast, are likely to cause people to file sooner by limiting the economic incentive of credit card issuers to continue lending.

The relative improvement for credit card lenders[23] has some obvious adverse consequences. Most obviously, credit card lenders are more able to adjust to evidence of distress than other unsecured creditors. Thus, in the current system, in which third parties bear a significant portion of the costs of financial distress, lenders have incentives to loan larger amounts without making adequate individualized assessments of the loans. If that is true, an appropriate response might be to alter the system so that the issuers will internalize more of the costs of the distress that arises from their loans, and thus determine the most sophisticated methods for minimizing risks. Therefore, for example, provisions that make credit card debts nondischargeable place lenders on an even playing field with child support and alimony claimants. Because the bill does nothing to increase the assets in bankruptcy estates,[24] even claimants with enhanced priority positions will be harmed.

This discussion suggests that an optimal bankruptcy/finance policy would alter the incentives of those creditors with the ability to control their borrowers. If credit card lenders are the plainest examples of such creditors and also the group whose lending most directly leads to financial distress, then reforms should go in the opposite direction. Any reform that transfers value from nonadjusting creditors to adjusting creditors only exacerbates the externalities of the bankruptcy process by imposing losses on creditors who have not had an opportunity to spread them over a mass of voluntarily priced transactions. Thus, it would make much more sense to expand the category of priority unsecured claims to include more comprehensively the categories of nonadjusting creditors who currently share priority with adjusting credit card lenders. The revisions that directly benefit credit card lenders reflect a move in the wrong direction.[25]

Conclusion

Looking back across the terrain of this project, I close with some surprise at the point to which I have come. My past academic work has been pervaded with my skepticism of government regulation and a general doubt that intervention in a market can succeed. That skepticism has fueled my long work on this project, as I have been driven to understand as much as I can about the effects of plastic cards on world economies.

In general, my recommendations are compelled by the view that the cost savings of plastic cards are counterbalanced by the tendency of the credit card to foster excessive borrowing. To limit the social costs of the distress that attends that borrowing, I have made a number of recommendations:

- Invalidating legal obstacles to credit card surcharging by merchants
- Invalidating unpriceable contract terms like universal default provisions
- Banning credit card marketing to minors and college students
- Banning rewards programs
- Shifting disclosure regimes to the point-of-sale
- Setting mandatory minimum repayment levels
- Taxing defaulted credit card debt
- Subordinating the debt of credit card lenders in cardholder bankruptcies.

My main hope, however, is not to see rapid enactment of any great share of those proposals. I am realistic enough to recognize the political implausibility of what I propose. My goal in writing is much more to work out for myself the implications of my views than it is to produce immediate legislative change. My short-term policy goals are much more modest, and I think realistic: to give policymakers, academics, and other interested parties an understanding of exactly how the card works and what it contributes to the U.S. economy and the economies of other countries around the world. If future policymakers act with an informed understanding, they are more likely to move in the right direction, at whatever speed. Compared to the recent legislative reforms in the United States – which I would characterize as firm steps in the wrong direction – that would be a signal improvement.

APPENDIX

Country-Level Data

Key

/C = Per Capita	**BIL** = Billions	**ConC** = Consumer Credit
LCU = Local Currency Unit	**Trxn** = Transaction	**CCV** = Credit Card Value
MIL = Millions	**CCD** = Credit Card Debt	**TCV** = Total Card Value
GDP = Gross Domestic Product	**M** = Million	**Bank** = Bankruptcy

Australia

Credit Card Data

Year	Credit Card Value (BIL US$)	Credit Card Value/C (US$)	Credit Card Value/GDP (%)	Credit Trxn (MIL)	Credit Trxn/C
1990	10.93	639.09	3.52		
1991	11.68	675.40	3.68		
1992	10.28	587.52	3.28		
1993	9.52	537.86	3.13		
1994	11.70	657.19	3.40	154.99	8.71
1995	13.34	737.18	3.58	246.98	13.65
1996	17.22	940.78	4.16	281.13	15.36
1997	18.55	1002.95	4.46	333.79	18.04
1998	17.59	935.63	4.72	427.58	22.74
1999	23.87	1256.41	5.91	553.60	29.14
2000	24.35	1268.24	6.24	677.72	35.30
2001	22.76	1173.06	6.15	787.43	40.59
2002	28.25	1434.12	6.90	862.92	43.80

Debit Card Data

Year	Debit Card Value (BIL US$)	Debit Card Value/C (US$)	Debit Card Value/GDP (%)	Debit Trxn (MIL)	Debit Trxn/C
1990					
1991					
1992					
1993					
1994	2.13	119.67	0.62	56.61	3.18
1995	10.62	586.49	2.85	267.89	14.80
1996	13.99	764.27	3.38	354.44	19.37
1997	18.56	1003.49	4.47	438.95	23.73
1998	21.42	1139.38	5.75	502.60	26.73
1999	19.89	1046.58	4.92	540.42	28.44
2000	22.43	1168.27	5.75	597.54	31.12
2001	22.23	1145.93	6.01	644.73	33.23
2002	21.56	1094.34	5.27	696.13	35.34

Total Card Data

Year	Total Card Value (BIL US$)	Credit Card Value/TCV (%)	Total Card Value/C (US$)	Total Card Value/GDP (%)	Total Card Trxn	Total Card Trxn/C	Credit Card Trxn/Total Trxn (%)
1990							
1991							
1992							
1993							
1994	13.83	84.60	776.86	4.02	211.60	11.89	73.2
1995	23.96	55.69	1323.66	6.43	514.86	28.45	48.0
1996	31.20	55.18	1705.05	7.54	635.58	34.73	44.2
1997	37.12	49.99	2006.44	8.93	772.73	41.77	43.2
1998	39.01	45.09	2075.01	10.48	930.18	49.48	46.0
1999	43.76	54.56	2302.99	10.83	1094.02	57.58	50.6
2000	46.78	52.05	2436.52	11.99	1275.26	66.42	53.1
2001	44.99	50.58	2318.99	12.15	1432.17	73.82	55.0
2002	49.81	56.72	2528.46	12.17	1559.05	79.14	55.3

Consumer and Card Debt Data

Year	CCD (BIL US$)	CCD/C (US$)	CCD/GDP (%)	CCD/CCV (%)	CONC (BIL US$)	CONC/C (US$)	CONC/GDP (%)	CCD/CONC (%)
1990	4.68	273.76	1.51	34	37.22	2176.87	12.0	12.6
1991	4.46	258.05	1.41	31	34.85	2014.46	11.0	12.8
1992	4.67	266.76	1.49	30	33.56	1917.77	10.7	13.9
1993	4.61	260.65	1.52	31	32.18	1818.29	10.6	14.3
1994	4.65	261.04	1.35	31	31.78	1785.42	9.2	14.6
1995	5.72	316.28	1.54	32	36.94	2040.81	9.9	15.5
1996	6.52	356.34	1.58	32	39.95	2182.90	9.6	16.3
1997	7.92	428.21	1.91	30	45.61	2465.48	11.0	17.4
1998	8.92	474.72	2.40	28	46.44	2470.48	12.5	19.2
1999	9.54	501.87	2.36	27	41.72	2195.75	10.3	22.9
2000	11.74	611.44	3.01	25	46.04	2397.73	11.8	25.5
2001	11.84	610.40	3.20	24	43.46	2240.39	11.7	27.2
2002	11.83	600.28	2.89	24	42.67	2165.99	10.4	27.7

Australia, *continued*

General Data

Year	Population (MIL)	GDP (BIL US$)	Exchange Rate (LCU/$)	Bank	Bank/M
1990	17.1	310.57	1.28		
1991	17.3	317.66	1.28	16301	942
1992	17.5	313.41	1.36	15328	876
1993	17.7	304.10	1.47	14754	834
1994	17.8	344.05	1.37	13647	767
1995	18.1	372.47	1.35	15380	850
1996	18.3	413.97	1.28	19803	1082
1997	18.5	415.73	1.35	23424	1266
1998	18.8	372.27	1.59	25411	1352
1999	19.0	403.89	1.55	25405	1337
2000	19.2	390.19	1.72	21453	1117
2001	19.4	370.14	1.93	26045	1342
2002	19.7	409.37	1.84	23067	1171

Belgium

Credit Card Data

Year	Credit Card Value (MIL US$)	Credit Card Value/C (US$)	Credit Card Value/GDP (%)	Credit Trxn (MIL)	Credit Trxn/C
1998	6614	648.85	2.4	56	5.5
1999	6917	678.76	2.5	62	6.1
2000	6301	612.16	2.6	66	6.5
2001	6337	615.39	2.7	69	6.7
2002	6868	667.26	2.8	70	6.8

Debit Card Data

Year	Debit Card Value (MIL US$)	Debit Card Value/C (US$)	Debit Card Value/GDP (%)	Debit Trxn (MIL)	Debit Trxn/C
1998	17373	1703.24	6.27	273	26.8
1999	19045	1867.16	7.03	327	32.1
2000	18553	1818.92	7.80	380	37.3
2001	19740	1916.50	8.44	433	42
2002	23641	2295.24	9.53	507	49.2

Total Card Data

Year	Total Card Value (MIL US$)	Credit Card Value/TCV (%)	Total Card Value/C (US$)	Total Card Value/GDP (%)	Total Card Trxn (MIL)	Total Card Trxn/C	Credit Card Trxn/Total Trxn (%)
1998	23987	27.57	2351.67	8.66	329	32.25	17.02
1999	25962	26.64	2545.29	9.58	389	38.14	15.94
2000	24854	25.35	2436.67	10.44	446	43.73	14.80
2001	26077	24.30	2531.75	11.14	502	48.74	13.75
2002	30509	22.51	2962.04	12.30	577	56.02	12.13

General Data

Year	Population (MIL)	GDP (BIL US$)	Exchange Rate (LCU/$)
1998	10.2	277	0.90
1999	10.2	271	0.94
2000	10.2	238	1.09
2001	10.3	234	1.12
2002	10.3	248	1.06

Canada

Credit Card Data

Year	Credit Card Value (BIL US$)	Credit Card Value/C (US$)	Credit Card Value/GDP (%)	Credit Trxn (BIL)	Credit Trxn/C
1990	45	1618.71	5.70		
1991	46	1631.21	5.91		
1992	46	1614.04	6.29		
1993	46	1597.22	6.66		
1994	49	1683.85	7.26	0.87	30
1995	53	1802.72	7.73	0.94	32
1996	57	1919.19	8.23	1.01	34
1997	62	2066.67	8.81	1.03	34
1998	63	2086.09	9.40	1.09	36
1999	68	2229.51	9.69	1.19	39
2000	77	2500.00	10.42	1.3	42
2001	80	2572.35	11.30	1.4	45
2002	86	2738.85	12.01		

Debit Card Data

Year	Debit Card Value (BIL US$)	Debit Card Value/C (US$)	Debit Card Value/GDP (%)	Debit Trxn (BIL)	Debit Trxn/C
1990					
1991					
1992					
1993					
1994	5.28	181.40	0.78	0.185	6.36
1995				0.394	13.40
1996	16.06	540.71	2.32	0.667	22.46
1997	23.37	779.14	3.32	1.00[iv]	33.33
1998	31.05	1028.09	4.63	1.36	45.03
1999	32.76	1074.14	4.67	1.7	55.74
2000	38.55	1251.51	5.22	1.96	63.64
2001	40.17	1291.71	5.67	2.2	70.74
2002					

Total Card Data

Year	Total Card Value (BIL US$)	Credit Card Value/TCV (%)	Total Card Value/C (US$)	Total Card Value/GDP (%)	Total Card Trxn (BIL)	Total Card Trxn/C (US$)	Credit Card Trxn/Total Trxn (%)
1990							
1991							
1992							
1993							
1994	54.28	90.3	1865	8.0	1.06	0.04	82.5
1995					1.33	0.05	70.5
1996	73.06	78.0	2460	10.5	1.68	0.06	60.2
1997	85.37	72.6	2846	12.1	2.03	0.07	50.7
1998	94.05	67.0	3114	14.0	2.45	0.08	44.5
1999	100.76	67.5	3304	14.4	2.89	0.09	41.2
2000	115.55	66.6	3752	15.6	3.26	0.11	39.9
2001	120.17	66.6	3864	17.0	3.60	0.12	38.9
2002							

Consumer and Card Debt Data

Year	CCD (BIL US$)	CCD/C (US$)	CCD/GDP (%)	CCD/CCV (%)	CONC (BIL US$)	CONC/C (US$)	CONC/GDP (%)	CCD/CONC (%)
1990	12	431.65	1.6	28	114	4100.72	15	10.5
1991	13	460.99	1.7	28	115	4078.01	15	11.3
1992	12	421.05	1.7	26	105	3684.21	14	11.4
1993	12	416.67	1.8	28	101	3506.94	15	11.9
1994	13	446.74	2	28	98	3367.70	15	13.3
1995	15	510.20	2.2	28	100	3401.36	15	15.0
1996	16	538.72	2.3	28	104	3501.68	15	15.4
1997	17	566.67	2.4	27	108	3600.00	15	15.7
1998	18	596.03	2.7	28	107	3543.05	16	16.8
1999	21	688.52	2.9	30	114	3737.70	16	18.4
2000	24	779.22	3.2	31	121	3928.57	16	19.8
2001	25	803.86	3.6	32	124	3987.14	17	20.2
2002	28	891.72	3.9	32	130	4140.13	18	21.5

Canada, *continued*

General Data

Year	Population (MIL)	GDP (BIL US$)	Exchange Rate (LCU/$)
1990	27.8	790	1.167
1991	28.2	778	1.146
1992	28.5	731	1.209
1993	28.8	691	1.29
1994	29.1	675	1.366
1995	29.4	686	1.372
1996	29.7	693	1.363
1997	30	704	1.385
1998	30.2	670	1.483
1999	30.5	702	1.486
2000	30.8	739	1.485
2001	31.1	708	1.549
2002	31.4	716	1.567

China

Credit Card Data

Year	Credit Card Value (BIL US$)	Credit Card Value/C (US$)	Credit Card Value/GDP (%)	Credit Trxn (MIL)	Credit Trxn/C
1996	17.64	16.63	2.16	21.50	0.018
1997	25.27	22.87	3.09	28.30	0.023
1998	25.21	22.29	3.07	34.40	0.028
1999	23.32	19.98	2.84	37.80	0.030
2000	32.25	25.91	3.93	47.60	0.037

Debit Card Data

Year	Debit Card Value (BIL US$)	Debit Card Value/C (US$)	Debit Card Value/GDP (%)	Debit Trxn (MIL)	Debit Trxn/C
1996	52.06	42.67	6.37	84.70	0.069
1997	73.56	59.32	8.98	88.70	0.072
1998	62.71	50.17	7.65	111.70	0.089
1999	81.69	64.83	9.96	291.30	0.231
2000	114.98	88.45	14.02	637.60	0.490

Total Card Data

Year	Total Card Value (BIL US$)	Credit Card Value/TCV (%)	Total Card Value/C (US$)	Total Card Value/GDP (%)	Total Card Trxn (MIL)	Total Card Trxn/C	Credit Card Trxn/Total Trxn (%)
1996	69.7	25.31	57.13	8.53	106.20	0.09	20.24
1997	98.83	25.57	79.70	12.07	117.00	0.09	24.19
1998	87.92	28.67	70.34	10.72	146.10	0.12	23.55
1999	105.01	22.21	83.34	12.81	329.10	0.26	11.49
2000	147.23	21.90	113.25	17.95	685.20	0.53	6.95

General Data

Year	Population (BIL)	GDP (BIL US$)	Exchange Rate (LCU/$)
1996	1.22	817.09	8.31
1997	1.24	819.06	8.29
1998	1.25	820.05	8.28
1999	1.26	820.05	8.28
2000	1.3	820.05	8.28

Finland

Credit Card Data

Year	Credit Card Value (BIL US$)	Credit Card Value/C (US$)	Credit Card Value/GDP (%)	Credit Trxn (MIL)	Credit Trxn/C
1993	4	784.31	4.64	72	14.12
1994	5	980.39	5.30	69	13.53
1995	6	1176.47	5.32	81	15.88
1996	6	1176.47	5.59	87	17.06
1997	6	1176.47	6.32	94	18.43
1998	7	1346.15	7.59	106	20.38
1999	6	1153.85	6.79	107	20.58
2000	6	1153.85	7.86	115	22.12
2001	6	1153.85	8.09	120	23.08
2002	6	1153.85	7.69	127	24.42

Debit Card Data

Year	Debit Card Value (BIL US$)	Debit Card Value/C (US$)	Debit Card Value/GDP (%)	Debit Trxn (MIL)	Debit Trxn/C
1993	7	1372.55	8.11	143	28.04
1994	8	1568.63	8.48	153	30.00
1995	11	2156.86	9.75	163	31.96
1996	10	1960.78	9.32	176	34.51
1997	9	1764.71	9.48	178	34.90
1998	10	1923.08	10.84	191	36.73
1999	11	2115.38	12.45	217	41.73
2000	9	1730.77	11.78	256	49.23
2001	11	2115.38	14.83	293	56.35
2002	13	2500.00	16.66	376	72.31

Total Card Data

Year	Total Card Value (BIL US$)	Credit Card Value/TCV (%)	Total Card Value/C (US$)	Total Card Value/GDP (%)	Total Card Trxn (MIL)	Total Card Trxn/C	Credit Card Trxn/Total Trxn (%)
1993	11	36.36	2156.86	12.75	215	42.16	33.49
1994	13	38.46	2549.02	13.78	222	43.53	31.08
1995	17	35.29	3333.33	15.06	244	47.84	33.20
1996	16	37.50	3137.25	14.91	263	51.57	33.08
1997	15	40.00	2941.18	15.80	272	53.33	34.56
1998	17	41.18	3269.23	18.43	297	57.12	35.69
1999	17	35.29	3269.23	19.25	324	62.31	33.02
2000	15	40.00	2884.62	19.64	371	71.35	31.00
2001	17	35.29	3269.23	22.92	413	79.42	29.06
2002	19	31.58	3653.85	24.35	503	96.73	25.25

General Data

Year	Population (MIL)	GDP (BIL US$)	Exchange Rate (LCU/$)
1993	5.1	86.29	0.96
1994	5.1	94.36	0.88
1995	5.1	112.88	0.73
1996	5.1	107.30	0.77
1997	5.1	94.95	0.87
1998	5.2	92.23	0.90
1999	5.2	88.32	0.94
2000	5.2	76.38	1.09
2001	5.2	74.18	1.12
2002	5.2	78.02	1.06

France

Credit Card Data

Year	Credit Card Value (BIL US$)	Credit Card Value/C (US$)	Credit Card Value/GDP (%)	Credit Trxn (BIL)	Credit Trxn/C
1991	77.45	1361.24	5.59	1.33	23.37
1992	88.08	1539.81	6.32	1.44	25.17
1993	90.23	1563.86	6.58	1.56	27.04
1994	96.18	1666.92	6.93	1.67	28.94
1995	118.21	2045.20	8.47	1.87	32.35
1996	126.95	2170.12	9.13	2.14	36.58
1997	120.22	2010.45	8.57	2.3	38.46
1998	134.62	2243.73	9.34	2.58	43.00
1999	143.68	2386.68	9.82	2.91	48.34
2000	140.90	2325.03	9.50	3.29	54.29
2001	152.13	2497.95	10.15	3.67	60.26

General Data

Year	Population (MIL)	GDP (BIL US$)	Exchange Rate (LCU/$)
1991	56.9	1386.21	5.64
1992	57.2	1392.99	5.39
1993	57.7	1371.57	5.66
1994	57.7	1387.88	5.55
1995	57.8	1395.11	4.99
1996	58.5	1389.87	0.79
1997	59.8	1402.39	0.89
1998	60	1441.24	0.90
1999	60.2	1463.28	0.94
2000	60.6	1483.64	1.09
2001	60.9	1498.91	1.12

Germany

Credit Card Data

Year	Credit Card Value (BIL US$)	Credit Card Value/C (US$)	Credit Card Value/GDP (%)	Credit Trxn (MIL)	Credit Trxn/C
1991	18.07	225.90	1.05	170	2.13
1992	22.88	283.93	1.25	214	2.66
1993	29.27	360.50	1.69	294	3.62
1994	35.31	433.77	2.01	351	4.31
1995	45.87	563.56	2.30	416	5.11
1996	59.11	721.78	1.64	504	6.15
1997	52.81	643.23	1.65	529	6.44
1998	78.11	952.57	2.47	993	12.11
1999	102.34	1246.53	3.38	1199	14.60
2000	100.73	1225.47	3.85	1391	16.92
2001	112.86	1371.29	4.44	1583	19.23

General Data

Year	Population (MIL)	GDP (BIL US$)	Exchange Rate (LCU/$)
1991	80	1716.87	1.66
1992	80.6	1826.92	1.56
1993	81.2	1727.27	1.65
1994	81.4	1759.26	1.62
1995	81.4	1993.01	1.43
1996	81.9	3607.59	0.79
1997	82.1	3202.25	0.89
1998	82	3166.67	0.9
1999	82.1	3031.91	0.94
2000	82.2	2614.68	1.09
2001	82.3	2544.64	1.12

Ireland

Credit Card Data

Year	Credit Card Value (BIL US$)	Credit Card Value/C (US$)	Credit Card Value/GDP (%)
1990	2.68	779.07	4.5
1991	2.76	793.10	5.0
1992	2.65	754.99	5.1
1993	2.71	761.24	4.9
1994	3.34	927.78	5.3
1995	4.11	1122.95	5.7
1996	4.79	1291.11	6.3
1997	5.07	1348.40	6.9
1998	4.61	1216.36	7.7
1999	5.62	1475.07	9.3
2000	6.02	1571.80	11.4
2001	6.79	1763.64	13.3
2002	8.24	2128.19	14.2

Consumer and Card Debt Data

Year	CCD (MIL US$)	CCD/C (US$)	CCD/GDP (%)	CCD/CCV (%)
1990				
1991				
1992				
1993				
1994				
1995				
1996				
1997				
1998	393.08	103.72	0.66	8.53
1999	473.64	124.31	0.78	8.43
2000	473.19	123.55	0.90	7.86
2001	516.44	134.14	1.01	7.61
2002	695.83	179.80	1.20	8.45

General Data

Year	Population (MIL)	GDP (BIL US$)	Exchange Rate (LCU/$)
1990	3.44	59.89	1.68
1991	3.48	55.66	1.73
1992	3.51	51.84	1.86
1993	3.56	54.84	1.85
1994	3.6	62.71	1.69
1995	3.66	72	1.52
1996	3.71	76.1	1.46
1997	3.76	73.93	1.51
1998	3.79	59.73	1.87
1999	3.81	60.5	1.89
2000	3.83	52.85	2.21
2001	3.85	51.18	2.38
2002	3.87	58.01	2.16

Italy

Credit Card Data

Year	Credit Card Value (BIL US$)	Credit Card Value/C (US$)	Credit Card Value/GDP (%)	Credit Trxn (MIL)	Credit Trxn/C
1996	13.08	227.79	1.12	116	2
1997	16.31	283.72	1.33	141	2.5
1998	18.19	315.81	1.43	175	3
1999	23.42	406.59	1.77	229	4
2000	26.63	461.61	1.91	272	4.7
2001	27.64	479.02	1.90	314	5.4

Italy, *continued*

Debit Card Data

Year	Debit Card Value (BIL US$)	Debit Card Value/C (US$)	Debit Card Value/GDP (%)	Debit Trxn (MIL)	Debit Card Trxn/C
1996	8.32	144.96	0.71	72	1.3
1997	13.80	240.07	1.13	124	2.2
1998	15.92	276.33	1.25	172	3
1999	21.19	367.87	1.60	248	4.3
2000	24.50	424.68	1.76	318	5.5
2001	26.72	463.05	1.84	423	7.3

Total Card Data

Year	Total Card Value (BIL US$)	Credit Card Value/TCV (%)	Total Card Value/C (US$)	Total Card Value/GDP (%)	Total Card Trxn	Total Card Trxn/C (%)	Credit Card Trxn/Total Trxn (%)
1996	21.40	61.11	372.75	1.83	188	3.3	61.70
1997	30.12	54.17	523.79	2.46	265	4.7	53.21
1998	34.11	53.33	592.14	2.68	347	6	50.43
1999	44.61	52.50	774.47	3.38	477	8.3	48.01
2000	51.14	52.08	886.28	3.67	590	10.2	46.10
2001	54.36	50.85	942.08	3.74	737	12.7	42.61

General Data

Year	Population (MIL)	GDP (BIL US$)	Exchange Rate (LCU/$)
1996	57	1169.05	0.84
1997	58	1226.19	0.80
1998	58	1273.81	0.88
1999	58	1321.43	0.90
2000	58	1392.86	0.94
2001	58	1452.38	1.09

Japan

Credit Card Data

Year	Credit Card Value (BIL US$)	Credit Card Value/C (US$)	Credit Card Value/GDP (%)
1990	109	882.33	3.6
1991	123	992.57	3.8
1992	132	1062.55	3.8
1993	147	1180.38	3.7
1994	161	1288.40	3.7
1995	184	1466.85	3.9
1996	177	1407.43	4.4
1997	168	1332.37	4.6
1998	160	1265.72	4.8
1999	191	1508.09	4.9
2000	211	1663.12	5.2
2001	194	1525.88	5.4

Consumer and Card Debt Data

Year	CCD (BIL US$)	CCD/C (US$)	CCD/GDP (%)	CCD/CCV (%)	CONC (BIL US$)	CONC/C (US$)	CONC/GDP (%)	CCD/CONC (%)
1990	16.86	99.13	0.55	15.47	375	3035.53	12.34	4.50
1991	16.17	98.79	0.49	13.15	395	3187.51	12.09	4.09
1992	15.91	99.91	0.46	12.05	406	3268.16	11.68	3.92
1993	15.52	100.13	0.39	10.56	456	3661.59	11.52	3.40
1994	16.38	107.96	0.38	10.17	501	4009.25	11.63	3.27
1995	17.16	115.93	0.37	9.33	537	4280.97	11.48	3.20
1996	14.61	101.27	0.36	8.25	457	3633.88	11.29	3.20
1997	12.77	90.35	0.35	7.60	403	3196.10	11.08	3.17
1998	11.57	82.91	0.34	7.23	363	2871.61	10.80	3.19
1999	12.37	90.47	0.32	6.48	378	2984.60	9.78	3.27
2000	12.6	95.05	0.31	5.97	378	2979.43	9.26	3.33
2001	10.68	82.68	0.29	5.51				

Japan, *continued*

General Data

Year	Population (MIL)	GDP (BIL US$)	Exchange Rate (LCU/$)	Bank	Bank/M
1990	123.537	3039.69	144.79	92.58	749.42
1991	123.921	3267.28	134.71	189.44	1528.74
1992	124.229	3475.09	126.65	347.15	2794.45
1993	124.536	3958.04	111.20	350.53	2814.67
1994	124.961	4306.18	102.21	324.91	2600.11
1995	125.439	4679.21	94.06	349.19	2783.76
1996	125.761	4046.04	108.78	450.81	3584.65
1997	126.091	3637.67	120.99	568.91	4511.92
1998	126.41	3362.16	130.91	837.05	6621.69
1999	126.65	3863.90	113.91	975.71	7703.98
2000	126.87	4084.10	107.77	1096.69	8644.23
2001	127.14	3621.56	121.53	1263.44	9937.40

The Netherlands

Credit Card Data

Year	Credit Card Value (BIL US$)	Credit Card Value/C (US$)	Credit Card Value/GDP (%)	Credit Trxn (MIL)	Credit Trxn/C
1991					
1992					
1993					
1994					
1995					
1996	2.37	152.70	0.74	43.9	2.83
1997	3.82	244.89	0.63	38.9	2.49
1998	4.33	276.01	0.72	42.1	2.68
1999	4.68	296.26	0.81	44.1	2.79
2000	4.77	300.04	0.96	46.8	2.94
2001	4.73	295.76	0.98	47.5	2.97

Debit Card Data

Year	Debit Card Value (BIL US$)	Debit Card Value/C (US$)	Debit Card Value/GDP (%)	Debit Trxn (MIL)	Debit Trxn/C
1991	1.07	70.83	0.37	32	2.1
1992	2.16	142.05	0.70	46.6	3.1
1993	3.66*	238.95	1.25	61.3	4
1994	7.91*	510.46	2.65	125.8	8.1
1995	6.83	440.79	2.03	255.9	16.5
1996	9.47	610.80	2.95	371	23.9
1997	23.60	1512.53	3.87	485.5	31.1
1998	28.67	1825.90	4.75	595	37.9
1999	34.04	2154.59	5.89	700.3	44.3
2000	34.22	2152.21	6.87	801.5	50.4
2001	39.46	2466.52	8.14	954.4	59.7

Total Card Data

Year	Total Card Value (BIL)	Credit Card Value/TCV (%)	Total Card Value/C (US$)	Total Card Value/GDP (%)	Total Card Trxn (MIL)	Total Card Trxn/C	Credit Card Trxn/Total Trxn (%)
1991							
1992							
1993							
1994							
1995							
1996	11.83	20.0	763.50	3.68	414.90	26.77	10.58
1997	27.42	13.9	1757.42	4.49	524.40	33.62	7.42
1998	33.00	13.1	2101.91	5.47	637.10	40.58	6.61
1999	38.72	12.1	2450.85	6.70	744.40	47.11	5.92
2000	38.99	12.2	2452.25	7.83	848.30	53.35	5.52
2001	44.20	10.7	2762.28	9.12	1001.90	62.62	4.74

The Netherlands, *continued*

General Data

Year	Population (MIL)	GDP (BIL US$)	Exchange Rate (LCU/$)
1991	15.1	290.37	1.87
1992	15.2	308.52	1.76
1993	15.3	291.94	1.86
1994	15.5	298.35	1.82
1995	15.5	337.27	1.61
1996	15.5	321.30	1.69
1997	15.6	610.11	0.89#
1998	15.7	603.33	0.9#
1999	15.8	577.66	0.94#
2000	15.9	498.17	1.09#
2001	16	484.82	1.12#

New Zealand

Credit Card Data

Year	Credit Card Value (BIL US$)	Credit Card Value/C (US$)	Credit Card Value/GDP (%)
1990	2.68	777.26	6.2
1991	2.76	789.68	6.5
1992	2.65	750.35	6.5
1993	2.71	758.64	6.2
1994	3.34	922.63	6.5
1995	4.11	1118.85	6.7
1996	4.79	1283.49	7.2
1997	5.07	1340.42	7.6
1998	4.61	1208.39	8.4
1999	5.64	1470.63	9.8
2000	6.02	1560.47	11.6
2001	6.79	1749.77	13.1
2002	8.24	2090.86	13.7

Consumer and Card Debt Data

Year	CCD (MIL US$)	CCD/C (US$)	CCD/GDP (%)	CCD/CCV (%)	CONC (MIL US$)	CONC/C (US$)	CONC/GDP (%)	CCD/CONC (%)
1990	779.16	225.97	1.79	29.1				
1991	784.88	224.57	1.86	28.4				
1992	727.99	206.13	1.80	27.5				
1993	759.78	212.69	1.72	28.0				
1994	926.58	255.95	1.79	27.7				
1995	1150.94	313.32	1.89	28.0				
1996	1355.49	363.21	2.04	28.3				
1997	1408.88	372.48	2.11	27.8				
1998	1219.95	319.78	2.23	26.5	3260.28	854.60	5.95	37.42
1999	1372.93	357.99	2.39	24.3	3446.89	898.77	6.00	39.83
2000	1296.68	336.12	2.50	21.5	3088.29	800.53	5.94	41.99
2001	1355.97	349.43	2.61	20.0	3049.99	785.98	5.87	44.46
2002	1633.80	414.76	2.72	19.8	3553.70	902.16	5.92	45.97

General Data

Year	Population (MIL)	GDP (BIL US$)	Exchange Rate (LCU/$)
1990	3.45	43.52	1.68
1991	3.50	42.15	1.73
1992	3.53	40.47	1.86
1993	3.57	44.06	1.85
1994	3.62	51.67	1.69
1995	3.67	60.97	1.52
1996	3.73	66.60	1.46
1997	3.78	66.71	1.51
1998	3.82	54.79	1.87
1999	3.84	57.44	1.89
2000	3.86	51.96	2.21
2001	3.88	51.99	2.38
2002	3.94	59.99	2.16

Singapore

Credit Card Data

Year	Credit Card Value (BIL US$)	Credit Card Value/C (US$)	Credit Card Value/GDP (%)
1997	5.3	1398.42	5.65
1998	5.11	1303.57	5.59
1999	5.8	1468.35	6.30
2000	6.37	1584.58	6.64
2001	6.49	1614.43	6.76
2002	6.89	1667.66	8.18

Debit Card Data

Year	Debit Card Value (BIL US$)	Debit Card Value/C (US$)	Debit Card Value/GDP (%)	Debit Trxn (MIL)	Debit Trxn/C
1997	2.3	606.86	2.45	50.86	13.42
1998	2.35	599.49	2.57	57.9	14.77
1999	2.66	673.42	2.89	65.74	16.64
2000	2.86	711.44	2.98	76.93	19.14
2001	3.21	798.51	3.35	87.73	21.24
2002	3.56	861.71	4.23	97.2	23.31

Total Card Data

Year	Total Card Value (BIL US$)	Credit Card Value/TCV (%)	Total Card Value/C (US$)	Total Card Value/GDP (%)
1997	7.60	69.74	2005.28	8.10
1998	7.46	68.50	1903.06	8.17
1999	8.46	68.56	2141.77	9.18
2000	9.23	69.01	2296.02	9.62
2001	9.70	66.91	2412.94	10.11
2002	10.45	65.93	2529.37	12.41

General Data

Year	Population (MIL)	GDP (BIL US$)	Exchange Rate (LCU/$)
1997	3.79	93.81	1.68
1998	3.92	91.36	1.66
1999	3.95	92.11	1.67
2000	4.02	95.96	1.73
2001	4.13	84.21	1.85
2002	4.17	89.68	1.74

South Africa

Credit Card Data

Year	Credit Card Value (BIL US$)	Credit Card Value/C (US$)	Credit Card Value/GDP (%)	Credit Trxn (MIL)	Credit Trxn/C
1990	4.91	139.49	4.4	88.3	2.51
1991	5.15	143.45	4.3	99	2.76
1992	5.49	149.59	4.2	105.3	2.87
1993	5.29	141.07	4.1	111.2	2.97
1994	5.44	142.04	4.0	118.1	3.08
1995	6.27	160.36	4.2	129.8	3.32
1996	6.49	162.66	4.5	149.7	3.75
1997	7.01	172.24	4.7	156.9	3.86
1998	6.79	164.01	5.1	162.1	3.92
1999	6.76	160.57	5.2	159.4	3.79
2000	7.05	164.72	5.5	167.9	3.92
2001	6.39	147.92	5.6	186.7	4.32
2002	5.98	137.23	5.7	193.2	4.43

South Africa, *continued*

Consumer and Card Debt Data

Year	CCD (BIL US$)	CCD/C (US$)	CCD/GDP (%)	CCD/CCV (%)
1990	12	431.65	1.6	28
1991	13	460.99	1.7	28
1992	12	421.05	1.7	26
1993	12	416.67	1.8	28
1994	13	446.74	2	28
1995	15	510.20	2.2	28
1996	16	538.72	2.3	28
1997	17	566.67	2.4	27
1998	18	596.03	2.7	28
1999	21	688.52	2.9	30
2000	24	779.22	3.2	31
2001	25	803.86	3.6	32
2002	28	891.72	3.9	32

General Data

Year	Population (MIL)	GDP (BIL US$)	Exchange Rate (LCU/$)
1990	35.2	111.97	2.59
1991	35.9	120.29	2.76
1992	36.7	130.53	2.85
1993	37.5	130.28	3.27
1994	38.3	135.77	3.55
1995	39.1	150.96	3.63
1996	39.9	143.72	4.3
1997	40.7	148.81	4.61
1998	41.4	133.63	5.53
1999	42.1	130.88	6.12
2000	42.8	127.77	6.95
2001	43.2	113.90	8.63
2002	43.6	104.47	10.52

South Korea

Credit Card Data

Year	Credit Card Value (BIL US$)	Credit Card Value/C (US$)	Credit Card Value/GDP (%)
1996	34.4	756.04	5.77
1997	31.38	682.17	5.87
1998	24.28	524.41	6.95
1999	38.87	834.12	8.87
2000	73.13	1555.96	15.17
2001	138.15	2920.72	31.86
2002	214	4500.60	44.94

Consumer and Card Debt Data

Year	CCD (BIL US$)	CCD/C (US$)	CCD/GDP (%)	CCD/CCV (%)	CONC (BIL US$)	CONC/C (US$)	CONC/GDP (%)	CCD/CONC (%)
1996								
1997								
1998	1.51	32.61	0.43	6.22				
1999	2.68	57.51	0.61	6.89	204.79	4394.63	46.75	1.31
2000	11.12	236.60	2.31	15.21	259.50	5521.38	53.82	4.29
2001	29.34	620.30	6.77	21.24	272.76	5766.50	62.89	10.76
2002	44.06	925.73	9.24	20.57	363.79	7642.63	76.31	12.11

General Data

Year	Population (MIL)	GDP (BIL US$)	Exchange Rate (LCU/$)
1996	45.5	596.09	805
1997	46	534.27	951
1998	46.3	349.34	1404
1999	46.6	438.01	1190
2000	47	482.18	1131
2001	47.3	433.68	1292
2002	47.6	476.74	1251

Sweden

Credit Card Data

Year	Credit Card Value (BIL US$)	Credit Card Value/C (US$)	Credit Card Value/GDP (%)	Credit Trxn (MIL)	Credit Trxn/C
1991	7.10	825.58	2.97	68	7.91
1992	7.40	850.57	2.97	62	7.13
1993	5.51	633.33	2.96	68	7.82
1994	5.58	634.09	2.97	97	11.02
1995	6.02	684.09	2.96	101	11.48
1996	6.41	728.41	2.5	44	5.00
1997	5.63	639.77	2.6	48	5.45
1998	5.41	607.87	2.7	53	5.96
1999	5.20	584.27	2.8	57	6.40
2000	4.69	526.97	3.2	67	7.53
2001	4.16	467.42	3.3	74	8.31

Debit Card Data

Year	Debit Card Value (BIL US$)	Debit Card Value/C (US$)	Debit Card Value/GDP (%)	Debit Trxn (MIL)	Debit Trxn/C
1991					
1992					
1993					
1994					
1995					
1996	8.49	965.32	3.93	88	10.00
1997	10.08	1145.29	5.31	121	13.75
1998	12.20	1370.93	6.69	160	17.98
1999	14.39	1616.78	8.21	198	22.25
2000	15.59	1752.17	9.86	256	28.76
2001	17.89	2010.30	12.76	326	36.63

Total Card Data

Year	Total Card Value (BIL US$)	Credit Card Value/TCV (%)	Total Card Value/C (US$)	Total Card Value/GDP (%)	Total Card Trxn (MIL)	Total Card Trxn/C	Credit Card Trxn/Total Trxn (%)
1991							
1992							
1993							
1994							
1995							
1996	14.90	43.01	1693.73	6.90	132	15.00	33.33
1997	15.71	35.84	1785.06	8.28	169	19.20	28.40
1998	17.61	30.72	1978.79	9.66	213	23.93	24.88
1999	19.59	26.55	2201.05	11.17	255	28.65	22.35
2000	20.28	23.12	2279.14	12.83	323	36.29	20.74
2001	22.05	18.86	2477.72	15.73	400	44.94	18.50

General Data

Year	Population (MIL)	GDP (BIL US$)	Exchange Rate (LCU/$)
1991	8.6	239.27	6.06
1992	8.7	249.57	5.81
1993	8.7	185.90	7.8
1994	8.8	188.07	7.71
1995	8.8	203.08	7.14
1996	8.8	216.10	6.71
1997	8.8	189.79	7.64
1998	8.9	182.39	7.95
1999	8.9	175.33	8.27
2000	8.9	158.12	9.17
2001	8.9	140.23	10.34

United Kingdom

Credit Card Data

Year	Credit Card Value (BIL US$)	Credit Card Value/C (US$)	Credit Card Value/GDP (%)	Credit Trxn (MIL)	Credit Trxn/C
1990					
1991					
1992	69	1193.78	5		
1993	62	1066.95	5.2	812	13.99
1994	70	1202.98	5.5	888	15.27
1995	80	1366.96	5.9	994	17.06
1996	90	1545.6	6.6	1126	19.30
1997	107	1827.02	7.2	1252	21.41
1998	119	2037.4	7.5	1362	23.24
1999	132	2248.21	8.4	1490	25.37
2000	135	2296.28	9	1618	27.48
2001	138	2349.57	9.6	1745	29.55

Debit Card Data

Year	Debit Card Value (BIL US$)	Debit Card Value/C (US$)	Debit Card Value/GDP (%)	Debit Trxn (MIL)	Debit Trxn/C
1990					
1991					
1992					
1993					
1994	64.16	1105.36	7.68	1215	20.93
1995	80.86	1390.34	9.48	1432	24.62
1996	101.27	1738.50	11.51	1727	29.65
1997	132.48	2270.34	15.24	2248	38.52
1998	162.54	2779.90	17.82	2539	43.42
1999	196.95	3361.23	21.34	2918	49.80
2000	229.57	3908.69	25.46	3466	59.01
2001	244.45	4151.73	28.99	3808	64.67
2002	283.85	4807.02	35.38	4381	74.19

Total Card Data

Year	Total Card Value (BIL US$)	Credit Card Value/TCV (%)	Total Card Value/C (US$)	Total Card Value/GDP (%)	Total Card Trxn (MIL)	Total Card Trxn/C	Credit Card Trxn/Total Trxn (%)
1990							
1991							
1992							
1993	126.16	49.1	2173.58	15.1	2027	34.92	40.1
1994	150.86	46.4	2593.99	17.7	2320	39.89	38.3
1995	181.27	44.1	3111.89	20.6	2721	46.71	36.5
1996	222.48	40.5	3812.64	25.6	3374	57.82	33.4
1997	269.54	39.7	4609.91	29.5	3791	64.84	33.0
1998	315.95	37.7	5392.11	34.2	4280	73.04	31.8
1999	361.57	36.5	6156.18	40.1	4956	84.38	30.1
2000	379.45	35.6	6444.53	45.0	5426	92.15	29.8
2001	421.85	32.7	7144.02	52.6	6126	103.74	28.5

Consumer and Card Debt Data

Year	CCD (MIL US$)	CCD/C (US$)	CCD/GDP (%)	CCD/CCV (%)	CONC (MIL US$)	CONC/C (US$)	CONC/GDP (%)	CCD/CONC (%)
1990								
1991	1803	30.38	0.13		126761	2184.69	9.3	1.4
1992	310	5.39	0.02	0.45	120368	2078.53	8.8	0.25
1993	1342	22.41	0.11	2.2	99514	1706.87	8.3	1.3
1994	2756	46.13	0.22	4	107844	1860.91	8.5	2.6
1995	3918	67.29	0.29	4.9	127057	2192.09	9.5	3.1
1996	13742	236.2	1	15.3	138626	2380.32	10	9.9
1997	16564	284.7	1.1	15.5	161658	2773.04	11	10
1998	21406	367.53	1.4	18.2	186843	3213.92	12	11
1999	19217	327.19	1.2	14.5	202939	3452.22	13	9.5
2000	20857	356.25	1.4	15.5	202384	3451.74	14	10
2001	23662	405.31	1.6	17.3	207233	4463.47	14	11

United Kingdom, *continued*

General Data

Year	Population (MIL)	GDP (BIL US$)	Exchange Rate (LCU/$)	Bank	Bank/M
1990	57.6	989.56421	0.56	13987	243
1991	57.7	982.87	0.57	25640	444
1992	57.9	978.11	0.57	36794	635
1993	58.0	835.84	0.67	36703	633
1994	58.2	852.89	0.65	30739	528
1995	58.3	879.48	0.63	26319	451
1996	58.4	869.48	0.64	26271	451
1997	58.5	912.36	0.61	24441	419
1998	58.6	922.95	0.60	24549	420
1999	58.7	901.70	0.62	28806	492
2000	58.9	843.20	0.66	29528	503
2001	59.1	802.27	0.69	29775	506
2002	59.2			30587	508

United States

Credit Card Data

Year	Credit Card Value (BIL US$)	Credit Card Value/C (US$)	Credit Card Value/GDP (%)	Credit Trxn (BIL)	Credit Trxn/C
1990	816.23	3269.85	14.18	10.36	41.50
1991	800.44	3164.03	13.46	10.88	43.01
1992	823.21	3209.22	13.09	11.49	44.79
1993	875.22	3367.28	13.25	12.34	47.48
1994	955.34	3630.73	13.61	13.41	50.96
1995	1036.43	3892.29	14.12	14.63	54.94
1996	1097.29	4073.18	14.14	15.78	58.58
1997	1141.05	4184.93	13.83	16.45	60.33
1998	1199.7	4349.04	13.80	17.06	61.84
1999	1296.88	4647.65	14.07	18.37	65.83
2000	1362.31	4827.05	13.95	19.82	70.23
2001	1339.85	4695.99	13.33	21.05	73.78
2002					

Debit Card Data

Year	Debit Card Value (BIL US$)	Debit Card Value/C (US$)	Debit Card Value/GDP (%)	Debit Trxn (BIL)	Debit Trxn/C
1990	11.45	45.87	0.20	0.25	1.00
1991	13.91	54.98	0.23	0.34	1.34
1992	16.67	64.99	0.27	0.45	1.75
1993	23.84	91.72	0.36	0.63	2.42
1994	33.55	127.51	0.48	0.91	3.46
1995	74.16	278.51	1.01	1.55	5.82
1996	83.9	311.44	1.08	2.21	8.20
1997	133.53	489.74	1.62	3.39	12.43
1998	224.16	812.60	2.58	5	18.13
1999	249.23	893.17	2.70	6.43	23.04
2000	327.33	1159.82	3.35	8.37	29.66
2001	393.02	1377.48	3.91	10.62	37.22
2002	480	1664.53	4.60	13.41	46.50

Total Card Data

Year	Total Card Value (BIL US$)	Credit Card Value/TCV (%)	Total Card Value/C (US$)	Total Card Value/GDP (%)	Total Card Trxn (BIL)	Total Card Trxn/C	Credit Card Trxn/Total Trxn (%)
1990	827.68	98.6	3315.72	14.4	10.61	42.50	97.6
1991	814.35	98.3	3219.02	13.7	11.22	44.35	97.0
1992	839.88	98.0	3274.21	13.4	11.94	46.55	96.2
1993	899.06	97.3	3459.00	13.6	12.97	49.90	95.1
1994	988.89	96.6	3758.24	14.1	14.32	54.42	93.6
1995	1110.59	93.3	4170.79	15.1	16.18	60.76	90.4
1996	1181.19	92.9	4384.62	15.2	17.99	66.78	87.7
1997	1274.58	89.5	4674.66	15.4	19.84	72.77	82.9
1998	1423.86	84.3	5161.64	16.4	22.06	79.97	77.3
1999	1546.11	83.9	5540.82	16.8	24.8	88.88	74.1
2000	1689.64	80.6	5986.88	17.3	28.19	99.89	70.3
2001	1732.87	77.3	6073.47	17.2	31.67	111.00	66.5
2002							

United States, *continued*

Consumer and Card Debt Data

Year	CCD (BIL US$)	CCD/C (US$)	CCD/GDP (%)	CCD/CCV (%)	CONC (BIL US$)	CONC/C	CONC/GDP	CCD/CONC (%)
1990	459.73	1343.4	4.2	56	1525.09	6109.57	26.49	30.14
1991	460.98	1386.89	4.5	58	1385.57	5476.97	23.30	33.27
1992	465.46	1423.3	4.5	56	1316.87	5133.72	20.95	35.35
1993	495.5	1543.78	4.9	57	1330.89	5120.40	20.15	37.23
1994	555.97	1748.02	5.4	58	1449.4	5508.39	20.65	38.36
1995	639.8	2018.56	6.3	62	1562.91	5869.47	21.29	40.94
1996	684.51	2224.38	6.9	62	1596.05	5924.59	20.56	42.89
1997	692.7	2275.37	6.7	61	1597.24	5858.06	19.36	43.37
1998	686.49	2262.55	6.5	57	1641.17	5949.42	18.88	41.83
1999	711.61	2364.83	6.6	55	1685.62	6040.78	18.29	42.22
2000	745.93	2528.21	7	55	1738.41	6159.68	17.80	42.91
2001	746.62	2580.16	7.2	56	1756.34	6155.73	17.48	42.51
2002					1762	6110.23	16.90	

General Data

Year	Population (MIL)	GDP (BIL US$)	Bank (K)	Bank/M
1990	250	5757.2	718	2884
1991	253	5946.9	872	3460
1992	257	6286.8	901	3533
1993	260	6604.3	813	3151
1994	263	7017.5	780	2989
1995	266	7342.3	875	3382
1996	269	7762.3	1125	4198
1997	273	8250.9	1350	4963
1998	276	8694.6	1398	5084
1999	279	9216.2	1282	4595
2000	282	9764.8	1218	4319
2001	285	10049	1452	5095
2002	288	10429	1539	5344

Notes

Introduction

1. "Oral Evidence Taken Before a Treasury Select Committee of the United Kingdom Parliament on Thursday 16 October 2003," at 28–29 [hereinafter UK Credit Card Hearing], available at http://www.parliament.the-stationery-office.co.uk/pa/cm200203/cmselect/cmtreasy/uc962-v/uc96202.htm.

1. Paper of Plastic? The Functionality of Payment Systems

1. 31 U.S.C. § 5103. Naturally, there is no requirement that a private business accept currency or coins as payment for goods or services. Thus, a convenience store may refuse to accept $50 bills, and a vending machine operator may refuse to accept pennies.
2. Chapter 9 discusses whether attitudes about crime affect payment system choice and the related question of whether substantial use of card-based payments within a society is likely to reduce violent crime.
3. Daniel D. Garcia-Swartz et al. "The Economics of a Cashless Society: An Analysis of the Costs and Benefits of Payment Instruments." AEI-Brookings Joint Center for Regulatory Studies, Related Publication 04-24 (September 2004), available at http://www.aei-brookings.org/publications/ abstract.php?pid=853. Daniel Garcia-Swartz offers varying estimates of between $1.18 and $1.40 for the total social costs consumed by each check transaction. Multiplied by about forty billion checks per year, this comes to something more than $500 billion per year, in an economy producing about $10 trillion each year.
4. Elizabeth Klee. "Paper or Plastic? The Effect of Time on Check and Debit Card Use at Grocery Stores." Board of Governors of the Federal Reserve, Finance and Economics Discussion Series, No. 2006-2 (March 2006), available at http://www.federalreserve.gov/pubs/FEDS/2006/200602/200602abs.html.

2. The Mechanics of Payment Card Transactions

1. Richard Mitchell, "The Future of Visa and MasterCard," *Credit Card Management*, June 2004, at 36, 38.
2. Dove Consulting, Debit Card Fraud and Performance Benchmarking (Oct. 2005 study).

3. Jennifer Bayot, "MasterCard Settles Case with Retailers Ahead of Trial," *New York Times*, Apr. 23, 2003, at C1; Jennifer Bayot, "Final Pact Approved in Long-Running Debit Card Litigation," *New York Times*, Dec. 20, 2003, at C4.
4. A countervailing force might be the growing pressure on banks to raise PIN-based debit fees to cover the costs of those transactions. One recent study suggests that the rise in those fees puts the all-in costs to a supermarket on a par with the costs of accepting checks. See "Hannaford Finds PIN Debit Is Now as Expensive as Checks," *Digital Transaction News*, Sept. 21, 2005.
5. See "MasterCard Reports Debit Increase Nearly Triple That of Credit," *Digital Transaction News*, Nov. 1, 2005 (noting that signature-based debit is far more popular in the United States than in most other regions of the world).
6. See Jennifer Kingson Bloom, "Visa Stands by Updated Debit Card, Though Banks' Response Is Cool," *Am. Banker*, July 28, 1999, at 1, 13.
7. See "Your Debit Card Is the Key To Protecting Your Money," *USA Today*, Oct. 5, 1999, at 14A (full-page advertisement for Visa debit cards, which neglects to mention the disadvantageous EFTA rules discussed in the text).
8. See id.

3. In Defense of Credit Cards

1. E.g., George Ritzer, *Expressing America* (1995); Juliet B. Schor, *The Overspent American* (1998).
2. Compare, e.g., Lawrence M. Ausubel, "The Failure of Competition in the Credit Card Market," 81 *Am. Econ. Rev.* 50, 71 (1991), with David Evans and Richard Schmalensee, *Paying with Plastic: The Digital Revolution in Buying and Borrowing* (2nd ed. 2005).
3. Dee Hock, *Birth of the Chaordic Age* (1999); Lewis Mandell, *The Credit Card Industry: A History* (1990).
4. See Klee, op. cit.
5. See ch. 1, note 3.
6. This data comes from Issue 850 of the *Nilson Report*, a periodical with detailed information about all aspects of credit and debit card transactions in the United States. Because the *Nilson Report* is proprietary, it is not clear exactly how the data is collected. In the absence of publicly available data, it is, however, the best source for the United States.
7. Federal Reserve System, Board of Governors, Report to the Congress on the Profitability of Credit Card Operations of Depositary Institutions 5 (June 2005) [hereinafter *Federal Reserve 2005 Report*], available at http://www.federalreserve.gov/boarddocs/rptcongress/creditcard/2005/ccprofit.pdf (noting that more than 6,000 depositary institutions issue Visa and MasterCard credit cards).
8. See "Financial Services Used by Small Businesses: Evidence from the 1998 Survey of Small Business Finances," *Fed. Res. Bull.*, Apr. 2001, at 183.

4. The Psychology of Card Payments: Card Spending and Consumer Debt

1. Diane Ellis, "The Effect of Consumer Interest Rate Deregulation on Credit Card Volumes, Charge-offs, and the Personal Bankruptcy Rate," *Bank Trends 98–05* (FDIC, Div. of Ins., Mar. 1998).
2. See Jim VandeHei, "Business Sees Gain in GOP Takeover; Political Allies Push Corporate Agenda," *Wash. Post*, Mar. 27, 2005, at A01 (MBNA was the fifth largest contributor to the two presidential campaigns).

3. See Gary Rivlin, "The Chrome-Shiny, Lights-Flashing, Wheel-Spinning, Touch-Screened, Drew-Carey-Wisecracking, Video-Playing, 'Sound Events'-Packed, Pulse-Quickening Bandit," *N.Y. Times*, May 9, 2004, at 42.
4. "McDonald's Confirms the Cashless Ticket Lift," *Cardflash*, July 22, 2005, available at www.cardweb.com (subscription required).
5. Brian Brus, "Credit Buyers Soaring, Restaurants Swallow Costs to Savor Benefits," *Okla. City Journal Record*, July 14, 2005.
6. "Card Payments at Vending Machines Boost Sales," *PR Newswire*, Nov. 19, 2004, available at http://www.epaynews.com/index.cgi?survey=&ref=browse&f=view&id=1100872637622215212&block.
7. See Isabelle Lindenmayer, "Fast Food Embraces Cards, Hesitant on Contactless," *American Banker*, Aug. 4, 2005 (reporting statistics on the rapidly growing acceptance of credit cards by fast food restaurants).
8. "Are Contactless Payments an Irresponsible Idea?," *Wisemarketer.com*, 26 Sept. 2005 (discussing research suggesting that contactless payments will lead to more compulsive purchasing behavior).
9. Robert Manning has written the most trenchant criticism of the marketing efforts of card issuers. See Robert D. Manning, *Credit Card Nation: The Consequences of America's Addiction to Credit* (2000).
10. Two such papers are Elizabeth C. Hirschman, "Differences in Consumer Purchase Behavior by Credit Card Payment System," 6 *J. Consumer Research* 58 (1979); Gillian Garcia, "Credit Cards: An Interdisciplinary Survey," 6 *J. Consumer Research* 327 (1980).
11. Richard A. Feinberg, "Credit Cards as Spending Facilitating Stimuli: A Conditioning Interpretation," 18 *J. Consumer Research* 348 (1986).
12. Feinberg, supra note 11.
13. Drazen Prelec & Duncan Simester, "Always Leave Home Without It: A Further Investigation of the Credit-Card Effect on Willingness to Pay," 12 *Marketing Letters* 5 (2001).
14. James M. Hunt et al., "Credit Cards as Spending-Facilitating Stimuli: A Test and Extension of Feinberg's Conditioning Hypothesis," 67 *Psychol. Rep.* 323 (1990); Richard A. Feinberg, "The Social Nature of the Classical Conditioning Phenomena in People: A Comment on Hunt, Florsheim, Chatterjee, and Kernan," 67 *Psychol. Rep.* 331 (1990).
15. Joydeep Srivastava & Priya Raghubir, "Debiasing Using Decomposition: The Case of Memory-Based Credit Card Expense Estimates," 12 *J. Consumer Psychology* 253 (2002).
16. Dilip Soman & Amar Cheema, "The Effect of Credit on Spending Decisions: The Role of the Credit Limit and Credibility," 21 *Marketing Sci.* 32 (2002).
17. Elizabeth Warren & Amelia Warren Tyagi, *The Two-Income Trap: Why Middle-Class Mothers and Fathers Are Broke* (2003); Christopher L. Peterson, *Taming the Sharks: Towards a Cure for the High Cost Credit Market* (2004).
18. Richard Hynes, "Non-Procrustean Bankruptcy," 2004 *Ill. L. Rev.* 301, 340–43; Thomas H. Jackson, "The Fresh-Start Policy in Bankruptcy Law," 98 *Harv. L. Rev.* 1393, 1419 (1985).
19. Melissa B. Jacoby, "Does Indebtedness Influence Health? A Preliminary Inquiry," 30 *J.L. Med. & Ethics* 560 (2002).
20. Eric Posner, "Contract Law in the Welfare State: A Defense of Usury Laws, the Unconscionability Doctrine, and Related Limitations on the Freedom to Contract," 24 *J. Legal Stud.* 283 (1995).
21. Hynes, supra note 18, at 340–43; Jackson, supra note 18, at 1422.
22. Jackson, supra note 18.

23. Jackson, supra note 18.
24. We know little about the prevalence of nonadjusting creditors in consumer bankruptcy cases. For evidence from business cases, see Elizabeth Warren and Jay L. Westbrook, "Contracting Out of Bankruptcy: An Empirical Intervention," 118 *Harv. L. Rev.* 1197 (2005).
25. The U.S. data come from the Nilson Report. See supra ch. 3, note 6, for a description of that periodical. Data for Australia come from the Royal Bank's Web site at www.rba.gov.au. For Canada, I rely on data about Visa and MasterCard transactions that the Bank of Canada has provided. The most general source of information for the United Kingdom is APACS (the Association for Payment Clearing Services), available at www.apacs.org.uk. I have relied on APACS's Plastic Card Review 2004 for information about the number and amount of credit and debit card transactions. For credit card debt, I use data provided by the Bank of England. Japanese data is from the yearbooks of the Japanese Consumer Credit Industry Association.
26. See the discussion of Japan in note 25, supra.
27. Todd J. Zywicki, Testimony Presented to the Judiciary Committee of the United States on Bankruptcy Reform (Feb. 10, 2005) [hereinafter *Zywicki, Testimony*].
28. Specifically, I calculated variance inflation factors of 22 and 58 for those runs, substantially more than the customary limit of 10.
29. For an interesting OECD study of the problem, see OECD Economics Department, "The Decline in Private Savings Rates in the 1990s in OECD Countries: How Much Can Be Explained by Non-Wealth Determinants?" (ECO/WKP(2002) Dec. 2002), available at http://www.olis.oecd.org/olis/2002doc.nsf/linkto/eco-wkp(2002)30.

5. Over the Brink: Credit Card Debt and Bankruptcy

1. Lawrence M. Ausubel, "Credit Card Defaults, Credit Card Profits, and Bankruptcy," 71 *Am. Bankr. L. J.* (1997); Joanna Stavins, "Credit Card Borrowing, Delinquency, and Personal Bankruptcy," *New England Econ. Rev.*, July/Aug. 2000.
2. Teresa Sullivan et al., *The Fragile Middle Class* (2000) [hereinafter SWW, *Fragile Middle Class*].
3. Edith H. Jones & Todd J. Zywicki, "It's Time for Means-Testing," 1999 *BYU L. Rev.* 177; Todd J. Zywicki, "An Economic Analysis of the Consumer Bankruptcy Crisis," 99 *Nw. U. L. Rev.* 1463 (2005) [hereinafter Zywicki, *Economic Analysis*]; Zywicki, Testimony.
4. Ian Domowitz & Robert L. Sartain, "Determinants of the Consumer Bankruptcy Decision," 54 *J. Fin.* 403 (1999).
5. Joseph Lupton & Frank Stafford, *Five Years Older: Much Richer or Deeper in Debt?* (Jan. 2000), available at http://psidonline.isr.umich.edu/Publications/Papers/FiveYearsOlder.pdf.
6. Warren & Tyagi, op. cit., at 212 n. 8.
7. Demos, "Borrowing to Make Ends Meet: The Growth of Credit Card Debt in the 90s," available at http://www.demos-usa.org/demos/debt_assets/borrowing.pdf.
8. Martin Wolf, *Why Globalization Works* 152–57 (2004).
9. David B. Gross & Nicholas S. Souleles, "An Empirical Analysis of Personal Bankruptcy and Delinquency," 15 *Rev. Fin. Stud.* 319 (2002); Carol C. Bertaut & Michael Haliassos, "Debt Revolvers for Self-Control" (University of Cyprus Working Papers in Economics No. 0208, June 2002), available at http://papers.ssrn.com/sol3/papers.cfm?abstract˙id=276052; Michael Haliassos & Michael Reiter, "Credit Card Debt Puzzles" (Center for Financial Studies Working Paper No. 2005/26), available at http:www/ifk-cfs.de/papers/05˙26.pdf.

10. Sandra E. Black & Donald P. Morgan, "Meet the New Borrowers," 5 *Current Issues in Econ. & Fin.*(Fed. Res. Bank of New York), Feb. 1999, at 1; Mark Furletti, "Credit Card Pricing Developments and Their Disclosure" (Fed. Res. Bank of Philadelphia, Payment Cards Center, Discussion Paper) (January 2003) [hereinafter Furletti, *Card Pricing*].
11. Teresa Sullivan et al., *As We Forgive Our Debtors* (1989) [hereinafter SWW, *As We Forgive*]; SWW, *Fragile Middle Class*, supra note 2; Warren & Tyagi, op. cit.; Teresa A. Sullivan et al., "Who Uses Chapter 13?," in *Consumer Bankruptcy in Global Perspective* 269 (J. Niemi-Kiesiläinen, I. Ramsay, & W. Whitford, eds. 2003).
12. Warren & Tyagi, op. cit.; Melissa B. Jacoby et al., "Rethinking the Debates over Health-Care Financing: Evidence from the Bankruptcy Courts," 76 *NYU L. Rev.* 375 (2001).
13. David U. Himmelstein et al., "MarketWatch: Illness and Injury as Contributors to Bankruptcy," *Health Affairs*, February 2005.
14. The Griffiths Commission on Personal Debt, "What Price Credit?" (2005) [hereinafter Griffiths Commission, *2005 Report*].
15. Id.
16. Evans & Schmalensee, op. cit.
17. Manning op. cit. ch. 5; Warren & Tyagi, op. cit.
18. Jones & Zywicki, supra note 3; Zywicki, *Economic Analysis*, supra note 53; Zywicki, *Testimony*.
19. I discuss in Chapter 17 some of the difficulties in empirically testing the relation between filing rates and specific changes in bankruptcy law.
20. Zywicki, *Testimony*.

6. Explaining the Pattern of Global Card Use

1. See CardData, Bank Credit Card Convenience Usage – Current, available at http://www.cardweb.com/carddata/charts/convenience_usage.amp (last visited Dec. 20, 2004) (subscription required).
2. See Mandell, op. cit.; see also Evans & Schmalensee, op. cit.; Manning, Ritzer, *Expressing America*.

7. The Introduction of the Payment Card

1. See Matty Simmons, *The Credit Card Catastrophe* (1995).
2. Bank One Chicago, N.A. v. Midwest Bank & Trust Co., 516 U.S. 264, 266 (1996); see Ronald J. Mann, *Payment Systems and Other Financial Transactions* 22-23 (3rd ed. 2006) [hereinafter Mann, *Payment Systems*].
3. Mandell, op. cit.; Simmons, supra note 1.
4. See Ronald J. Mann, "A Payments Policy for the Information Age," 93 *Geo. L.J.* 633 (2005) [hereinafter Mann, *Payments Policy*].
5. See Peter Z. Grossman, *American Express: The Unofficial History of the People Who Built the Great Financial Empire* (1987); Mandell, op. cit.; Simmons, supra note 1.
6. See Joint Committee on Check Collection System, Study of Check Collection System (1954) (presented to American Bankers Association, Association of Reserve City Bankers, and Conference of Presidents of the Federal Reserve Banks).
7. See Mark J. Roe, *Strong Managers, Weak Owners: The Political Roots of American Corporate Finance* (1994).
8. See R. Alton Gilbert, "The Advent of the Federal Reserve and the Efficiency of the Payments Systems: The Collection of Checks, 1915–1930," 37 *Explorations in Econ. Hist.* 121 (2000).

9. See Harold van B. Cleveland, *Citibank: 1812–1970* (1986) (emphasizing the relative effects of deposit insurance on different types of financial institutions); James Grant, *Money of the Mind: Borrowing and Lending in America from the Civil War to Michael Milken* (1992).
10. Duncan McDowall, *Quick to the Frontier: Canada's Royal Bank* (1993).
11. See APACS, "Plastic Cards–History of Plastic Cards." Available at http://www.apacs.org.uk.
12. Mandell, op. cit. (presenting statistics on check guarantee cards in the United States).

8. Revolving Credit

1. See Timothy Wolters, "Carry Your Credit in Your Pocket: The Early History of the Credit Card at Bank of America and Chase Manhattan," 1 *Enterprise & Society* 315 (2000) (detailed history based on archival research of early credit card programs at Chase Manhattan and Bank of America); see also Hock, op. cit. (original founder of Visa provides an insider's account of Visa's inception and its early conflicts with MasterCard).
2. E.g., Hock, op. cit.; see also Evans & Schmalensee, op. cit. (providing a more sympathetic view of the effect of that decision on the competitive landscape).
3. See National Bank of Canada v. Interbank Card Association, 507 F. Supp. 1113 (S.D.N.Y. 1980) (rejecting an attempt by the National Bank of Canada to issue cards under both MasterCard and Visa brands).
4. See Robert Hendrickson, *The Cashless Society* (1972).
5. See Mandell, op. cit.; Grant, op. cit.
6. See Mandell, op. cit.
7. See Wolters, supra note 1.
8. See Lendol Calder, *Financing the American Dream: A Cultural History of Secured Credit* (1999); Martha Olney, *Buy Now, Pay Later: Advertising, Credit, and Consumer Durables in the 1920s* (1991).
9. See Evans & Schmalensee, op. cit.
10. See Cleveland, op. cit.; Grant, op. cit.; Wolters, supra note 1.
11. See Hock, op. cit.; Mandell, op. cit.; Wolters, supra note 1.
12. See Wolters, supra note 1.
13. See Mandell, op. cit.; Manning, op. cit.; Wolters, supra note 1.
14. See Simmons, op. cit.; Jon Friedman & John Meehan, *House of Cards: Inside the Troubled Empire of American Express* (1992).
15. See Ronald J. Mann, "Credit Cards and Debit Cards in the United States and Japan," 55 *Vand. L. Rev.* 1055 (2002) [hereinafter Mann, *Japanese Cards*].
16. See Hock, op. cit.
17. See Mann, *Japanese Cards*, supra note 15.
18. See Anne Segall, "Retail Banking in Britain: The Neglected Consumer," *The Economist*, Dec. 8, 1979, at 5 (discussing the restrictions on consumer lending by the large "clearing" banks before 1971, which led to consumer lending by "hire purchase companies" and "fringe ba[n]ks").
19. See Margaret Ackrill & Leslie Hannah, *Barclay's: The Business of Banking 1690–1996*, 188–89, 250 (2001) (discussing the termination of restrictions).
20. See Ackrill & Hannah, supra note 19, at 188–89.
21. See Mann, *Japanese Cards*, supra note 15.
22. See Matt Ablott, "French Banks Accused of Cards Cartel Carve-up," *Cards International*, Issue 322 (2004), at 3.

23. "Debit Cards Dominate Belgian Market," *Cards International*, Issue 299 (2003), at 17 [hereinafter *Belgian Debit Cards*].
24. See "Eurocard," *The Economist*, Apr. 29, 1978.
25. "Portugal Offers Growth Potential," *Cards International*, Issue 322 (2004), at 20 [hereinafter *Portuguese Potential*].
26. See "Slovenia – A Small Market with Big Potential," *Cards International*, Issue 328 (2004), at 12.

9. Point-of-Sale Debit

1. For a general account of debit cards worldwide, see Arnold Rosenberg, "Better than Cash? Global Proliferation of Payment Cards and Consumer Protection Policy" 44 Col. J. Transnat'l L. 520 (2006).
2. See "Card Transactions a Sure Bet for the Future," *Credit Union J.*, Mar. 28, 2005, at 28 (suggesting that consumers who are worried about the loss of float induced by Check 21 should use credit cards instead of checks).
3. TILA §133; EFTA §909; see Mann, *Payments Policy*.
4. TILA §170.
5. See Howard Strong, *What Every Credit Card User Needs to Know: How To Protect Yourself and Your Money* (1999).
6. See Consumer Credit Act §§75 (parallel to TILA §170), 83–84 (parallel to TILA §133). See Office of Fair Trading v. Lloyds TSB Bank, [2006] EWCA Civ 268 (CA (Civ Div)) (holding that the Consumer Credit Act protections extend to transactions in which cards are used outside the United Kingdom); Graham Stephenson, *Credit, Debit and Cheque Cards: Law and Practice* (1993).
7. Cost of Borrowing Regulations §12; see Benjamin Geva, "Consumer Liability in Unauthorized Electronic Funds Transfers," 38 *Canadian Bus. L.J.* 207 (2003).
8. Japan's protection against unauthorized transactions (parallel to TILA §133) appears in Article 30 of the Installment Sales Law [Kappu hanbaihō], Law No. 159 of 1961. That law, however, only applies to *kappu* transactions (a legal category that involves extended borrowing); it excludes the overwhelming majority of transactions that are accomplished through *ikkai barai* (payment in the first month). See Mann, *Japanese Cards*. The distinction is not accidental. The Japanese press report continued pressure (unsuccessful to date) to convince issuers to offer protections similar to those available to American cardholders. See Isabel Reynolds, "Glimmer of Hope for Japan's Card Fraud Victims," *Reuters*, Feb. 21, 2005.
9. Voluntary codes among banks in Australia, Canada, and the United Kingdom provide protection for unauthorized debit card transactions where the cardholder is not negligent, but assign responsibility to negligent cardholders. See Geva, supra note 7; Stephenson, supra note 6; see also Rosenberg, supra note 1 (noting that consumer protections for debit cards worldwide are minimal).
10. See Mann, *Payments Policy*.
11. See id.
12. See Demos, op. cit.
13. See Ronald J. Mann, "Regulating Internet Payment Intermediaries," 82 *Texas L. Rev.* 681 (2004) [hereinafter Mann, *Payment Intermediaries*].
14. Nilson Report 818.
15. See Dina ElBoghdady, "For Some, No Purchase Is Too Small for Plastic," *Washington Post*, Feb. 23, 2005, at A01; Robin Sidel, "Cash? What's Cash?," *Wall St. J.*, Jan. 31, 2005, at R3.
16. See Richard Thaler, *Quasi-Rational Economics* (1991).

17. The empirical evidence appears to be equivocal. See Jonathan Zinman, "Debit or Credit?" (Oct. 2005 working paper), available at http://www.dartmouth.edu/~jzinman.
18. See Calder, op. cit.
19. See Dove Consulting, op. cit.
20. See Mann, *Japanese Cards*.
21. See id.
22. See id.
23. See Euromonitor, *World Market for Financial Cards* (2002).
24. Academically, this hypothesis generally is associated with the work of David Humphrey. See David B. Humphrey et al., 28 *J. Money, Credit & Banking* 914 (1996).
25. See Sara Sun Beale, "The Political, Social, Psychological and Other Non-Legal Factors Influencing the Development of (Federal) Criminal Law," 1 *Buffalo Crim. L. Rev.* 23 (1997).
26. See UNICRI, *Understanding Crime: Experiences of Crime and Crime Control* (1993).
27. See Mandell, op. cit.
28. See Curtis J. Milhaupt & Mark D. West, "The Dark Side of Private Ordering: An Institutional and Empirical Analysis of Organized Crime," 67 *U. Chi. L. Rev.* 41 (2000).
29. See Euromonitor, supra note 23.
30. See "India's Banks Join the Party," *Cards International*, Newsletter 483 (2002).
31. See Jose L. Negrin, The Regulation of Payment Cards: The Mexican Experience, 4 *Rev. Network Econ*. 243, 245 (2005).
32. See "Global Report on Crime and Justice" (G. Newman, ed. 1999) (noting that problem).
33. See "Global Report on Crime and Justice," supra note 32 (noting that problem).
34. Because each value in a time series is likely to be related to the present and future values, there is a possibility that statistical tests will report spurious correlations. The Durbin-Watson statistic is a standard test for determining whether this problem afflicts a particular data set. The first model in the Humphrey paper (which includes a much larger number of variables, including country dummies and variables for the prices of various products) produces a Durbin-Watson statistic ranging from 1.714 to 2.321. Because a value of 2 indicates that there is not undue autocorrelation, the values indicate that the analysis is only marginally reliable. That model, however, did not indicate a significant relationship for the crime variable. The authors ran a second set of models that excluded the dummy and price variables. In that analysis, the variable for crime was significant, at the 5% level. Unfortunately, the Durbin-Watson coefficient for that model is 0.194, far too low to make the analysis reliable. Accordingly, on its face the analysis suggests that their data tell us little about the relation between crime and card use.
35. The data include thirteen countries: Belgium, Canada, France, Germany, Hong Kong, Italy, Japan, the Netherlands, Singapore, Sweden, Switzerland, the United Kingdom, and the United States. Those countries account for significantly more than two-thirds of world use of plastic cards. With significant gaps, the data currently available run from 1996 to 2003, providing fifty-four observations.
36. The authors state only that their data comes "from BIS reports [and] other published sources."
37. Like the analysis in Chapters 4 and 5, the analysis here uses StataSE9, running ordinary least squares regressions, with robust clusters to control for autocorrelation in the time series. The credit card variable reflects current U.S. dollars per capita. Homicide and violent crime reflect crimes per 100,000 population.
38. See Hendrickson, op. cit.

10. Convergence and Exceptionalism in the Use of Cards

1. Mann, *Japanese Cards*, at 1080–81.
2. See "New Entrants Shake Up Irish Market," *Cards International*, Issue 319 (2004), at 23 (Ireland).
3. See "Debit Cards Dominate Belgian Market," *Cards International*, Issue 299 (2003), at 17 [hereinafter *Belgian Debit Cards*]; "Portugal Offers Growth Potential," *Cards International*, Issue 322 (2004), at 20 [hereinafter *Portuguese Potential*].
4. See "Cards Slowly Overcoming Barriers in Indonesia," *Cards International*, Issue 316 (2004), at 19 [hereinafter *Indonesian Cards Barriers*] (discussing Citibank's general business model in Asia); Wayne Arnold, "Boom Time for Credit in Southeast Asia," *N.Y. Times*, Nov. 12, 2004 (discussing Citibank's success in Malaysia, the Philippines, and Indonesia); "Cards Jump on Consumer Credit Bandwagon in Poland," *Cards International*, Issue 296 (2003), at 19 (discussing Citibank's business model in Poland).
5. See "Culture Clash for Chinese Cards," *Cards International*, Issue 325 (2004), at 2; Matt Ablott, "Citibank's Chinese Head-Start," *Cards International*, Issue 298 (2003), at 10; "South Korea Takes Action over Credit Debt Crisis," *Cards International*, Issue 294/295 (2003), at 9 [hereinafter *South Korean Action*].
6. See Shawn W. Crispin, "Thailand Acts to Slow Down Some Lending," *Wall St. J.*, Mar. 25, 2004, at A15 (discussing Thai rules that cap interest rates at 18% and require a minimum salary of about $4,500 a month for cardholders); Arnold, supra note 4 (discussing role of GECC).
7. See George Ritzer, *The Globalization of Nothing* (2004).
8. See "Adib Launches Credit Card that Complies with Sharia," *Gulf News*, Jul. 5, 2004, available at www.zawya.com (last visited July 30, 2004) [hereinafter *Adib's Sharia Card*].
9. See Euromonitor, supra note (discussing southern Europe).
10. See "Dutch Revolve, But Not on Cards," *Cards International*, Issue 318 (2004), at 24.
11. See Euromonitor, supra note (discussing Saudi Arabia); *Indonesian Cards Barriers*, supra note 5 (discussing Indonesia).
12. See *Adib's Sharia Card*, supra note 8 (discussing "Sharia-compliant" credit card issued in 2004 in Abu Dhabi); "The Risk-Reward Challenge of Credit Cards in the Middle East," *Cards International*, Issue 319 (2004), at 14 [hereinafter *Middle East Credit Cards*] (discussing business problems in fostering cards in the Middle East).
13. See *Indonesian Cards Barriers*, supra note 5 (discussing efforts by Citibank to foster use of revolving credit by Muslim population in Indonesia); Arnold, supra note 4 (discussing Citibank's success in Indonesia).
14. See "Japanese Consumer Debt; Less Thrifty Than They Seemed," *The Economist*, Feb. 8, 1992 (making that point with 1990s data); Mann, *Japanese Cards* (discussing 2000-era data with similar implications).
15. See Raghuram G. Rajan & Luigi Zingales, *Saving Capitalism from the Capitalists* (2003).
16. See Nuria Diez Guardia, "Consumer Credit in the European Union" (ECRI Research Report No. 1) (Feb. 2000) (an older empirical study of the distribution of consumer credit in the EU).
17. For details, see Mark D. West, *Law in Everyday Japan: Sex, Sumo, Suicide, and Statutes* 228–30 (2005). See also Arnold, supra note 4 (suggesting that recent Thai limits on credit cards might have a similar effect, driving lower-income borrowers to "loan sharks").
18. See 2003 A.T. Kearney/FOREIGN POLICY Magazine Globalization Index, available at http://www.foreignpolicy.com/wwwboard/g-index.php (last visited Nov. 11, 2005).

19. See Marco Pagano & Tullio Jappelli, "Information Sharing in Credit Markets," 48 *J. Fin.* 1693 (1993) (discussing the rise of credit bureaus).
20. See Robert M. Hunt, "Development and Regulation of Consumer Credit Reporting in the US," in *The Economics of Consumer Credit: European Experience and Lessons from the U.S.* (Giuseppe Bertola et al. eds. forthcoming); Amparo San José Riestra, "Credit Bureaus in Today's Credit Markets" (ECRI Research Report No. 4) (Sept. 2002).
21. See Hock, op. cit.
22. Peter L. McCorkell, "The Impact of Credit Scoring and Automated Underwriting on Credit Availability," in *The Impact of Public Policy on Consumer Credit* 209 (Thomas A. Durkin & Michael E. Staten eds. Kluwer 2002).
23. See Hunt, supra note 20.
24. See Evans & Schmalensee, op. cit.
25. 15 U.S.C. §§1681 et seq.
26. See Bill Grady, *Credit Card Marketing* (1992) (discussing how American issuers use data for marketing).
27. See Ronald J. Mann & Jane Kaufman Winn, *Electronic Commerce* 208–16 (2nd ed. 2005).
28. See Data Protection Directive arts. 7, 15.
29. See Nicola Jentzsch, "The Regulation of Financial Privacy: The United States vs. Europe" (ECRI Research Report No. 5) (June 2003).
30. See Hunt, supra note 20.
31. See Tullio Jappelli & Marco Pagano, "The Role and Effects of Credit Information Sharing," in *The Economics of Consumer Credit: European Experience and Lessons from the U.S.* (Giuseppe Bertola et al. eds. forthcoming) (March 2000); Tullio Jappelli & Marco Pagano, "Information Sharing, Lending, and Defaults: Cross-Country Evidence," 26 J. Banking & Finance 2017 (2002); Nicola Jentzsch & Amparo San Jose Riestra, "Consumer Credit Markets in the United States and Europe," in *The Economics of Consumer Credit: European Experience and Lessons from the U.S.* (Giuseppe Bertola et al. eds. forthcoming 2006); Jorge A. Padilla & Marco Pagano, "Sharing Default Information as a Borrower Discipline Device," 44 *European Economics Review* 1951 (2000).
32. See "Overindebtedness in the Enlarged EU," *Cards International*, Issue 319 (2004), at 20.
33. See "Proposal for a Directive of the European Parliament and of the Council on the Harmonization of the Law, Regulations and Administrative Provisions of the Member States Concerning Credit for Consumers," *COM* (2002) 443 (Sept. 11, 2002).
34. See APACS, "The Proposed Consumer Credit Directive (*COM* (2002) 443) & Its Potential Consequences for the UK Credit Card Market" (Apr. 23, 2003) (providing an industry perspective).
35. See MBNA's 2004 10-K at 3–6 (discussing arrangements with affinity sponsors, underwriting techniques, and collection practices); see also Michael E. Staten & Fred H. Cate, "The Impact of Opt-in Privacy Rules on Retail Credit Markets: A Case Study of MBNA," 52 *Duke Law Journal* 745 (2003) (arguing that a rigorous application of fair information practices would undermine those techniques).
36. For details, see Chapter 16.
37. See "Snap!," *The Economist*, Jan. 10, 2004 (discussion of the South Korean government's vigorous encouragement of credit card borrowing); "Hangover Cure: South Korea's Banks," *The Economist*, June 5, 2004 (same).
38. See "The Korea Credit Card Meltdown – What Happened and What Lessons Are Relevant?," *Cards International*, Issue 318 (2004), at 13; "Korean Card Company Blacklist

Reaches 3m," *Cards International*, Issue 297 (2003), at 11 [hereinafter *Korean Card Blacklist*].

39. See "Korean Rescue Programmes Unveiled," *Cards International*, Issue 298 (2003), at 23; *Korean Card Blacklist*, supra note 38; "Investors Nervous over South Korean Card Debts," *Cards International*, Issue 296 (2003), at 11; *South Korean Action*, supra note 5.
40. See Na Jeong-Ju, South Korean Households' Debt Reach an All-Time High Last Year, Korea Times, Mar. 2, 2006.
41. See "Regulators Tighten South Korea's Belt," *Cards International*, Issue 290 (2003); see also "The New Spendthrifts," *The Economist*, Apr. 20, 2002 (attributing high default rates in Hong Kong to reliance on credit bureaus that contain only "blacklist" information); "Taiwan Takes Action over Credit Crunch Fears," *Cards International*, Issue 319 (2004), at 9 (attributing stability of Taiwanese market, as compared to Korean market, to capabilities of national credit bureau).
42. See "Turkish Card Growth Accelerates," *Cards International*, Issue 321 (2004), at 16; see also *Portuguese Potential*, supra note 3 (describing recent similar effort in Portugal).
43. See Tony Morbin, "Chinese to Launch National Credit Bureau in 2005," *Cards International*, Issue 325 (2004), at 3 (China); "India Credit Bureau Set for Launch in 2005," *Cards International*, Issue 327 (2004), at 10 (India); "India Unveils First National Credit Bureau," *Cards International*, Issue 319 (2004), at 8 (India).
44. See "Hong Kong Returns to Profitability," *Cards International*, Issue 320 (2004), at 12; see also "Singaporean Credit Bureau Promotes Positive Data Sharing," *Cards International*, Issue 334 (2005), at 6 (discussing similar plan in Singapore).
45. See "From Communism to Consumerism," *The Economist*, Mar. 1, 2003 (discussing plans for credit bureaus and use of credit scoring in Poland and the Czech Republic).
46. See *Middle East Credit Cards*, supra note 12 (discussing actions of central banks in Oman, Kuwait, UAE, Saudi Arabia, Bahrain, and Qatar).

11. Indirect Approaches: Regulating Interchange and Encouraging Surcharges

1. See "Office of Fair Trading, MasterCard Interchange Fees: Preliminary Conclusions" (Feb. 2003); Reserve Bank of Australia, "Reform of Credit Card Schemes in Australia: Final Reforms and Regulatory Impact Statement" (Aug. 2002); European Commission Decision of 24 July 2002 (Case No. COMP/29.373); European Commission Decision of 9 August 2001 (Case No. COMP/29.373) (the Visa litigation). The EU Commission recently initiated a similar case against MasterCard. See "Now It's MasterCard's Turn for Interchange over Fees, *European Banker*," November 30, 2003, at 1. Issuers report that interchange fees are being reviewed in a number of other jurisdictions, including Poland, Spain, New Zealand, Portugal, Mexico, Colombia, South Africa, and Switzerland. See MasterCard Incorporated 10-K for year ending December 31, 2004, at 14. In addition, the Federal Reserve Bank of Kansas City recently held a conference to consider the propriety of similar regulations in the United States. http://www.kc.frb.org/FRFS/PSR/2005/05prg.htm. Although regulators in the United States have been less aggressive in challenging interchange fees, merchants have raised challenges, largely on antitrust grounds, targeting the fees as the product of collusion either between MasterCard and Visa or among the member banks of those organizations. See Eric Dash, "7 Big Retail Chains Sue Visa, Saying Its Fees Are a Form of Price Fixing," *N.Y. Times*, July 16, 2005 (discussing merchant lawsuits). See generally Stuart E. Weiner & Julian Wright, "Interchange Fees in Various Countries: Developments and Determinants," 4 *Rev. Network Econ.* 290 (2005).

2. "RBA: Gresham's Law of Payments," *Cards International*, Issue 337, (2005), at 10 (reporting speech by Ian J Macfarlane, Governor, Reserve Bank of Australia and chairman of the Council of Financial Regulators).
3. See Howard Chang et al., "The Effect of Regulatory Intervention in Two-Sided Markets: An Assessment of Interchange-Fee Capping in Australia," 4 *Rev. Network Economics* 328 (2005).
4. See John Simon, "Payment Systems Are Different: Shouldn't Their Regulation Be Too?," 4 *Rev. Network Econ.* 364 (2005).
5. See David B. Humphrey et al., "Realizing the Gains from Electronic Payments: Costs, Pricing, and Payment Choice," 33 *J. Money, Credit & Banking* 216 (2001).
6. See Gerard Lysaght, "Swimming Successfully Against the Tide," *Cards International*, Issue 345 (2005), at 14.
7. See Food Marketing Institute, "A Retailer's Guide to Electronic Payment Systems" (1998); Fumiko Hayashi, "A Puzzle of Card Payment Pricing: Why Are Merchants Still Accepting Card Payments?" 5 *Rev. Network Econ.* 144 (2006); Swartz et al., op. cit.
8. Mann, *Japanese Cards*.
9. Interviews with British regulators and credit card executives. For the EU generally, the rates are discussed in the Commission Decisions of 24 July 2002 and 9 August 2001 (both in Case No. COMP/29.373).
10. See Isabelle Lindenmayer, "Warnings of a Downside for Amex in Bank Cards," *American Banker*, Mar. 22, 2005.
11. See Evans & Schmalensee, op. cit.
12. See Gwendolyn Bounds & Robin Sidel, "Merchants Balk at Higher Fees for Credit Cards," *Wall St. J.*, Apr. 12, 2005, at B1.
13. See Dennis W. Carlton & Alan S. Frankel, "The Antitrust Economics of Credit Card Networks," 63 *Antitrust L.J.* 643 (1995); Alan S. Frankel, "Monopoly and Competition in the Supply and Exchange of Money," 66 *Antitrust L.J.* 313 (1998).
14. See Adam J. Levitin, "America's Payment Systems, No-Surcharge Rules, and the Hidden Costs of Credit," 3 *Berk. Bus. L. J.* 69 (2006).
15. See Levitin, supra note 14.
16. See Frankel, supra note 13.
17. See Levitin, supra note 14.
18. See Edmund W. Kitch, "The Framing Hypothesis: Is It Supported by Credit Card Issuer Opposition to a Surcharge on a Cash Price?," 6 *J.L., Econ. & Org.* 217 (1990).
19. See Kitch, supra note 18.
20. See Irvin Molotsky, "The Hidden Costs of the Cashless Society," *N.Y. Times*, Mar. 4, 1984, § 4, at 3.
21. See Robert White, "The Impact of Australia's Credit Card Reform on the Nation's Payment Value Chain" (Aug. 2004 white paper), available at edgardunn.com; "Australian Market Tackles Regulation," *Cards International*, Nov. 2004 (Issue 329), at 16, 17. Recent evidence, however, suggests that more and more merchants may be surcharging as cardholders become accustomed to the practice. "More Aussie Retailers Plan Surcharges for Credit Card Payments," digitaltransactionsnews, Mar. 21, 2006.
22. See Matt Ablott, "MasterCard and Visa Go Separate Ways on Surcharging," *Cards International*, Issue 325 (2004), at 10.
23. See Peter Lucas, "PIN Debit: Grounded," *Credit Card Management*, May 2005, at 16.

12. Contract Design

1. See Alan M. White & Cathy Lesser Mansfield, "Literacy and Contract," 13 *Stan. L. & Pol'y Rev.* 233, 235–41 (2002) (discussing incomprehensibility of financial disclosures); William R. Emmons, "Consumer-Finance Myths and Other Obstacles to Financial Literacy," 24 *St. Louis U. Public L. Rev.* 335 (2005).
2. See Nilson Report, Issue 843 (2005).
3. Federal Reserve, 2005 Report, supra note (discussing industry study that shows that an estimated 5.23 billion direct mail solicitations were sent by issuers during 2004, up 22% from 4.29 billion in 2003, with 71% of U.S. households receiving an average of 5.7 offers per month).
4. Id. (noting that the response rate on credit card solicitations in 2004 was estimated to be 0.4%).
5. See Robert D. Cooter & Edward L. Rubin, "A Theory of Loss Allocation for Consumer Payments," 66 *Texas L. Rev.* 63 (1987); Clayton Gillette, "Rolling Contracts as an Agency Problem," 2004 *Wis. L. Rev.* 679 (2004); Russell Korobkin, "Bounded Rationality, Standard Form Contracts, and Unconscionability," 70 *U. Chi. L. Rev.* 1203 (2003); see also Restatement of Contracts (Second) § 211 cmt. b ("A party who makes regular use of a standardized form of agreement does not ordinarily expect his customers to understand or even to read the standard terms.").
6. See Arthur R. Gaudio, "Electronic Real Estate Records: A Model for Action," 24 *W. New Eng. L. Rev.* 271, 284–85 (2002) (discussing the development of the standard residential real estate mortgage by the Federal National Mortgage Association [Fannie Mae]); Ronald J. Mann, "Searching for Negotiability in Payment and Credit Systems," 44 *UCLA L. Rev.* 951, 971 (1997) (same).
7. See, e.g., Kenneth S. Abraham, *Insurance Law and Regulation* 32 (3rd ed. 2000) ("[S]tandardization in insurance * * * involves * * * an offer of the same policy, to all customers, by all companies. Competition in insurance markets, therefore, often tends to be over price, quality of service, or reliability, but rarely over the terms of coverage itself.").
8. See Badie v. Bank of America, 79 Cal. Rptr. 2d 273 (Ct. App. 1998) (declining to enforce "bill-stuffer" amendment that added arbitration term even though cardholder did not close or stop using account upon receipt of amendment with bill). For statutory references, see, e.g., Del. Code Ann. Tit. 5 §952; Ga. Code Ann. §7–5-4(c); Proposed Consumer Credit Code Amendments, S.B. 252 (Utah 2006) (authorizing lenders to contract for class action waivers through unilateral amendments to consumer credit card contracts); see also Strand v. U.S. Bank Nat'l Ass'n ND, 693 N.W.2d 918 (N.D. 2005) (holding that bill-stuffer amendment waiving the right to file a class action was procedurally unconscionable, but enforceable because the term was not substantively unconscionable).
9. See, e.g., Shea v. Household Bank, 105 Cal. App. 4th 85 (2003) (holding that failure to repay outstanding balance was not sufficient "use" to support bilateral modification); Rossman v. Fleet Bank Nat'l Ass'n, 280 F.3d 384 (3d Cir. 2002) (noting that interest rate would increase from 7.99% to 24.99% upon closure of account).
10. To give context: one major issuer recently amended its agreement to provide that it can charge its default rate to any cardholder that is late or over the limit twice in a single year. Thus, a cardholder with a $12,000 annual limit that makes two $50 over-the-limit transactions on a single day thus might be exposed to a default rate on the existing $12,000 of debt, even if that type of conduct would not have been an event of default at the time the funds were borrowed. This seemingly minor amendment reflects a shift from a model in which issuers welcome over-the-limit

transactions (as an identifier of borrowers likely to pay interest) to a model in which issuers rely on cognitive difficulties that cardholders face in tracking their outstanding balances to collect fees on accidental over-the-limit transactions by liquid borrowers.

11. Some courts have rejected the argument that payment of an annual fee precludes the issuer from modifying or terminating the agreement for that period. E.g. Gaynoe v. First Union Direct Bank, N.A., 2001 WL 34000142 (N.C. Super. Ct. Jan. 18, 2001) (holding that annual fees are not fees paid for services to be performed over time, but rather in consideration of issuing a card).
12. Regulation Z, 12 C.F.R. §226.1 et seq. requires a credit card issuer to give fifteen days' written notice of a change in terms if the term was required to be disclosed initially under 12 C.F.R. §226.6 or if the required minimum payment is increased. 12 C.F.R. §226.9(c)(1). The timing requirement does not apply if a rate or fee is increased due to the customer's default, and the notice requirement does not apply if the change involves late payment charges, over-the-limit charges, or other specified occurrences.
13. See James J. White, "Autistic Contracts," 45 *Wayne L. Rev.* 1693, 1700–01 (2000) (asserting that modification of credit card agreements following notice and use is consistent with the objective theory of contracts and practical necessity).
14. See Garber v. Harris Trust & Savings Bank, 104 Ill. App. 3d 675 (1982) (holding that a separate contract was created each time the card was used according to the terms of the cardholder agreement at the time of such use).
15. See David M. Grether et al., "The Irrelevance of Information Overload: An Analysis of Search and Disclosure," 59 S. *Cal. L. Rev.* 277, 296–97 (1986); James R. Bettman, *An Information-Processing Theory of Consumer Choice* (1979); Herbert A. Simon, "Rationality as Process and as Product of Thought," *American Economic Review*, May 1978, at 1, 13; see also Susan Block-Lieb & Edward Janger, "The Myth of the Rational Borrower: Rationality, Behaviorism, and the Misguided "Reform" of Bankruptcy Law," 84 *Texas L. Rev.* (forthcoming) (reviewing the literature).
16. Jeffrey Davis, "Protecting Consumers from Overdisclosure and Gobbledygook: An Empirical Look at the Simplification of Consumer-Credit Contracts," 63 *Va. L. Rev.* 841 (1977).
17. The agreement is set forth in 63 *Va. L. Rev.* at 908–11. It is perhaps one-quarter the length of a modern credit cardholder agreement.
18. See Davis, supra note 16, at 854–56.
19. See Philip Schuchman, "Consumer Credit by Adhesion Contracts," 35 *Temple L.Q.* 125, 134–35 (1962) (discussing some of the detailed legal acumen required for understanding consumer credit contracts).
20. Jinkook Lee & Jeanne M. Hogarth, "Relationships Among Information Search Activities When Shopping for a Credit Card," 34 *J. Consumer Affairs* 330 (2000) (documenting rarity with which consumers evaluate anything other than the most basic financial terms).
21. See Jon D. Hanson & Kyle D. Logue, "The First Party Insurance Externality: An Economic Justification for Enterprise Liability," 76 *Cornell L. Rev.* 129, 154–58 (1990) (discussing lack of competitive pressure on terms not examined by consumers); Korobkin, supra note 5 (explaining incentive of drafters to include one-sided terms regardless of whether the terms are efficient when terms are not within the limited number of attributes that consumers are expected to price).
22. See Jackson, op. cit.
23. See Xavier Gabaix & David Laibson, "Shrouded Attributes, Consumer Myopia, and Information Suppression in Competitive Markets," 121 *Quarterly Journal of Economics* (forthcoming) (summarizing literature).

24. See, e.g., Jon D. Hanson & Douglas A. Kysar, "Taking Behavioralism Seriously: The Problem of Market Manipulation," 74 *NYU L. Rev.* 630, 654–58 (1999); James R. Bettman et al., *Cognitive Considerations in Presenting Risk Information, in Learning About Risk: Consumer and Worker Responses to Hazard Information* 15, 17 (1987); Neil D. Weinstein, "Unrealistic Optimism About Future Life Events," 39 *J. Personality & Soc. Psychol.* 806, 809–12 (1980).
25. See, e.g., Amos Tversky & Daniel Kahneman, "Availability: A Heuristic for Judging Frequency and Probability," 5 *Cognitive Psychol.* 207, 208 (1973); Amos Tversky & Daniel Kahneman, "Judgment Under Uncertainty: Heuristics and Biases," 185 *Science* 1124 (1974); Jon Hanson & David Yosifon, "The Situational Character: A Critical Realist Perspective on the Human Animal," 93 *Geo. L.J.* 1, 40 (2004); Cass R. Sunstein, "Group Judgments: Statistical Means, Deliberation, and Information Markets," 80 *NYU L. Rev.* 962, 991 (2005).
26. See George Ainslie & Nick Haslam, "Hyperbolic Discounting," in *Choice over Time* 57, 69 (George Loewenstein & Jon Elster, eds. 1992); Stefano Dellavigna & Ulrike Malmendier, "Contract Design and Self-Control: Theory and Evidence," 199 *Quarterly Journal of Economics* 353 (2004); Christine Jolls et al., "A Behavioral Approach to Law and Economics," 50 *Stan. L. Rev.* 1471, 1539–40 (1998); David Laibson, "Golden Eggs and Hyperbolic Discounting," 112 *Quarterly Journal of Economics* 443 (1997).
27. Oren Bar-Gill, "Seduction by Plastic," 98 *Nw. U. L. Rev.* 1373 (2004); Dellavigna & Malmendier, supra note 26.
28. See Hanson & Kysar, supra note 24; Jon D. Hanson & Douglas A. Kysar, "Taking Behavioralism Seriously: Some Evidence of Manipulation," 112 *Harv. L. Rev.* 1420 (1999); Todd Rakoff, "Contracts of Adhesion: An Essay In Reconstruction," 96 *Harv. L. Rev.* 1174, 1230 (1983) (noting that "intense competition will, if anything, make the situation worse, for it tends toward degradation of any [consumer]-protective provisions of the contract").
29. See Gabaix & Laibson, supra note 23 (presenting model that explains why firms shroud the negative attributes of their products, particularly high prices for complementary add-ons, and shows why competition will not induce firms to reveal information that would improve market efficiency).
30. Stewart Macaulay, "Private Legislation and the Duty to Read – Business Run by IBM Machine, the Law of Contracts and Credit Cards," 19 *Vand. L. Rev.* 1051, 1069–74 (1966).
31. See Bar-Gill, supra note 27.
32. See Gaibaix & Laibson, supra note 23 (pointing out that it is difficult for any single firm to capture the profits from debiasing consumers).
33. See Gabaix & Laibson, supra note 23 (noting that sophisticated credit card users take advantage of "free miles" and avoid interest rate charges and late payment fees).
34. Jeffrey Green, Profitability 2006, Cards and Payments, May 2006, at 31.
35. See Gabaix & Laibson, supra note 23 (noting that innovation creates new opportunities for shrouding and undermines the effects of education).
36. The card issuer also might receive a higher interchange fee for these cards, which (in theory) would be passed back to consumers at the point-of-sale in the form of higher prices.
37. The emphasis here is on rationalization, not rational calculation. Stewart Macaulay's early study compared contracts for gasoline cards (issued primarily to less wealthy individuals) and T&E cards issued to more wealthy individuals. He provides some interesting empirical evidence suggesting that the wealthy are no more likely to be "debiased" than the impecunious – perhaps because a sense that their time is more valuable decreases the likelihood that they will pay attention to details of small transactions. See Macaulay, supra note 30, at 1086–1107.

38. MBNA's annual reports explain the valuable uses it makes of that information.
39. See Lizabeth Cohen, *A Consumers' Republic: The Politics of Mass Consumption in Postwar America* 292–309 (2003).
40. See Alan Schwartz & Louis L. Wilde, "Imperfect Information in Markets for Contract Terms: The Examples of Warranties and Security Interests," 69 *Va. L. Rev.* 1387 (1983); Gillette, supra note 5, at 691–693.
41. See Steven P. Croley & Jon D. Hanson, "Rescuing the Revolution: The Revived Case for Enterprise Liability," 91 *Mich. L. Rev.* 683, 772–79 (1993); Gillette, supra note 5, at 691–693; Hanson & Logue, supra note 21; see also Rakoff, supra note 28, at 1231 (1983) (results of competition say nothing about consumer preferences when consumers do not in fact understand contracts).
42. Lawrence Friedman, *Contract Law in America*, ch. 4 (1965). I write consciously in a line of recent scholarship that analyzes how responses to social problems that traditionally are characterized as "public" and "private" in fact are closely intertwined and interdependent. E.g., Jacob S. Hacker, *The Divided Welfare State: The Battle over Public and Private Social Benefits in the United States* (2002); David A. Moss, *When All Else Fails: The Government as Ultimate Risk Manager* (2002).
43. Macaulay, supra note 30, at 1056.
44. 16 CFR Part 435.
45. The Uniform Commercial Code does not cover payment cards. See 4–104(a)(9) ("'Item' * * * does not include * * * a credit or debit card slip."). But see Broadway Nat'l Bank v. Barton-Russell Corp., 585 N.Y.S.2d 933, 938 (Sup. Ct. 1992) (reaching a contrary conclusion under pre-revision Article 4). Although some states have enacted statutes that govern certain aspects of the issuer/cardholder relationship, it seems fair to say that none of those statutes has any significant impact, largely because the National Bank Act would preempt any substantial regulation. See Mark Furletti, "The Debate over the National Bank Act and the Preemption of State Efforts to Regulate Credit Cards," 77 *Temp. L. Rev.* 425 (2004) [hereinafter Furletti, *Preemption*]. To the extent there is any substantive regulation by the states, it is in the form of statutes authorizing specific business practices, like the Delaware bill-stuffer statute discussed earlier.
46. Regulation Z requires that a bank issuing a credit card provide the consumer a written disclosure that summarizes the applicable legal rules. Regulation Z §226.5, 226.6. Appendix G to Regulation Z contains model disclosures.
47. TILA §132; Regulation Z, §226.12(a).
48. TILA §§133, 161 and 170. Oddly enough, those provisions might be counterproductive if they encourage consumers to use credit cards instead of debit cards.
49. That is not to say that I think the existing disclosure regime is sensible, see White & Mansfield, supra note 1, at 260–62 (arguing that the disclosures are too complex to be comprehensible to typical consumers), or that it could not be improved. I argue in Chapter 13 that the existing disclosure regime should focus on disclosure at the point of purchase.
50. See Richard Craswell, "Property Rules and Liability Rules in Unconscionability and Related Doctrines," 60 *U. Chi. L. Rev.* 1, 49–50 (1993) (explaining that problems in market competition for contract terms do not justify administrative promulgation of terms if the administrative terms will not be better than the market terms).
51. See Colin Camerer et al., "Regulation for Conservatives: Behavioral Economics and the Case for 'Asymmetric Paternalism,'" 151 *U. Pa. L. Rev.* 1211 (2003); Macaulay, supra note 30.
52. See Friedrich Kessler, "Contracts of Adhesion – Some Thoughts About Freedom of Contract," 43 *Colum. L. Rev.* 629 (1943).

53. Jim White's discussion of the cases interpreting Section 211 is excellent. James J. White, "Form Contracts Under Revised Article 2," 75 *Wash. U.L.Q.* 315 (1997). See also Gillette, supra note 5, at 712–14; White & Mansfield, supra note 1, at 254–56.
54. See, e.g., statutes cited supra note 8.
55. See Jean Sternlight, "Creeping Mandatory Arbitration: Is It Just?," 57 *Stan. L. Rev.* 1631 (2005).
56. See Discover Bank v. Boehr, 30 Cal. Rptr. 3d 76 (S. Ct. 2005) (invalidating such a clause in Discover's cardholder agreement); Samuel Issacharoff & Erin F. Delaney, "Credit Card Accountability," 73 *U. Chi. L. Rev.* 157 (2006) (arguing that functional judicial review of arbitration clauses would curtail unscrupulous behavior by card issuers by allowing the class-action lawyer to be an agent for myopic consumers).
57. I rely here on the pleadings in Ross v. Bank of America, No. 05 CV 7116 (S.D.N.Y.).
58. A survey of reported opinions in credit card-related class actions suggests that the great majority involve either challenges under TILA for disclosure violations or claims that issuers are imposing improper fees. There are other, more unusual cases – my favorite is Cie v. Comdata Network, Inc., 656 NE2d 123 (Ill. Ct. App. 1995) (challenging the enforceability of gambling claims on a Discover card) – but it is safe to say that class actions have not been a major device for bringing substantive change to the credit card industry.
59. This is the core allegation, as yet unproven, in Ross v. Bank of America, No. 05 CV 7116 (S.D.N.Y.).
60. Again, this has been alleged in Ross v. Bank of America, No. 05 CV 7116 (S.D.N.Y.).
61. See James J. White, "Contracting Under Amended 2–207," 2004 *Wis. L. Rev.* 723, 742 ("For a nickel or a dime, almost all of us would *** agree to arbitrate."). Cf. Carnival Cruise Lines, Inc. v. Shute, 499 U.S. 585, 594 (1991) ("[I]t stands to reason that passengers who purchase tickets containing a forum clause like that at issue in this case benefit in the form of reduced fares reflecting the savings that the cruise line enjoys by limiting the fora in which it may be sued.").
62. Council Directive 93/13/EEC of 5 April 1993 on Unfair Terms in Consumer Contracts.
63. As Larry Bates has shown, several other countries have developed administrative approaches under which bureaucrats generally approve form contracts. See Larry Bates, "Administrative Regulation of Terms in Form Contracts: A Comparative Analysis of Consumer Protection," 16 *Emory Int'l L. Rev.* 1 (2002). For example, consider Israel's Standard Contract Law of 1964, which allows users of form contracts to obtain government approval of "restrictive terms." Approval immunizes the terms from court challenge for five years. Standard Contracts Law (Isr.) 1964, 18 L.S.I. 51 (1963–1964).
64. See Annex to Unfair Terms Directive ¶¶1(j), 1(q).
65. See, e.g., W. David Slawson, "The New Meaning of Contract: The Transformation of Contracts Law by Standard Forms," 46 *U. Pitt. L. Rev.* 21, 49–50 (1984); Tex. Property Code §§ 92.006, 92.052 (establishing a nonwaivable warranty of habitability).
66. The most obvious reason is that the Federal National Mortgage Association (FNMA or Fannie Mae) will not purchase a mortgage that includes such a provision. E.g., Fannie Mae, Announcement 04–06 (Sept. 28, 2004), available at http://www.mortgagebankers.org/resident/2004/fannie-04–06.pdf.
67. As I discuss in Part V, the retroactivity concern arguably poses an objection to the entirety of the consumer bankruptcy provisions in the Bankruptcy Abuse and Consumer Protection Act of 2005.
68. Todd Rakoff refers more elegantly to "invisible" terms – terms the consumer does not notice. See Rakoff, supra note 28, at 1250–55. I have in mind here a narrower

category – terms that not only are invisible in practice, but that are all but impossible for a consumer to assess (generally, because they operate ex post facto).

69. See Schwartz & Wilde, supra note 39, at 1457–85; see Camerer et al., supra note 50.
70. Regulation Z (12 C.F.R. §226.9(c)(1)).
71. See supra note 9 and accompanying text.
72. See Linda Punch, "Getting Tough?," *Credit Card Management*, Feb. 2005, at 42 (discussing Comptroller proposals).
73. A bill has been introduced that would ban these provisions entirely, by prohibiting any alteration of interest rates based on events "wholly unrelated to the consumer's credit card account." Consumer Credit Card Protection Act of 2005, H.R. 3492, 109th Cong., 1st Sess., §2. For discussion, see Kathy M. Kristof, "Late on One Card? Rates Can Rise on All of Them," *L.A. Times*, Aug. 7, 2005, at C2.
74. I discount the possibility that the clause provides signaling benefits by sorting customers that do not expect to default (who would not be concerned about such a clause) from those that do expect to default (who would be concerned). Tolerance of a clause that goes unread can send no signal.
75. See Furletti, *Card Pricing*.
76. See Ronald J. Mann, "Strategy and Force in the Liquidation of Secured Debt," 96 *Mich. L. Rev.* 159 (1997).
77. National banks dominate the major card issuers, because only national banks are entitled to the preemptive provisions of the National Bank Act. Because the OCC regulates all national banks, the OCC would be in a position to regulate major credit card issuers if it chose to do so. See Furletti, *Preemption*, supra note 44. To date, however, the OCC for the most part has limited itself to safety and soundness regulation – criticizing practices that might undermine the solvency of the institution (such as unduly risky lending practices).
78. See White & Mansfield, supra note 1, at 258–59.
79. See W. David Slawson, "Standard Form Contracts and Democratic Control of Lawmaking Power," 84 *Harv. L. Rev.* 529, 530 (1971).
80. See Schuchman, supra note 19, at 130.
81. See Arthur Alan Leff, "Contract as Thing," 19 *Am. U. L. Rev.* 131, 144 (1970).
82. See Jean Braucher, "Defining Unfairness: Empathy and Economic Analysis at the Federal Trade Commission," 68 *B.U. L. Rev.* 349 (1988).
83. See Leff, supra note 80; Gillette, supra note 5, at 717–719.
84. Jeffrey Davis made a similar proposal two decades ago. See Jeffrey Davis, "Revamping Consumer-Credit Contract Law," 68 *Va. L. Rev.* 1333 (1982).
85. The phenomenon is not new. For early discussion, see Nathan Isaacs, "The Standardizing of Contracts," 27 *Yale L.J.* 34, 37–40 (1917); Rakoff, supra note 28, at 1182.
86. See Abraham, supra note 7, at 32–33; Macaulay, supra note 30, at 1062; Slawson, supra note 64, at 50–52.
87. See, e.g., Texas Prop. Code ch. 5 (articulating various provisions and notices that must be used in residential real estate transactions).
88. In many geographic areas, a residential real estate transaction proceeds on a form prepared by a group of real estate brokers. That group might not be biased in favor of consumers – their primary interest doubtless is to prod the transaction toward consummation (so that a brokerage commission is due) – but that interest typically results in a reasonably balanced form.
89. See Grether et al., supra note 15, at 296–97.
90. See Grether et al., supra note 15, at 298–99.
91. See Camerer et al., supra note 50. The most obvious potential harm to consumers would be a contraction of the credit markets in response to limitations on ex post

facto terms. My analysis here assumes that the likely contraction will affect, for the most part, consumers that are already in serious financial distress. To the extent lenders stop lending to those people sooner, a strong argument can be made that the contraction in fact is desirable.

92. Andrew P. Morriss & Jason Korosec, "Automating Dispute Resolution: Credit Cards, Debit Cards, and Private Law," *J.L. Econ. & Pol'y* (forthcoming).
93. See Kathy Chu, "Credit Cards Quitting Rate-Bumping Game," *USA Today*, Oct. 19, 2005 (discussing effect that public scrutiny has had on policies of Chase, CitiBank, American Express, and Discover).
94. See Consent Order, In re Providian National Bank, Office of the Comptroller of the Currency #2000-53, available at http://www.occ.gov/ftp/release/2000-49b.pdf; see also Michele Heller & Laura Mandaro, Providian's $300M Pact with Regulators Is One for the Books, *American Banker*, June 29, 2000, at 4; Sam Zuckerman, How Providian Misled Card Holders, *S.F. Chron.*, May 5, 2002, at A1; see also Edmund Sanders, CitiBank to Set up Fund for Improper Late Fees, *L.A. Times*, Aug. 4, 2000, at C2 (discussing $18 million settlement of claims that CitiBank charged late fees for payments received at 10 a.m. on the due date).
95. See Andrew Ellson, "OFT Says Credit Card Charges Are 'Unfair,'" Times Online, Apr. 5, 2006.
96. See CardFlash (May 18, 2005) (discussing Federal Reserve consideration of such a proposal).
97. Credit Card Accountability Responsibility and Disclosure Act of 2005 §213, S. 499, 109th Cong., 1st Sess.
98. See UK Credit Card Hearing, at 3 (testimony of CEO of MBNA Europe).

13. Regulating Information

1. See Camerer et al., op. cit.; Robert E. Scott, "Error and Rationality in Individual Decisionmaking: An Essay on the Relation Between Cognitive Illusions and the Management of Choices," 59 *S. Cal. L. Rev.* 329 (1986).
2. See William M. Sage, "Regulating Through Information: Disclosure Laws and American Health Care," 99 *Colum. L. Rev.* 1701 (1999).
3. See Gabaix & Laibson, op. cit.
4. See Cass R. Sunstein, "Boundedly Rational Borrowing," 73 *University of Chicago Law Review* 249 (2006) (recommending campaign that would disseminate "vivid narratives of possible harm").
5. Cohen, op. cit., at 121.
6. See id. at 121 (quoting William Whyte of *Fortune* Magazine).
7. See Schor, op. cit.
8. Some states have extended similar rules to credit cards. For example, Mont. Code Ann. §31-1-115 bars the issuance of a credit card to a minor without first obtaining consent from the minor's parent or legal guardian.
9. See Stephenson, supra note.
10. The problem is not limited to the United States. See "The New Spendthrifts," supra (discussing a "Hello Kitty" card marketed to teenage girls in Hong Kong); "Indian Card Growth Exceeds 50% Per Annum," *Cards International*, Issue 333 (2005), at 15 (explaining that "Indian teens drive card growth").
11. See Laurie A. Lucas, "Integrative Social Contracts Theory: Ethical Implications of Marketing Credit Cards to U.S. College Students," 38 *Am. Bus. L. J.* 413 (2001).
12. James A. Roberts & Eli Jones, "Money Attitudes, Credit Card Use, and Compulsive Buying Among American College Students," 35 *J. Consumer Affairs* 213 (2001).

13. See Ark. Code Ann. §§4–104–201 et seq. (barring face-to-face solicitation on college campuses); Calif. Educ. Code §99030 (requiring colleges to regulate card marketing and stating the "intent of the Legislature" that the regulations should prohibit offering gifts in exchange for card applications); Hawaii Act of January 24, 2003 (requiring colleges to regulate card marketing and requiring that "consideration be given to" a prohibition on offering gifts in exchange for card applications); Kentucky Act of Mar. 5, 2004 (invalidating card applications from college students unless authorized in writing by a parent); La. Rev. Stat. Ann. §9:3577.2 et seq. (barring solicitation on college campuses unless accompanied by debt education brochures); N.Y. Educ. Law 6437 (requiring colleges to prohibit marketing of credit cards on campuses); Pa. Stat. 24 PS §2301-A (requiring colleges to regulate card marketing and requiring that colleges "consider" a prohibition on offering gifts in exchange for card applications); W. Va. Code §18B-14–10 (requiring colleges to adopt rules regulating card marketing that must, among other things, prohibit offering tangible gifts in exchange for a card application); "U.S. State to Restrict Card Marketing on Campus," *Cards International*, Issue 321 (2004), at 11 (discussing additional statutes and proposals in Illinois, Missouri, New Mexico, and Virginia).
14. See Office of the Comptroller of the Currency, Bank Activities, and Operations; Real Estate Lendings and Appraisals, 69. Fed.Reg. 1895 (Jan. 13, 2004) (to be codified in scattered sections of 12 CFR parts 7 & 34) (broad preemption of state regulation of national banks); Furletti, *Preemption*.
15. Manning, op. cit., ch. 6.
16. See Nellie Mae, *Undergraduate Students and Credit Cards* in 2004: "An Analysis of Usage Rates and Trends" (May 2005), available at http://www.nelliemae.com/library/research_12.html (last visited May 27, 2005).
17. See Nellie Mae, "Credit Card Use Among Graduate Students 2003" (May 2004), available at http://www.nelliemae.com/library/ccstudy_2003.pdf (last visited May 27, 2005).
18. See Kate Fitzgerald, "They're Baaaaack: Card Marketers on Campus," *Credit Card Management*, June 2003, at 18.
19. Jill M. Norvilitis et al., "Factors Influencing Level of Credit-Card Debt in College Students," 33 *J. Applied Social Psychology* 935 (2003).
20. See Nellie Mae, "College on Credit: How Students Perceive Their Education Debt" 9 tbl. 5 (Feb. 2003), available at http://www.nelliemae.com/library/nasls_2002.pdf (last visited May 27, 2005).
21. See Eileen Ambrose, "Judges Start with Young to Head off Bankruptcy," *Chi. Trib.*, Apr. 24, 2005.
22. See Ron Lieber, "A Bonus for Blowing Off Your Bills," *Wall St. J.*, Sept. 16, 2003, at D1. I propose in Chapter 14 that such products be prohibited.
23. As Chapter 16 discusses, Britain formerly had a rule requiring cardholders to repay 15% of their credit card debt each month. Issuers responded to the removal of the rule by rapidly lowering minimum-repayment requirements to 5% per month. "The Plastic-Money Would-Be Pre-Election Boom," *The Economist*, Sept. 9, 1978, at 107 (discussing rule imposed in 1973 and lifted in 1978).
24. See Sage, supra note 2.
25. 15 U.S.C. §1637(c), 12 CFR §226.5a(b).
26. See "Q&A: Why Do We Need New Credit Laws," BBC (Dec. 8, 2003), available at http://news.bbc.co.uk/2/hi/business/3293707.stm (last visited May 27, 2005).
27. See UK Credit Card Hearing, supra note, at 3.

28. See Regulation Z, 12 CFR §226.5a (describing requirements for applications and solicitations), 226.6 (describing required initial disclosures).
29. Compare Regulation E, 12 CFR §205.9(a) (requiring contemporaneous receipt in electronic point-of-sale transactions).
30. Compare Sage, supra note 2 (suggesting that should be the goal of health-industry disclosures).
31. 15 U.S.C. §1637(b), 12 CFR §226.7.
32. For example, as this book goes to press there is a simple calculator at the www.CNNMoney.com Web site, http://cgi.money.cnn.com/tools/debtplanner/debtplanner.jsp.
33. General Accounting Office, Credit Cards: Customized Minimum Payment Disclosures Would Provide More Information to Consumers, But Impact Could Vary (Report GAO-06-434) (April 2006). The GAO study contemplated a customized disclosure of how long it would take for a cardholder to repay the balance with a minimum payment. I contemplate a more carefully tailored disclosure: how long it would take to repay the balance if the cardholder continued to pay at the rate paid the previous month.
34. See U.S. Overlimit Fees Monthly Averages Among > $100M Portfolios – Current, available at http://www.cardweb.com/carddata/charts/overlimit_fees.amp (subscription only) (last visited April 13, 2006) ($31.29 average in December 2005 for issuers with portfolios greater than $100 million). That amount is 42% larger than the comparable 1998 figure and 141% higher than the comparable 1993 figure. See Dec. 5, 2003, CardFlash.
35. We have little empirical data about the operation of the card system in the United States. The regulatory authorities in other countries (Australia and the United Kingdom in particular) have considerably more accurate historical and current information about payment systems than we have in the United States.
36. See Ellson, op. cit.
37. See Regulation E, 12 CFR §205.9(a).
38. See Feinberg, supra note; Feinberg, supra note.
39. See Srivastava & Raghubir, supra note.
40. Federal Reserve System, Board of Governors Report to the Congress on the Disclosure of Point-of-Sale Debit Fees 34–35 (November 2004).
41. The rough calculations in the text assume a total cost of $6 billion, an annual volume of about $1,200 billion, and an outstanding debt of about $800 billion.
42. Given the benefits of electronic authorization, it is not likely that networks would route transactions away from electronic authorization in order to avoid such a requirement.
43. Pub. L. No. 108-159 (codified in scattered sections of 15 & 20 U.S.C.).
44. See FACT Act §113 (codified as Fair Credit Reporting Act §605(g), 15 U.S.C. §1681c(g)).
45. For such proposals, see Sunstein, supra note 4; Oren Bar-Gill, "Consumer Misperceptions and Market Reactions: The Case of Competitive Bundling," 73 *U. Chi. L. Rev.* 33 (2006) (recommending the unbundling of payment and credit functions on cards).
46. Mann, *Payments Policy*.
47. For an introductory discussion of some ideas for reform, see Mann, *Payments Policy*.
48. See UK Credit Card Hearing, at 14–16 (testimony by credit card issuers attempting to justify higher rates in the United Kingdom).

14. Product Design: Affinity and Rewards Programs and Teaser Rates

1. See Jennifer Bayot, "Credit Card Lets Democrats Shop with Party Loyalty," *N. Y. Times*, Jan. 20, 2004, at C8.
2. See Linda Punch, "The Cash-Rebate Card, Part II," *Credit Card Management*, Oct. 2002, at 54.
3. Airline miles are one of the most successful benefits. See Zack Martin, "Still Flying High After All These Years," *Credit Card Management*, Dec. 2001, at 50; Burney Simpson, "Weathering Severe Turbulence," *Credit Card Management*, May 2003, at 14. To get a sense for their value, airline miles are sold in a secondary market at about 2.75 cents per mile. See Martin, supra.
4. See Kelly Shermach, "The Vibrant World of Loyalty," *Credit Card Management*, Aug. 2002, at 30. Seventy-seven out of eighty-four (92%) banks responding to the most recent installment of the Federal Reserve's biennial Survey of Credit Card Plans have such a program. See www.federalreserve.gov/pubs/shop/survey.htm.
5. Discussed in Chapter 9.
6. See Steve Worthington, "Down Under," *Eur. Card Rev.*, Jan./Feb. 2005, at 16.
7. See Ronald G. Mazursky & F. Alan Schultheis, "The Evolving Role of Credit Cards in Consumers' Wallets" (April 2004), available at www.edgardunn.com/eletter/2004–04 (last visited September 3, 2004).
8. "Loyalty Drive Revolving Credit," *Cards International*, Aug. 2005, at 9.
9. See Burney Simpson, "The Case for Easier Redemptions," *Card Management*, Aug. 2004, at 13.
10. See Peter Lucas, "A Big Lift for Loyalty," *Credit Card Management*, June 2002, at 26 (discussing benefits provided at the register based on the profile of the particular customer).
11. See Rachelle Garbarine, "Paying Rent by Credit Card, and Dreaming of Waikiki," *N. Y. Times*, Dec. 29, 2003, at A17.
12. See Howard Strong, *What Every Credit Card User Needs to Know: How To Protect Yourself and Your Money* (1999) (discussing the economic value of and the secondary market for airline miles).
13. See Richard Rolfe, "Europe's Cobranding Boom," *Credit Card Management*, Jan. 2003, at 16 (statement of Visa executive that "Germany is going loyalty-mad since [the repeal of the so-called Rabattgesetz law]").
14. Unfortunately, despite correspondence with the German central bank, I have not been able to obtain data about credit card debt in Germany.
15. See Lieber, op. cit.
16. See Punch, supra note 2.
17. See Joshua S. Gans & Stephen P. King, "The Role of Interchange Fees in Credit Card Associations: Competitive Analysis and Regulatory Issues," 20 *Australian Bus. Law Rev.* 94 (2001).
18. The most persuasive empirical evidence is an analysis of the cost efficiency of credit card banks, which suggests that they are generally as competitive as other American banks. See Sivakumar Kulasekaran & Sherrill Shaffer, "Cost Efficiency Among Credit Card Banks," 54 *J. Econ. & Bus.* 54 (2002). Studies relying on data from industry profits and pricing practices have drawn markedly inconsistent conclusions. Compare Dagobert L. Brito & Per R. Hartley, "Consumer Rationality and Credit Cards," 103 *J. Pol. Econ.* 400 (1995) (favorable assessment of competitiveness of American credit card industry); Jones & Zywicki, supra note (same); Todd J. Zywicki, "The Economics of Credit Cards," 3 *Chapman L. Rev.* 79 (2000) (same), with Ausubel, op. cit. (reasoning that the American credit card industry is not competitive

because credit card interest rates do not drop when the cost of funds in the industry falls).

19. See Gans & King, supra note 17.

Part V. Optimizing Consumer Credit Markets and Bankruptcy Policy

1. A. N. Wilson, *The Laird of Abbotsford* 4, 185 (1980).
2. Jones & Zywicki, op. cit., at 221.
3. Id. at 216.
4. Wilson, supra note 1, at 158 (quoting Scott's comments that *Anne of Geierstein* had turned out "more trashy than I expected" and that he "hated[d] Anne").

15. Causation, Consumer Credit, and Bankruptcy

1. Barry Adler et al., "Regulating Consumer Bankruptcy: A Theoretical Inquiry," 29 *J. Legal Stud.* 585 (2000) [hereinafter APS, *Regulating Consumer Bankruptcy*].
2. Michelle J. White, "Personal Bankruptcy: Insurance, Work Effort, Opportunism, and the Efficiency of the 'Fresh Start'" (unpublished 2005 manuscript), available at http://econ.ucsd.edu/~miwhite/ [hereinafter White, *Personal Bankruptcy*].
3. Jackson, op. cit.
4. Jason Kilborn, "The Innovative German Approach to Consumer Debt Relief: Revolutionary Changes in German Law, and Surprising Lessons for the United States," 24 *Nw. J. Int'l L. & Bus.* 257 (2004); Jason Kilborn, "Continuity, Change, and Innovation in Emerging Consumer Bankruptcy Systems: Belgium and Luxembourg," 14 Am. Bankr. Inst. L. Rev. (forthcoming) [hereinafter Kilborn, *Belgium and Luxembourg*]; Jason Kilborn, "La Responsabilisation de l'Economie: What the U.S. Can Learn from the New French Law on Consumer Overindebtedness," 26 *Mich. J. Int'l L.* 619 (2005); Johanna Niemi-Kiesiläinen, "Changing Directions in Consumer Bankruptcy Law and Practice in Europe and USA," 20 *J. Consumer Pol'y* 133 (1997); Jay Westbrook, "Local Legal Culture and the Fear of Abuse," 6 *American Bankr. Inst. L. Rev.* 25 (1998); SWW, The Fragile Middle Class.
5. Rajan & Zingales, op. cit. (asserting that thesis). Mark Roe has made the most detailed explication of this point in the legal context. Mark J. Roe, "Backlash," 98 *Colum. L. Rev.* 217 (1998); Mark J. Roe, *Political Determinants of Corporate Governance: Political Context, Corporate Impact* (2003).
6. For a thoughtful discussion of the extent to which the systems are and are not converging, see Charles Jordan Tabb, "Lessons from the Globalization of Consumer Bankruptcy," 30 *Law & Social Inquiry* 763 (2005).
7. For representative citations, compare the more optimistic views in Dean M. Maki, "The Growth of Consumer Credit and the Household Debt Service Burden," in *The Impact of Public Policy on Consumer Credit* (Thomas A. Durkin & Michael E. Staten, eds. 2002), with the more pessimistic findings in Philippe Bacchette & Stefan Gerlach, "Consumption and Credit Constraints: International Evidence," 40 *J. Monetary Econ.* 207 (1997); Sydney Ludvigson, "Consumption and Credit: A Model of Time-Varying Liquidity Constraints," 81 *Rev. Econ. Stat.* 434 (1999).
8. For example, in the United States, consumer spending represents about 70% of the GDP. U.S. Department of Commerce, Bureau of Economic Analysis, Gross Domestic Product First Quarter 2005, available at http://www.bea.doc.gov/bea/newsrelarchive/2005/gdp105a.pdf. Thus, substantial increases in consumer spending should directly cause an increase in GDP. The premise of

current Federal Reserve policymaking is that reductions of interest rates will lead directly to increased consumer spending, and thus in turn to an increase in GDP.

9. Finance for Small and Medium-Sized Enterprises: A Report on the 2004 UK Survey of SME Finances, available at http://www.wbs.ac.uk/downloads/research/sme-report-may-2005.cfm (showing substantial small business use of personal credit cards, particularly by start-ups); Board of Governors of the Federal Reserve, Report to Congress on the Availability of Credit to Small Businesses (Sept. 2002), available at http://www.federalreserve.gov/boarddocs/RptCongress/sbfreport 2002.pdf (same).
10. Bruce Mann's historical work shows that this impulse has a lengthy pedigree in the United States. Bruce H. Mann, *Republic of Debtors: Bankruptcy in the Age of American Independence* (2002). For more general discussions of the relation between bankruptcy policy and productivity, see Rafael Efrat, "Global Trends in Personal Bankruptcy," 76 *Am. Bankr. L.J.* 81 (2002); Nicholas L. Georgakopoulos, "Bankruptcy Law for Productivity," 37 *Wake Forest L. Rev.* 51 (2002); Richard Hynes, "Overoptimism and Overborrowing," 2004 *BYU L. Rev.* 127; Hynes, supra note.
11. Insolvency Act 1986 §279 (as amended by Enterprise Act 2002 §256).
12. John Armour, "Personal Insolvency Law and the Demand for Venture Capital," 5 *Eur. Bus. Org'n L. Rev.* 87 (2004).
13. See Wei Fan & Michelle J. White, "Personal Bankruptcy and the Level of Entrepreneurial Activity," 46 *J.L. & Econ.* 543 (2003).
14. See White, *Bankruptcy and Consumer Credit*, supra note 6.
15. Robert M. Lawless & Elizabeth Warren, "The Myth of the Disappearing Business Bankruptcy," 93 *Calif. L. Rev.* 743 (2005).
16. Mortgage lending markets – in particular, some of the newer home equity loan products – have many of the same structural characteristics as credit cards and are likely to contribute in similar ways to the excessive debt problem.
17. APS, *Regulating Consumer Bankruptcy*, supra note 5; Samuel A. Rea, Jr., "Arm-Breaking, Consumer Credit, and Personal Bankruptcy," 22 *Econ. Inquiry* 188 (1984); Richard Hynes, "Why (Consumer) Bankruptcy?," 56 *Ala. L. Rev.* 121, 159–62 (2004).
18. E.g., Jones & Zywicki, op. cit.; Zywicki, *Economic Analysis*; Zywicki, *Testimony*.
19. It is not clear, for example, whether older people suffer more or less in bankruptcy than younger people.
20. SWW, *As We Forgive*; SWW, *The Fragile Middle Class*; Himmelstein et al., op. cit.; Katherine Porter & Deborah Thorne, "Going Broke and Staying Broke: The Realities of the Fresh Start in Chapter 7 Bankruptcies" 92 *Cornell Law Review* (forthcoming).
21. Lynn LoPucki provides a contrary account based on his experiences as a lawyer in consumer bankruptcy cases. See Lynn LoPucki, "Common Sense Consumer Bankruptcy," 71 *Am. Bankr. L.J.* 461 (1997). The experiences he recounts, however, are difficult to reconcile with the empirical evidence.
22. See Li Gan & Tarun Sabarwal, A Simple Test of Adverse Events and Strategic Timing Theories of Consumer Bankruptcy (NBER Working Paper 11763) (Nov. 2005 draft) (concluding that the financial benefit from bankruptcy filing is exogenous to the bankruptcy decision, consistent with an "adverse events" explanation of bankruptcy filing).
23. See Nathalie Martin, "The Role of History and Culture in Developing Bankruptcy and Insolvency Systems: The Perils of Legal Transplantation," 28 *Boston College Int'l & Comp. L. Rev.* 1 (2005).

24. Ellis, op. cit. I discount the argument of F.H. Buckley, "The American Fresh Start," 4 *S. Cal. Interdis. L.J.* 67 (1994) [hereinafter Buckley, *The American Fresh Start*], because his comparative econometric analysis of the causes of U.S. and Canadian bankruptcy filings includes no data on debt levels in the two countries.
25. Jacob S. Ziegel, *Comparative Consumer Insolvency Regimes: A Canadian Perspective* 27–31, 38–39 (2003).
26. Insolvency Act 1986 §279 (as amended by Enterprise Act 2002 §256).
27. West, op. cit., ch. 8.
28. The point is underscored by the conflicting empirical assessments of the effects of the enactment of the Bankruptcy Code of 1978. Compare, e.g., Lawrence Shepherd, "Personal Failures and the Bankruptcy Reform Act of 1978," 27 *J.L. & Econ.* 419 (1984) (finding a significant effect), with Jagdeep S. Bhandari & Lawrence A. Weiss, "The Increased Bankruptcy Filing Rate: An Historical Analysis," 67 *Am. Bankr. L.J.* 1 (1993) (finding no significant effect). From my perspective, it would be surprising if we could find strong quantitative links between reform measures and filing rates, because so many external factors are likely to influence filing rates. One such example, discussed in Chapter 16, is the concurrent change to minimum payment requirements – a change that issuers expect to increase bankruptcy filing rates substantially, at least in the short term.
29. See Michelle J. White, "Why It Pays to File for Bankruptcy: A Critical Look at Incentives Under U.S. Bankruptcy Laws and a Proposal for Change," 65 *U. Chi. L. Rev.* 685 (1998) [hereinafter White, *Why It Pays*]; Michelle J. White, "Why Don't More Households File for Bankruptcy?," 14 *J.L. Econ. & Org'n* 205 (1998) [hereinafter White, *Why Don't More Households File?*].
30. E.g., Scott Fay et al., "The Household Bankruptcy Decision," 2002 *Am. Econ. Rev.* 92; Gross & Souleles, op. cit.
31. See F. H. Buckley & Margaret F. Brinig, "The Bankruptcy Puzzle," 27 *J. Legal Stud.* 187 (1998) [hereinafter Buckley & Brinig, *The Bankruptcy Puzzle*]. They argue that correlations between lower bankruptcy filings and greater population shares of urban residents, Catholics, and the elderly indicate that bankruptcy filings are a sign of the breakdown of social networks.
32. Gross & Souleles, op. cit.
33. Because their data set includes two different credit scores for each borrower, it is possible that information about outstanding borrowing is included indirectly (as a component of the credit score). Nothing in the paper, however, discusses whether that is true or how the variables they use are likely to relate to credit card use.
34. See, e.g., Buckley & Brinig, *The Bankruptcy Puzzle*, supra note 35 (expressing doubt that lending variables could explain the variation and noting that they did not use lending data in their models); Buckley, *The American Fresh Start*, supra note 28 (econometric model designed to test differences between Canadian and American filing rates that does not include any data related to debt in the two countries).
35. See Jones & Zywicki, op. cit., at 217 (treating the decline of the stigma of divorce and bankruptcy as parallel social problems).
36. E.g., Anita Bernstein, "For and Against Marriage: A Revision," 102 *Mich. L. Rev.* 129, 194–95 (2003); Amy L. Wax, "Bargaining in the Shadow of the Market: Is There a Future for Egalitarian Marriage?," 84 *Va. L. Rev.* 509, 668 (1998). For empirical support, consider Paul Amato's research on the effect of divorce on children. He suggests that efforts to reduce the stigma of divorce have limited the harm divorce creates for the children of divorcing parents. Paul R. Amato, "Life-Span Adjustment of Children to Their Parents' Divorce," 4 *Future Child* 143 (1994).
37. West, op. cit.

16. Regulating Consumer Credit Markets

1. In the United Kingdom, a disproportionately large amount of the debt is in the form of home mortgages. For general discussion of the problem, see Griffiths Commission, 2005 Report.
2. Warren & Tyagi, op. cit.; Posner, op. cit.; see Peterson, op. cit.
3. James J. White, "The Usury Trompe L'Oeil," 51 S.C. L. Rev. 445 (2000).
4. Furletti, supra note. For similar analysis of events in the United Kingdom and France, see Department of Trade and Industry, The Effect of Interest Rate Controls in Other Countries (2004) [hereinafter *DTI Report*].
5. *DTI Report*, supra note 4.
6. See White, supra note 3.
7. See Mann, *Japanese Cards*.
8. See Mann, *Payment Intermediaries* (discussing benefits of keeping consumer transactions in the hands of banks rather than smaller and less reputationally constrained entities).
9. For the classic model of the demand for extralegal enforcement of consumer credit contracts, see Rea, op. cit. In that model, the problem is moral hazard; borrowers agree to harsh consequences to reveal their intention to repay.
10. Cleveland, op. cit.; Grant, op. cit.
11. Christopher C. DeMuth, "The Case Against Credit Card Interest Rate Regulation," 3 *Yale J. on Regulation* 201 (1986).
12. See Ackrill & Hannah, op. cit., at 188–89; McDowall, op. cit.
13. Mark Flannery & Katherine Samolyk, "Payday Lending: Do the Costs Justify the Price?" (FDIC Center for Financial Research, Working Paper No. 2005–09).
14. DeMuth, supra note 11, at 228, reports a Federal Reserve study indicating that about 60% of the costs of consumer lending are administrative costs unrelated to the cost of funds. For a detailed discussion of this problem in the United Kingdom, see Griffiths Commission, 2005 Report.
15. See Robert Elder, "Payday Lenders Hope Bill Will Reverse Their Fortunes," *Austin American Statesman*, Apr. 22, 2005, at C1.
16. *DTI Report*, supra note 4; Griffiths Commission, 2005 Report.
17. See *DTI Report*, supra note 4.
18. For a thorough discussion of the systemic problems in providing financial services to the poor, see Michael Barr, "Banking the Poor," 21 *Yale J. on Reg.* 121 (2004).
19. UK policymakers in the last few years have rejected interest rate caps after a series of detailed studies of subprime lending markets suggested that caps would do more harm than good. *DTI Report*, supra note 4; Griffiths Commission, 2005 Report.
20. See Ackrill & Hannah, op. cit., at 188–89; "The Plastic-Money Would-Be Pre-Election Boom," *The Economist*, Sept. 9, 1978, at 107 (discussing rule imposed in 1973 and lifted in 1978). Similarly, in the context of hire purchase agreements (roughly equivalent to retail installment sales in the United States), the United Kingdom and other Commonwealth countries have had a long tradition of imposing minimum down payments and maximum repayment terms. See R.M. Goode & Jacob S. Ziegel, *Hire-Purchase and Conditional Sale: A Comparative Survey of Commonwealth and American Law*, ch. 21 (1965).
21. The Federal Reserve press release is available at http://www.federalreserve.gov/boarddocs/press/bcreg/2003/20030108/.
22. MBNA reports, for example, that it has changed its standard procedure from requiring a repayment of 2.25% (a shade above the interest accruing at 18% each month) to a requirement that each borrower repay 1% of the principal each month in

addition to all interest and fees. This is not a requirement that each borrower repay the principal in 100 months. As described in the annual report, a borrower who made the minimum payments under that plan, and never made any future purchases, would never repay the outstanding debt, because the minimum payment would decline steadily as the outstanding balance declined. See MBNA 2004 Annual Report at 33. The requirement is expected to reduce the interest income available to issuers, which might cause issuers to raise fees. See Tom Ramstack, "Fees Put Squeeze on Credit Cards," *Washington Times*, July 4, 2005, at A01 (attributing recent fee increases of U.S. Bank and JPMorgan Chase to increased minimum payment requirement).

23. See Calder, op. cit.
24. See, e.g., Bank of America 2004 Annual Report 30, 35, 43, 69 (noting an increase in charge-offs and provisions for losses on credit card lending because of the change); Citigroup 2004 Annual Report 55 (predicting increased losses and delinquencies because of the change); JPMorgan Chase 2004 Annual Report 21 (predicting that the change will cause increased delinquency and charge-off rates); "MBNA Profits Plunge Among Record Results for U.S. Banks," *Cards International*, Apr. 29, 2005 (Issue 337) (reporting 94% decline in profits for MBNA, apparently related to higher minimum-payment obligations). As other lenders raise their minimum payment levels, the costs should spread. See Tom Ramstack, "Fees Put Squeeze on Credit Cards," *Washington Times*, July 4, 2005 (predicting that Citibank, Bank of America, and MBNA will raise their minimum payment levels to 4%).
25. This idea is derived from a tax on defaulted credit obligations that is part of the new Belgic bankruptcy system. See Kilborn, *Belgium and Luxembourg*.
26. Compared to usury regulation, a tax also has the important benefit that it probably could be applied to national banks without risk of preemption or evasion under the National Bank Act, something that is not true for usury regulation. Furletti, *Preemption*.
27. I use that example because Furletti's data indicate that segmentation of borrowing pools by FICO scores provides a useful benchmark for the rapidly increasing differentiation of interest rates within a single creditor's portfolio. Furletti, *Card Pricing*.

17. Consumer Bankruptcy Reform

1. See Jackson, op. cit. For a broader discussion founded on empirical investigation, see SWW, *The Fragile Middle Class*.
2. Jackson, op. cit.
3. APS, *Regulating Consumer Bankruptcy*.
4. See White, *Why It Pays*; White, *Why Don't More Households File?*
5. A fundamental aspect of much of the work of Professors Sullivan, Warren, and Westbrook is that bankruptcy is exogenous. E.g., SWW, *As We Forgive*; SWW, *The Fragile Middle Class*; Warren & Tyagi, op. cit.
6. The Griffiths Commission Report argues that consumer bankruptcy in the United Kingdom (where household indebtedness is even higher than it is in the United States) generally follows upon a "trigger" (such as loss of a job or change in family circumstances) followed by a "spiral" into debt that cannot be repaid. Griffiths Commission, 2005 Report. The Griffiths Commission Report is particularly interesting because it offers a rare glance at what seems to be reliable household-level information about consumer credit.
7. White, *Personal Bankruptcy*.

8. Moss, op. cit.
9. Cohen, op. cit.
10. E.g., Jackson, op. cit.; APS, *Regulating Consumer Bankruptcy.*
11. The idea is not a new one. For example, writing in 1985, Tom Jackson presciently acknowledged the possibility that experienced lenders might develop the ability to monitor borrowing more adeptly than borrowers might. Jackson, op. cit., at 1400; see also Theodore Eisenberg, "Bankruptcy Law in Perspective," 28 *UCLA L. Rev.* 953, 976–91 (1981).
12. As a glance at any annual report for a monoline credit card issuer will show, this is an oversimplification. Delinquencies on credit card accounts show a distinct time trend as the portfolio ages. The science of controlling delinquency and charge-off rates involves management over time of classes of accounts of differing ages and risk profiles. See, for example, Providian's discussion of its careful efforts to lower the delinquency rate in its portfolio since 2001 by shifting to higher quality borrowers. Providian 2004 Annual Report 3–5.
13. As Tom Jackson noted twenty years ago in comparing the relative ability of borrowers and lenders to bear risks, consumer borrowers (unlike, perhaps, publicly traded corporations) are much less able to diversify the risk of financial distress than lenders. Jackson, op. cit., at 1400.
14. See Elizabeth Warren, "The Phantom $400," 13 *J. Bankr. L. & Pr.* (2004) (describing that conventional syllogism and the implausibility of the notion that the increased charges amount to $400 per year per family).
15. See the discussion in Chapter 12 of the reasons why cardholders often become more attractive to their card issuers as they enter financial distress.
16. Paul S. Calem et al., "Switching Costs and Adverse Selection in the Market for Credit Cards: New Evidence," *J. Banking & Finance* (forthcoming).
17. Mann, *Payments Policy.*
18. I discern such a perspective in Jones & Zywicki, op. cit., LoPucki, op. cit., and Marcus Cole, "A Modest Proposal for Bankruptcy Reform," 5 *Green Bag* 269 (2002) (proposing the revival of debtors' prisons). The instinct that harsh punishment is necessary calls to mind the cadena temporal condemned as cruel by the Supreme Court in Weems v. United States, 217 U.S. 349 (1910).
19. After struggling with bankruptcy reform for eight years, Congress passed the Bankruptcy Abuse Prevention and Consumer Protection Act in April 2005, and President Bush signed the act a few days later. The act substantially amends the bankruptcy laws of the United States and will have its greatest impact in consumer bankruptcy cases. The legislation relating to consumer bankruptcy will make it more difficult for individuals to seek relief under Chapter 7 of the Bankruptcy Code. Among other changes, the act imposes on consumer debtors who are above the median income a complex mathematical "means testing" formula to determine whether the case should be dismissed for an abuse of Chapter 7. The act also will require the payment of greater amounts under a Chapter 13 plan for many consumer debtors and will alter provisions on exempt assets, reaffirmation of debts, and discharge of indebtedness for individuals.
20. For a more detailed discussion of BAPCPA and credit card lenders, see Ronald J. Mann, Bankruptcy Reform and the "Sweat Box" of Credit Card Debt, 2007 *Illinois L. Rev.* (forthcoming).
21. The revisions do not alter the provisions in Bankruptcy Code §707 that limit the chapter-shifting rules to debtors with "primarily consumer debts." Thus, chapter-shifting rules by their terms will not affect individuals who have incurred debts for business purposes. The empirical evidence discussed earlier does suggest good

reasons for the differential treatment of business-related lending. Still, there is considerable insincerity in the juxtaposition of the public policy to encourage that borrowing (and the related spending) with the subsequent harsh treatment of that borrowing in bankruptcy.

22. The reforms may not substantially reduce filing rates over time. If filings are almost entirely attributable to serious distress, then the likely effect will only be a deferral, which would be evidenced by a short-term downturn in filings. Only time will tell.
23. Several statutes that might have limited the prerogatives of credit card lenders received little attention from Congress. Consider, for example, Credit CARD Act of 2005, S. 499, 109th Cong. (prohibiting various credit card practices, enhancing disclosures, and the like); Bankruptcy Fairness Act, S. 329, 109th Cong. (increasing priority claims for nonadjusting creditors); Medical Bills Interest Rate Relief Act, H.R. 1238, 109th Cong. (amending TILA with respect to credit card transactions related to medical bills). In addition, an amendment that would have exempted victims of natural disasters from means testing was not seriously considered, an oversight that caused some to push for renewed consideration of an exemption following Hurricane Katrina. Peter G. Gosselin, "New Bankruptcy Law Could Exact a Toll on Storm Victims," *Los Angeles Times*, Sept. 7, 2005.
24. Congress did not include the Billionaire's Loophole Elimination Act, H.R. 1278, 109th Cong., which would have limited the use of asset protection trusts.
25. The "reforms" designed to protect consumers are likely to be useless or even counterproductive, as discussed in Chapter 13. With respect to minimum payment disclosures, the legislation requires that credit card companies provide the consumer examples of the estimated time for repayment under hypothetical conditions and a toll-free number to call to obtain an estimate of the time it would take to repay the actual balance. With respect to teaser rates, it requires boilerplate warnings designed to ensure that the temporary nature of the rate is disclosed.

Bibliography

Cases

Badie v. Bank of America, 79 Cal. Rptr. 2d 273 (Ct. App. 1998).
Bank One Chicago, N.A. v. Midwest Bank & Trust Co., 516 U.S. 264, 266 (1996).
Broadway Nat'l Bank v. Barton-Russell Corp., 585 N.Y.S.2d 933, 938 (Sup. Ct. 1992).
Carnival Cruise Lines, Inc. v. Shute, 499 U.S. 585, 594 (1991).
Cie v. Comdata Network, Inc., 656 NE2d 123 (Ill. Ct. App. 1995).
Discover Bank v. Boehr, 30 Cal. Rptr. 3d 76 (S. Ct. 2005).
Garber v. Harris Trust & Savings Bank, 104 Ill. App. 3d 675 (1982).
National Bank of Canada v. Interbank Card Association, 507 F. Supp. 1113 (S.D.N.Y. 1980).
Office of Fair Trading v. Lloyds TSB Bank, [2006] EWCA Civ 268 (CA (Civ Div))
Ross v. Bank of America, No. 05 CV 7116 (S.D.N.Y.).
Rossman v. Fleet Bank Nat'l Ass'n, 280 F.3d 384 (3d Cir. 2002).
Shea v. Household Bank, 105 Cal. App. 4th 85 (2003).
Strand v. U.S. Bank Nat'l Ass'n ND, 693 N.W.2d 918 (N.D. 2005).
Weems v. United States, 217 U.S. 349 (1910).

* * * * *

Federal Statutes and Regulations

Bankruptcy Abuse Prevention and Consumer Protection Act of 2005.
Fair and Accurate Credit Transactions Act of 2003.
EFTA §909.
TILA §132.
TILA §133.
TILA §161.
TILA §170.
15 U.S.C. §1637.
15 U.S.C. §§1681 et seq.
31 U.S.C. §5103.
12 CFR §205.9(a).

12 CFR 226.1 et seq.
12 CFR 226.5.
12 CFR §226.5a.
12 CFR 226.6.
12 CFR §226.7.
12 CFR §226.9(c)(1).
16 CFR Part 435.

* * * * *

Federal Bills

Bankruptcy Fairness Act, S. 329, 109th Cong.
Billionaire's Loophole Elimination Act, H.R. 1278, 109th Cong.
Consumer Credit Card Protection Act of 2005, H.R. 3492, 109th Cong., 1st Sess., §2.
Credit CARD Act of 2005, S. 499, 109th Cong.
Medical Bills Interest Rate Relief Act, H.R. 1238, 109th Cong.

* * * * *

European and British Materials

Annex to Unfair Terms Directive ¶¶ 1(j), 1(q).
Consumer Credit Act §75.
Cost of Borrowing Regulations §12.
Council Directive 93/13/EEC of 5 April 1993 on Unfair Terms in Consumer Contracts.
Data Protection Directive arts. 7, 15.
European Commission Decision of 24 July 2002. (Case No. COMP/29.373).
European Commission Decision of 9 August 2001. (Case No. COMP/29.373).
Insolvency Act 1986 §279 (as amended by Enterprise Act 2002 §256).
Office of Fair Trading, "MasterCard Interchange Fees: Preliminary Conclusions." (Feb. 2003).
"Oral Evidence Taken Before a Treasury Select Committee of the United Kingdom Parliament." (16 Oct. 2003) <http://www.parliament.the-stationery-office.co.uk/pa/cm200203/cmselect/cmtreasy/uc962-v/uc96202.htm>.
Proposal for a Directive of the European Parliament and of the Council on the Harmonization of the Law, Regulations and Administrative Provisions of the Member States Concerning Credit for Consumers. COM (2002) 443, (Sept. 11, 2002).

* * * * *

State Statutes

Ark. Code Ann. §§4-104-201 et seq.
Calif. Educ. Code §99030.
Del. Code Ann. Tit. 5 §952

Ga. Code Ann. §7-5-4(c).
La. Rev. Stat. Ann. §9:3577.2 et seq.
Mont. Code Ann. §31-1-115.
N.Y. Educ. Law 6437.
Pa. Stat. 24 PS §2301-A.
Tex. Property Code §§92.006, 92.052.
Proposed Consumer Credit Code Amendments, S.B. 252 (Utah 2006)
W. Va. Code §18B-14-10.

* * * * *

Books, News Stories, Periodicals, and Other Materials

Ablott, Matt: "Citibank's Chinese Head-Start." *Cards International*: 298 (2003): 10.

Ablott, Matt: "French Banks Accused of Cards Cartel Carve-up." *Cards International*: 322 (2004): 3.

Ablott, Matt: "MasterCard and Visa Go Separate Ways on Surcharging." *Cards International*: 325 (2004): 10.

Abraham, Kenneth S.: *Insurance Law and Regulation*. (3rd ed. 2000).

Ackrill, Margaret, and Leslie Hannah: *Barclay's: The Business of Banking 1690–1996*. 2001.

"Adib Launches Credit Card that Complies with Sharia." *Gulf News*: (5 Jul. 2004) <http://www.zawya.com>.

Adler, Barry, et al.: "Regulating Consumer Bankruptcy: A Theoretical Inquiry." *J. Legal Stud.*: 29 (2000): 585.

Ainslie, George, and Nick Haslam: *Hyperbolic Discounting, in Choice over Time*. 57, 69 (George Loewenstein & Jon Elster eds. 1992).

Amato, Paul R.: "Life-Span Adjustment of Children to Their Parents' Divorce." *4 Future Child*. (1994): 143.

Ambrose, Eileen: "Judges Start with Young to Head off Bankruptcy." *Chicago Tribune*: (24 Apr. 2005).

APACS: "Plastic Cards – History of Plastic Cards." Available at http://www.apacs.org.uk

APACS: The Proposed Consumer Credit Directive (Com (2002) 443) & Its Potential Consequences for the UK Credit Card Market (Apr. 23, 2003) (providing an industry perspective).

"Are Contactless Payments an Irresponsible Idea?" *Wisemarketer.com*: (26 Sept. 2005).

Armour, John: "Personal Insolvency Law and the Demand for Venture Capital." *Eur. Bus. Org'n L. Rev.*: 5 (2004): 87.

Arnold, Wayne: "Boom Time for Credit in Southeast Asia." *New York Times*: (12 Nov. 2004).

"Australian Market Tackles Regulation." *Cards International*: 329 (Nov. 2004): 16.

Ausubel, Lawrence M.: "Credit Card Defaults, Credit Card Profits, and Bankruptcy." *American Bankruptcy Law Journal*: 71 (1997).

Bacchette, Philippe, and Stefan Gerlach: "Consumption and Credit Constraints: International Evidence." *J. Monetary Econ.*: 40 (1997): 207.

Bank of America 2004 Annual Report.

Bar-Gill, Oren: "Seduction by Plastic." *Northwestern University Law Review*: 98 (2004): 1373.

Bar-Gill, Oren: "Consumer Misperceptions and Market Reactions: The Case of Competitive Bundling." *U. Chi. L. Rev.* 73 (2006): 33.

Barr, Michael: "Banking the Poor." *Yale J. on Reg.*: 21 (2004): 121.

Bates, Larry: "Administrative Regulation of Terms in Form Contracts: A Comparative Analysis of Consumer Protection." *Emory International Law Review*: 16 (2002): 1.

Bayot, Jennifer: "Credit Card Lets Democrats Shop with Party Loyalty." *New York Times*: (20 Jan. 2004): C8.

Bayot, Jennifer: "Final Pact Approved in Long-Running Debit Card Litigation." *New York Times*: (20 Dec. 2003): C4.

Bayot, Jennifer: "MasterCard Settles Case With Retailers Ahead of Trial." *New York Times*: (23 Apr. 2003): C1.

Beale, Sara Sun: "The Political, Social, Psychological and Other Non-Legal Factors Influencing the Development of (Federal) Criminal Law." *Buffalo Criminal Law Review*: 1 (1997): 23.

Bernstein, Anita: "For and Against Marriage: A Revision." *Mich. L. Rev.*: 102 (2003): 129, 194–95.

Bertaut, Carol C., and Michael Haliassos: "Debt Revolvers for Self-Control." (University of Cyprus Workingn Papers in Economics No. 0208, June) <http://papers.ssrn.com/sol3/papers.cfm?abstract_id=276052>.

Bettman, James R. *An Information Processing Theory of Consumer Choice*. (1979).

Bettman, James R. et al. *Cognitive Considerations in Presenting Risk Information, in Learning About Risk: Consumer and Worker Responses to Hazard Information*. (1987).

Black, Sandra E., and Donald P. Morgan: "Meet the New Borrowers, Current Issues in Econ. & Fin." *Federal Reserve Bank of New York*: 5 (Feb. 1999): 1.

Block-Lieb, Susan and Edward Janger: "The Myth of the Rational Borrower: Rationality, Behaviorism, and the Misguided "Reform" of Bankruptcy Law." *Texas Law Review*: 84 (forthcoming).

Bloom, Jennifer Kingson: "Visa Stands by Updated Debit Card, Though Banks' Response Is Cool." *American Banker*: (28 July 1999).

Bounds, Gwendolyn, and Robin Sidel: "Merchants Balk at Higher Fees for Credit Cards." *Wall Street Journal*: (12 Apr. 2005): B1.

Braucher, Jean: "Defining Unfairness: Empathy and Economic Analysis at the Federal Trade Commission." *B.U. L. Rev*: 68 (1988): 349.

Brito, Dagobert L., and Per R. Hartley: "Consumer Rationality and Credit Cards." *J. Pol. Econ. 400*: 103 (1995).

Brus, Brian: "Credit Buyers Soaring, Restaurants Swallow Costs To Savor Benefits." *Oklahoma City Journal Record*: (14 July 2005).

Buckley, F. H., and Margaret F. Brinig: "The Bankruptcy Puzzle." *J. Legal Stud.*: 27 (1998): 187.

Calder, Lendol. *Financing the American Dream: A Cultural History of Secured Credit*. (1999).

Calem, Paul S., et al. "Switching Costs and Adverse Selection in the Market for Credit Cards: New Evidence." *Journal of Banking & Finance* (forthcoming).

Camerer, Colin, et al.: "Regulation for Conservatives: Behavioral Economics and the Case for 'Asymmetric Paternalism.'" *University of Pennsylvania Law Review*: 151 (2003): 1211.

"Card Payments at Vending Machines Boost Sales." *PR Newswire*: (19 Nov. 2004) <http://www.epaynews.com/index.cgi?survey=&ref=browse&f=view&id=1100872637622215212&block>.

"Card Transactions a Sure Bet for the Future." *Credit Union Journal*: (28 Mar. 2005): 28.

CardData, "Bank Credit Card Convenience Usage." (20 Dec. 2004) <http://www.cardweb.com/carddata/charts/convenience_usage.amp>.

CardFlash (May 18, 2005).

"Cards Jump on Consumer Credit Bandwagon in Poland." *Cards International*: 296 (2003): 19.

"Cards Slowly Overcoming Barriers in Indonesia." *Cards International*: 316 (2004): 19.

Carlton, Dennis W., and Alan S. Frankel: "The Antitrust Economics of Credit Card Networks." *Antitrust Law Journal*: 63 (1995): 643.

Chang, Howard et al.: "The Effect of Regulatory Intervention in Two-Sided Markets: An Assessment of Interchange-Fee Capping in Australia." *Rev. Network Economics*: 4 (2005): 328.

Chu, Kathy: "Credit Cards Quitting Rate-Bumping Game." *USA Today*: (19 Oct. 2005).

Citigroup 2004 Annual Report.

Cleveland, Harold van B.: *CitiBank: 1812–1970*. (1986).

Cohen, Lizabeth. *A Consumers' Republic: The Politics of Mass Consumption in Postwar America*. (2003).

Cole, Marcus: "A Modest Proposal for Bankruptcy Reform." *Green Bag*: 5 (2002): 269.

Cooter, Robert D., and Edward L. Rubin: "A Theory of Loss Allocation for Consumer Payments." *Texas Law Review*: 66 (1987): 63.

Craswell, Richard: "Property Rules and Liability Rules in Unconscionability and Related Doctrines." *University of Chicago Law Review*: 60 (1993): 1.

Crispin, Shawn W.: "Thailand Acts to Slow Down Some Lending." *Wall Street Journal:* (25 Mar. 2004): A15.

Croley, Steven P., and Jon D. Hanson: "Rescuing the Revolution: The Revived Case for Enterprise Liability." *Michigan Law Review*: 91 (1993): 683.

"Culture Clash For Chinese Cards." *Cards International*: 325 (2004): 2.

Dash, Eric: "7 Big Retail Chains Sue Visa, Saying Its Fees Are a Form of Price Fixing." *New York Times*: (16 July 2005).

Davis, Jeffrey: "Protecting Consumers from Overdisclosure and Gobbledygook: An Empirical Look at the Simplification of Consumer-Credit Contracts." *Virginia Law Review*: 63 (1977).

Davis, Jeffrey: "Revamping Consumer-Credit Contract Law." *Virginia Law Review*: 68 (1982): 1333.

"Debit Cards Dominate Belgian Market." *Cards International*: 299 (2003): 17.

Dellavigna, Stefano, and Ulrike Malmendier: "Contract Design and Self-Control: Theory and Evidence." *Quarterly Journal of Economics*: 199 (2004): 353.

Demos: "Borrowing to Make Ends Meet: The Growth of Credit Card Debt in the 90's." <http://www.demos-usa.org/demos/debt_assets/borrowing.pdf>.

DeMuth, Christopher C.: "The Case Against Credit Card Interest Rate Regulation." *Yale J. on Regulation*: 3 (1986): 201.

Domowitz, Ian, and Robert L. Sartain: "Determinants of the Consumer Bankruptcy Decision." *Journal of Finance*: 54 (1999): 403.

Dove Consulting: "Debit Card Fraud and Performance Benchmarking." (Oct. 2005).

"Dutch Revolve, But Not on Cards." *Cards International*: 318 (2004): 24.

Efrat, Rafael: "Global Trends in Personal Bankruptcy." *Am. Bankr. L.J.*: 76 (2002): 81.

Eisenberg, Theodore: "Bankruptcy Law in Perspective." *UCLA L. Rev.*: 28 (1981): 953.

ElBoghdady, Dina: "For Some, No Purchase Is Too Small for Plastic." *Washington Post*: (23 Feb. 2005): A01.

Elder, Robert: "Payday Lenders Hope Bill Will Reverse Their Fortunes." *Austin American Statesman*: (22 Apr. 2005): C1.

Ellis, Diane: "The Effect of Consumer Interest Rate Deregulation on Credit Card Volumes, Charge-offs, and the Personal Bankruptcy Rate." *Bank Trends*: (May 1998).

Emmons, William R.: "Consumer-Finance Myths and Other Obstacles to Financial Literacy." *St. Louis University Public Law Review*: 24 (2005): 335.

"Eurocard." *The Economist*: (29 Apr. 1978).

Euromonitor, World Market for Financial Cards. (2002).

Fan, Wei, and Michelle J. White: "Personal Bankruptcy and the Level of Entrepreneurial Activity." *J.L. & Econ.*: 46 (2003): 543.

Fannie Mae, Announcement 04-06 (Sept. 28, 2004) <http://www.mortgagebankers.org/resident/2004/fannie-04-06.pdf>.

Fay, Scott, et al.: "The Household Bankruptcy Decision." *Am. Econ. Rev.*: 92 (2002).

Federal Reserve System, Board of Governors of, "Report to the Congress on the Disclosure of Point-of-Sale Debit Fees" 34–35 (November 2004).

Federal Reserve System, Board of Governors of, "Report to the Congress on the Profitability of Credit Card Operations of Depositary Institutions" Volume 5 (June 2005) <http://www.federalreserve.gov/boarddocs/rptcongress/creditcard/2005/ccprofit.pdf>.

Federal Reserve System, Board of Governors of, "Report to Congress on the Availability of Credit to Small Businesses" (Sept. 2002) <http://www.federalreserve.gov/boarddocs/RptCongress/sbfreport2002.pdf>.

Feinberg, Richard A.: "Credit Cards as Spending Facilitating Stimuli: A Conditioning Interpretation." *J. Consumer Research:* 18 (1986): 348.

Feinberg, Richard A.: "The Social Nature of the Classical Conditioning Phenomena in People: A Comment on Hunt, Florsheim, Chatterjee, and Kernan." *Psychology Report*: 67 (1990): 331.

"Financial Services Used by Small Businesses: Evidence from the 1998 Survey of Small Business Finances." *Federal Reserve Bulletin*: (Apr. 2001): 183.

Fitzgerald, Kate: "They're Baaaaack: Card Marketers on Campus." *Credit Card Management*: (June 2003): 18.

Flannery, Mark, and Katherine Samolyk. *Payday Lending: Do the Costs Justify the Price*. (FDIC Center for Financial Research, Working Paper No. 2005–09).

Food Marketing Institute, A Retailer's Guide to Electronic Payment Systems. (1998).

Frankel, Alan S.: "Monopoly and Competition in the Supply and Exchange of Money." *Antitrust Law Journal*: 66 (1998): 313.

Friedman, Jon, and John Meehan. *House of Cards: Inside the Troubled Empire of American Express*. (1992).

Friedman, Lawrence. *Contract Law in America*. (1965).

"From Communism to Consumerism." *The Economist*: (1 Mar. 2003).

Furletti, Mark: "Credit Card Pricing Developments and Their Disclosure." *Federal Reserve Bank of Philadelphia*: (January 2003).

Furletti, Mark: "The Debate over the National Bank Act and the Preemption of State Efforts to Regulate Credit Cards." *Temple Law Review*: 77 (2004): 425.

Gabaix, Xavier, and David Laibson: *Shrouded Attributes, Consumer Myopia, and Information Suppression in Competitive Markets*. *Quarterly Journal of Economics*: 121 (forthcoming).

Gan, Li & Tarun Sabarwal: "A Simple Test of Adverse Events and Strategic Timing Theories of Consumer Bankruptcy" (NBER Working Paper 11763) (Nov. 2005 draft).

Gans, Joshua S., and Stephen P. King: "The Role of Interchange Fees in Credit Card Associations: Competitive Analysis and Regulatory Issues." *Australian Bus. Law Rev.*: 20 (2001): 94.

Garbarine, Rachelle: "Paying Rent by Credit Card, and Dreaming of Waikiki." *New York Times*: (29 Dec. 2003): A17.

Gaudio, Arthur R.: "Electronic Real Estate Records: A Model for Action." *W. New Eng. L. Rev.*: 24 (2002): 271.

Georgakopoulos, Nicholas L.: "Bankruptcy Law for Productivity." *Wake Forest L. Rev.*: 37 (2002): 51.

Geva, Benjamin: "Consumer Liability in Unauthorized Electronic Funds Transfers." *Canadian Business Law Journal*: 38 (2003): 207.

Gilbert, R. Alton: "The Advent of the Federal Reserve and the Efficiency of the Payments Systems: The Collection of Checks, 1915–1930." *Explorations in Economic History*: 37 (2000): 121.

Gillette, Clayton: "Rolling Contracts as an Agency Problem." *Wisconsin Law Review*: 679 (2004).

Global Report on Crime and Justice. G. Newman, ed. 1999.

Gosselin, Peter G.: "New Bankruptcy Law Could Exact a Toll on Storm Victims." *Los Angeles Times*: (7 Sept. 2005).

Grady, Bill. *Credit Card Marketing*. (1992).

Grant, James. *Money of the Mind: Borrowing and Lending in America from the Civil War to Michael Milken*. (1992).

Green, Jeffrey: "Profitability 2006." *Cards and Payments*: (May 2006): 31.

Grether, David M. et al.: "The Irrelevance of Information Overload: An Analysis of Search and Disclosure." *Southern California Law Review*: 59 (1986): 277.

The Griffiths Commission on Personal Debt, "What Price Credit?" (2005).

Gross, David B., and Nicholas S. Souleles: "An Empirical Analysis of Personal Bankruptcy and Delinquency." *Review of Financial Studies*: 15 (2002): 319.

Grossman, Peter Z. *American Express: The Unofficial History of the People Who Built the Great Financial Empire*. (1987).

Guardia, Nuria Diez: "Consumer Credit in the European Union." *ECRI Research Report*: 1 (Feb. 2000).

Hacker, Jacob S. *The Divided Welfare State: The Battle over Public and Private Social Benefits in the United States*. (2002).

Haliassos, Michael, and Michael Reiter. *Credit Card Debt Puzzles*. (Center for Financial Studies Working Paper No. 2005/26), available at http:www/ifk-cfs.de/papers/05_26.pdf.

"Hangover Cure: South Korea's Banks." *The Economist*: (5 June 2004).

"Hannaford Finds PIN Debit Is Now as Expensive as Checks." *DigitalTransactionNews*: (21 Sept. 2005).

Hanson, Jon D., and Douglas A. Kysar: "Taking Behavioralism Seriously: The Problem of Market Manipulation." *New York University Law Review*: 74 (1999): 630.

Hanson, Jon D., and Douglas A. Kysar: "Taking Behavioralism Seriously: Some Evidence of Manipulation." *Harvard Law Review*: 112 (1999): 1420.

Hanson, Jon D., and Kyle D. Logue: "The First Party Insurance Externality: An Economic Justification for Enterprise Liability." *Cornell Law Review*: 76 (1990): 129.

Hanson, Jon, and David Yosifon: "The Situational Character: A Critical Realist Perspective on the Human Animal." *Georgetown Law Journal*: 93 (2004): 1.

Hayashi, Fumiko. "A Puzzle of Card Payment Pricing: Why Are Merchants Still Accepting Card Payments." *Rev. Network Econ.*: 5 (2006): 144.

Hendrickson, Robert. *The Cashless Society*. (1972).

Himmelstein, David U: "MarketWatch: Illness and Injury as Contributors to Bankruptcy, Health Affairs." (February 2005).

Hock, Dee. *Birth of the Chaordic Age*. (1999).

"Hong Kong Returns to Profitability." *Cards International*: 320 (2004): 12.

Humphrey, David B., et al.: "Realizing the Gains from Electronic Payments: Costs, Pricing, and Payment Choice." *Journal Money, Credit & Banking*: 33 (2001): 216.

Hunt, James M., R. A. Florsheim, and Jerome B. Kernan: "Credit Cards as Spending-Facilitating Stimuli: A Test and Extension of Feinberg's Conditioning Hypothesis." *Psychology Report*: 67 (1990): 323.

Hunt, Robert M.: "Development and Regulation of Consumer Credit Reporting in the US," in *The Economics of Consumer Credit: European Experience and Lessons from the U.S.* (Guiseppe Bertola et al. eds. forthcoming).

Hynes, Richard: "Non-Procrustean Bankruptcy." *Illinois Law Review*: (2004): 301.

Hynes, Richard: "Overoptimism and Overborrowing." *BYU L. Rev.*: (2004): 127.

Hynes, Richard: "Why (Consumer) Bankruptcy?" *Ala. L. Rev.*: 56 (2004): 121.

"India Credit Bureau Set for Launch in 2005." *Cards International*: 327 (2004): 10 (India).

"India Unveils First National Credit Bureau." *Cards International*: 319 (2004): 8.

"India's Banks Join the Party." *Cards International*: 483 (2002).

"Investors Nervous over South Korean Card Debts." *Cards International*: 296 (2003): 11.

Isaacs, Nathan: "The Standardizing of Contracts." *Yale L.J*: 27 (1917): 34.

Issacharoff, Samuel, and Erin F. Delaney: "Credit Card Accountability." *University of Chicago Law Review*: 73 (2006): 157.

Jackson, Thomas H.: "The Fresh-Start Policy in Bankruptcy Law." *Harvard Law Review*: 98 (1985): 1393.

Jacoby, Melissa B.: "Does Indebtedness Influence Health? A Preliminary Inquiry." *J.L. Med. & Ethics*: 30 (2002): 560.

Jacoby, Melissa B.: "Rethinking the Debates over Health-Care Financing: Evidence from the Bankruptcy Courts." *New York University Law Review*: 76 (2001): 375.

"Japanese Consumer Debt; Less Thrifty Than They Seemed." *The Economist*: (8 Feb. 1992).

Jappelli, Tullio, and Marco Pagano. "The Role and Effects of Credit Information Sharing," in *The Economics of Consumer Credit: European Experience and Lessons from the U.S.* (Guiseppe Bertola et al. eds. forthcoming).

Jappelli, Tullio, and Marco Pagano. *Information Sharing, Lending and Defaults: Cross Country Evidence. Journal of Banking & Finance*: 26 (2002): 2017.

Jentzsch, Nicola, and Amparo San Jose Riestra. "Consumer Credit Markets in the United States and Europe," in *The Economics of Consumer Credit: European Experience and Lessons from the U.S.* (Giuseppe Bertola et al. eds. forthcoming).

Jentzsch, Nicola. *The Regulation of Financial Privacy: The United States vs. Europe.* (ECRI Research Report No. 5) (June 2003).

Jeong-Ju, Na.: South Korean Households' Debt Reach an All-Time High Last Year, Korea Times, Mar. 2, 2006.

Joint Committee on Check Collection System, "Study of Check Collection System." (1954).

Jolls, Christine et al.: "A Behavioral Approach to Law and Economics." *Stanford Law Review*: 50 (1998): 1471.

Jones, Edith H., and Todd J. Zywicki: "It's Time for Means-Testing." *Brigham Young Law Review*: 177 (1999).

J. P. Morgan Chase 2004 Annual Report.

Kessler, Friedrich: "Contracts of Adhesion – Some Thoughts About Freedom of Contract." *Columbia Law Review*: 43 (1943): 629.

Kilborn, Jason. "Continuity, Change, and Innovation in Emerging Consumer Bankruptcy Systems: Belgium and Luxembourg." *American Bankruptcy Institute Law Review*: 14 (forthcoming).

Kilborn, Jason: "La Responsabilisation de l'Economie: What the U.S. Can Learn from the New French Law on Consumer Overindebtedness." *Mich. J. Int'l L.*: 26 (2005): 619.

Kilborn, Jason: "The Innovative German Approach to Consumer Debt Relief: Revolutionary Changes in German Law, and Surprising Lessons for the United States." *Nw. J. Int'l L. & Bus.*: 24 (2004): 257.

Kitch, Edmund W.: "The Framing Hypothesis: Is It Supported by Credit Card Issuer Opposition to a Surcharge on a Cash Price?" *J.L. Econ. & Org.*: 6 (1990): 217.

Klee, Elizabeth: "Paper or Plastic? The Effect of Time on Check and Debit Card Use at Grocery Stores." Board of Governors of the Federal Reserve, Finance and Economics Discussion Series, No. 2006-2 (March 2006), available at http://www.federalreserve.gov/pubs/FEDS/2006/200602/200602abs.html

"The Korea Credit Card Meltdown – What Happened and What Lessons Are Relevant?" *Cards International*: 318 (2004): 13.

"Korean Card Company Blacklist Reaches 3m." *Cards International*: 297 (2003): 11.

"Korean Rescue Programmes Unveiled." *Cards International*: 298 (2003): 23.

Korobkin, Russell: "Bounded Rationality, Standard Form Contracts, and Unconscionability." *University of Chicago Law Review*: 70 (2003): 1203.

Kristof, Kathy M.: "Late on One Card? Rates Can Rise on All of Them." *L.A. Times*: (7 Aug. 2005): C2.

Kulasekaran, Sivakumar, and Sherrill Shaffer: "Cost Efficiency Among Credit Card Banks." *J. Econ. & Bus*: 54 (2002): 54.

Laibson, David: "Golden Eggs and Hyperbolic Discounting." *Quarterly Journal of Economics*: 112 (1997): 443.

Lawless, Robert M., and Elizabeth Warren: "The Myth of the Disappearing Business Bankruptcy:" *Calif. L. Rev.*: 93 (2005): 743.

Lee, Jinkook, and Jeanne M. Hogarth: "Relationships Among Information Search Activities When Shopping for a Credit Card." *J. Consumer Affairs*: 34 (2000): 330.

Leff, Arthur Alan: "Contract as Thing." *American University Law Review*: 19 (1970): 131.

Levitin, Adam J.: "America's Payment Systems, No-Surcharge Rules, and the Hidden Costs of Credit." *Berkeley Business Law Journal*: 3 (2006): 69.

Lieber, Ron: "A Bonus for Blowing Off Your Bills." *Wall Street Journal*: (16 Sept. 2003): D1.

Lindenmayer, Isabelle: "Fast Food Embraces Cards, Hesitant on Contactless." *American Banker*: (4 Aug. 2005).

Lindenmayer, Isabelle: "Warnings of a Downside for Amex in Bank Cards." *American Banker:* (22 Mar. 2005).

LoPucki, Lynn: "Common Sense Consumer Bankruptcy." *Am. Bankr. L.J.*: 71 (1997): 461.

"Loyalty Drive Revolving Credit." *Cards International*: (Aug. 2005): 9.

Lucas, Laurie A.: "Integrative Social Contracts Theory: Ethical Implications of Marketing Credit Cards to U.S. College Students." *Am. Bus. L. J.*: 38 (2001): 413.

Lucas, Peter: "A Big Lift for Loyalty." *Credit Card Management*: (June 2002): 26.

Lucas, Peter: "PIN Debit: Grounded, Credit Card Management." (May 2005): 16.

Ludvigson, Sydney. *Consumption and Credit: A Model of Time-Varying Liquidity.*

Lupton, Joseph, and Frank Stafford: "Five Years Older: Much Richer or Deeper in Debt?" (Jan. 2000), available at http://psidonline.isr.umich.edu/Publications/Papers/FiveYearsOlder.pdf.

Lysaght, Gerard: "Swimming Successfully Against the Tide." *Cards International*: 345 (2005): 14.

Macaulay, Stewart: "Private Legislation and the Duty to Read – Business Run by IBM Machine, the Law of Contracts and Credit Cards." *Vanderbilt Law Review*: 19 (1966): 1051.

Mae, Nellie. *College on Credit: How Students Perceive Their Education Debt 9 tbl. 5.* (Feb. 2003) <http://www.nelliemae.com/library/nasls_2002.pdf>, (last visited May 27, 2005).

Mae, Nellie. *Credit Card Use Among Graduate Students 2003.* (May 2004) <http://www.nelliemae.com/library/ccstudy_2003.pdf>, (last visited May 27, 2005).

Mae, Nellie. *Undergraduate Students and Credit Cards in 2004: An Analysis of Usage Rates and Trends.* (May 2005) <http://www.nelliemae.com/library/research_12.html>, (last visited May 27, 2005).

Maki, Dean M. *The Growth of Consumer Credit and the Household Debt Service Burden, in The Impact of Public Policy on Consumer Credit.* (Thomas A. Durkin & Michael E. Staten eds. 2002).

Mandell, Lewis. *The Credit Card Industry: A History.* (1990).

Mann, Bruce H. *Republic of Debtors: Bankruptcy in the Age of American Independence.* (2002).

Mann, Ronald J. *Payment Systems and Other Financial Transactions.* (3rd ed. 2006).

Mann, Ronald J., and Jane Kaufman Winn. *Electronic Commerce.* (2d ed. 2005).

Mann, Ronald J.: "A Payments Policy for the Information Age." *Georgetown Law Journal*: 93 (2005): 633.

Mann, Ronald J.: "Bankruptcy Reform and the 'Sweat Box' of Credit Card Debt." *Illinois L. Rev.* (forthcoming).

Mann, Ronald J.: "Credit Cards and Debit Cards in the United States and Japan." *Vanderbilt Law Review*: 55 (2002): 1055.

Mann, Ronald J.: "Regulating Internet Payment Intermediaries." *Texas Law Review*: 82 (2004): 681.

Mann, Ronald J.: "Searching for Negotiability in Payment and Credit Systems." *UCLA Law Review*: 44 (1997): 951.

Mann, Ronald J.: "Strategy and Force in the Liquidation of Secured Debt." *Michigan Law Review*: 96 (1997): 159.

Manning, Robert D. *Credit Card Nation: The Consequences of America's Addiction to Credit.* (2000).

Martin, Nathalie: "The Role of History and Culture in Developing Bankruptcy and Insolvency Systems: The Perils of Legal Transplantation." *Boston College Int'l & Comp. L. Rev.*: 28 (2005): 1.

Martin, Zack: "Still Flying High After All These Years." *Credit Card Management*: (Dec. 2001): 50.

"MasterCard Reports Debit Increase Nearly Triple That of Credit." *DigitalTransactionNews*: (1 Nov. 2005).

Mazursky, Ronald G., and F. Alan Schultheis. *The Evolving Role of Credit Cards in Consumers' Wallets*. (April 2004) <http://www.edgardunn.com/eletter/2004--04> (last visited September 3, 2004).

MBNA 2004 10-K.

"MBNA Profits Plunge Among Record Results for US Banks." *Cards International*: 337 (29 Apr. 2005).

McCorkell, Peter L.: "The Impact of Credit Scoring and Automated Underwriting on Credit Availability," in *The Impact of Public Policy on Consumer Credit* 209 (Thomas A. Durkin & Michael E. Staten eds. Kluwer 2002).

"McDonalds Confirms the Cashless Ticket Lift." *Cardflash*: (22, July 2005) <http://www.cardweb.com>.

McDowall, Duncan. *Quick to the Frontier: Canada's Royal Bank*. (1993).

Milhaupt, Curtis J., and Mark D. West: "The Dark Side of Private Ordering: An Institutional and Empirical Analysis of Organized Crime." *University Chicago Law Review*: 67 (2000): 41.

Mitchell, Richard: "The Future of Visa and MasterCard, Credit Card Management." (June 2004).

Molotsky, Irvin: "The Hidden Costs of the Cashless Society." *New York Times*: 4 (4 Mar. 1984): 3.

Morbin, Tony: "Chinese to Launch National Credit Bureau in 2005." *Cards International*: 325 (2004): 3.

"More Aussie Retailers Plan Surcharges for Credit Card Payments." digitaltransactionsnews, Mar. 21, 2006.

Morriss, Andrew P., and Jason Korosec. "Automating Dispute Resolution: Credit Cards, Debit Cards, and Private Law." *Journal of Law, Econ. & Pol'y* (forthcoming).

Moss, David A. *When All Else Fails: The Government as Ultimate Risk Manager*. (2002).

Negrin, Jose L.: "The Regulation of Payment Cards: The Mexican Experience." *Rev. Network Econ.*: 4 (2005): 243.

"New Entrants Shake Up Irish Market." *Cards International*: 319 (2004): 23.

"The New Spendthrifts." *The Economist*: (20 Apr. 2002).

Niemi-Kiesiläinen, Johanna: "Changing Directions in Consumer Bankruptcy Law and Practice in Europe and USA." *J. Consumer Pol'y*: 20 (1997): 133.

Nilson Report.

Norvilitis, Jill M, et al.: "Factors Influencing Level of Credit-Card Debt in College Students." *J. Applied Social Psychology*: 33 (2003): 935.

OECD Economics Department: "The Decline in Private Savings Rates in the 1990s in OECD Countries: How Much Can Be Explained by Non-Wealth

Determinants?" (ECO/WKP(2002) Dec. 2002), available at http://www.olis.oecd.org/olis/2002doc.nsf/linkto/eco-wkp(2002)30.

Office of the Comptroller of the Currency, Bank Activities and Operations; Real Estate Lendings and Appraisals, 69. Fed.Reg. 1895 (Jan. 13, 2004).

Olney, Martha. *Buy Now, Pay Later: Advertising, Credit and Consumer Durables in the 1920's*. (1991).

"Overindebtedness in the Enlarged EU." *Cards International*: 319 (2004): 20.

Padilla, Jorge A., and Marco Pagano. "Sharing Default Information as a Borrower Discipline Device." *European Econ. Rev.*: 44 (2000): 1951.

Pagano, Marco, and Tullio Jappelli: "Information Sharing in Credit Markets." *Journal of Finance*: 48 (1993): 1693.

Peterson, Christopher L. *Taming the Sharks: Towards a Cure for the High Cost Credit Market*. (2004).

"The Plastic-Money Would-Be Pre-Election Boom." *The Economist*: (Sept. 9 1978): 107.

Porter, Katherine, and Deborah Thorne. "Going Broke and Staying Broke: The Realities of the Fresh Start in Chapter 7 Bankruptcies." *Cornell Law Review*: 92 (forthcoming).

"Portugal Offers Growth Potential." *Cards International*: 322 (2004): 20.

Posner, Eric: "Contract Law in the Welfare State: A Defense of Usury Laws, the Unconscionability Doctrine, and Related Limitations on the Freedom to Contract." *Journal of Legal Studies*: 24 (1995): 283.

Prelec, Drazen, and Duncan Simester: "Always Leave Home Without It: A Further Investigation of the Credit-Card Effect on Willingness to Pay." *Marketing Letters*: Volume 12 (2001): 5.

Providian 2004 Annual Report.

Punch, Linda: "Getting Tough?" *Credit Card Management*: (Feb. 2005): 42.

Punch, Linda: "The Cash-Rebate Card, Part II." *Credit Card Management*: (Oct. 2002): 54.

"Q&A: Why Do We Need New Credit Laws." *BBC* (8 Dec. 2003) <http://news.bbc.co.uk/2/hi/business/3293707.stm>, (last visited May 27, 2005).

Rajan, Raghuram G., and Luigi Zingales. *Saving Capitalism from the Capitalists*. (2003).

Rakoff, Todd: "Contracts of Adhesion: An Essay In Reconstruction." *Harvard Law Review*: 96 (1983): 1174.

Ramstack, Tom: "Fees Put Squeeze on Credit Cards." *Washington Times*: (4 July 2005): A01.

"RBA: Gresham's Law of Payments." *Cards International*: 337 (2005): 10.

Rea, Jr., Samuel A.: "Arm-Breaking, Consumer Credit and Personal Bankruptcy." *Econ. Inquiry*: 22 (1984): 188.

"Regulators Tighten South Korea's Belt." *Cards International*: 290 (2003).

Reserve Bank of Australia, Reform of Credit Card Schemes in Australia: Final Reforms and Regulatory Impact Statement. (Aug. 2002).

Restatement of Contracts (Second).

Reynolds, Isabel: "Glimmer of Hope for Japan's Card Fraud Victims." *Reuters*: (21 Feb. 2005).

Riestra, Amparo San José: "Credit Bureaus in Today's Credit Markets." *ECRI Research Report*: 4 (Sept. 2002).

"The Risk-Reward Challenge of Credit Cards in the Middle East." *Cards International*: 319 (2004): 14.

Ritzer, George. *Expressing America*. (1995).

Ritzer, George. *The Globalization of Nothing*. (2004).

Rivlin, Gary: "The Chrome-Shiny, Lights-Flashing, Wheel-Spinning, Touch-Screened, Drew-Carey-Wisecracking, Video-Playing, 'Sound Events'-Packed, Pulse-Quickening Bandit." *New York Times*: (9 May 2004): 42.

Roberts, James A., and Eli Jones: "Money Attitudes, Credit Card Use, and Compulsive Buying Among American College Students." *J. Consumer Affairs*: 35 (2001): 213.

Roe, Mark J. *Political Determinants of Corporate Governance: Political Context, Corporate Impact*. (2003).

Roe, Mark J. *Strong Managers, Weak Owners: The Political Roots of American Corporate Finance*. (1994).

Roe, Mark J.: "Backlash." *Colum. L. Rev.*: 98 (1998): 217.

Rolfe, Richard: "Europe's Cobranding Boom." *Credit Card Management*: (Jan. 2003): 16.

Rosenberg, Arnold: "Better than Cash? Global Proliferation of Payment Cards and Consumer Protection Policy." *Columbia Journal of Transnational Law*: 44 (2006): 520.

Sage, William M.: "Regulating Through Information: Disclosure Laws and American Health Care." *Columbia Law Review*: 99 (1999): 1701.

Schor, Juliet B. *The Overspent American*. (1998).

Schuchman, Philip: "Consumer Credit by Adhesion Contracts." *Temple L.Q.*: 35 (1962): 125.

Schwartz, Alan, and Louis L. Wilde: "Imperfect Information in Markets for Contract Terms: The Examples of Warranties and Security Interests." *Virginia. Law Review*: 69 (1983): 1387.

Scott, Robert E.: "Error and Rationality in Individual Decisionmaking: An Essay on the Relation Between Cognitive Illusions and the Management of Choices." *Southern California Law Review*: 59 (1986): 329.

Segall, Anne: "Retail Banking in Britain: The Neglected Consumer." *The Economist*: (Dec. 8 1979): 5.

Shermach, Kelly: "The Vibrant World of Loyalty." *Credit Card Management*: (Aug. 2002): 30.

Simmons, Matty. *The Credit Card Catastrophe*. (1995).

Simon, Herbert A.: "Rationality as Process and as Product of Thought." *Am. Econ. Rev.*: (May 1978): 1, 13.

Simon, John: "Payment Systems Are Different: Shouldn't Their Regulation Be Too?," *Rev. Network Econ.*: 4 (2005): 364.

Simpson, Burney: "The Case for Easier Redemptions." *Card Management*: (Aug. 2004): 13.

Simpson, Burney: "Weathering Severe Turbulence." *Credit Card Management*: (May 2003): 14.

"Singaporean Credit Bureau Promotes Positive Data Sharing." *Cards International*: 334 (2005): 6.

Slawson, W. David: "Standard Form Contracts and Democratic Control of Lawmaking Power." *Harvard Law Review*: 84 (1971): 529, 530.

Slawson, W. David: "The New Meaning of Contract: The Transformation of Contracts Law by Standard Forms." *University of Pittsburgh Law Review*: 46 (1984): 21.

"Slovenia – A Small Market with Big Potential." *Cards International*: 328 (2004): 12.

"Snap!" *The Economist*: (10 Jan. 2004).

Soman, Dilip, and Amar Cheema: "The Effect of Credit on Spending Decisions: The Role of the Credit Limit and Credibility." *Marketing Science*: 32 (2002).

"South Korea Takes Action over Credit Debt Crisis." *Cards International*: 294/295 (2003): 9.

Srivastava, Joydeep, and Priya Raghubir: "Debiasing Using Decomposition: The Case of Memory-Based Credit Card Expense Estimates." *J. Consumer Psychology:* 12 (2002): 253.

Standard Contracts Law (Isr.) 1964, 18 L.S.I. 51 (1963–1964).

Staten, Michael E., and Fred H. Cate: "The Impact of Opt-in Privacy Rules on Retail Credit Markets: A Case Study of MBNA." *Duke Law Journal*: 52 (2003): 745.

Stavins, Joanna: "Credit Card Borrowing, Delinquency, and Personal Bankruptcy." *New England Economic Review*: (July/Aug. 2000).

Stephenson, Graham. *Credit, Debit & Cheque Cards: Law & Practice*. (1993).

Sternlight, Jean: "Creeping Mandatory Arbitration: Is It Just?" *Stanford Law Review*: 57 (2005): 1631.

Strong, Howard. *What Every Credit Card User Needs to Know: How To Protect Yourself and Your Money*. (1999).

Sullivan, Teresa, Elizabeth Warren, and Jay Lawrence Westbrook. *The Fragile Middle Class*. (2000).

Sunstein, Cass R.: "Boundedly Rational Borrowing." *University of Chicago Law Review*: 73 (2006): 249.

Sunstein, Cass R.: "Group Judgments: Statistical Means, Deliberation, and Information Markets." *New York University Law Review*: 80 (2005): 962.

Swartz, Daniel, D. Garcia, Robert W. Hahn, and Anne Layne-Farrar: "The Economics of a Cashless Society: An Analysis of the Costs and Benefits of Payment Instruments." AEI-Brookings Joint Center for Regulatory Studies, Related Publication 04-24 (Sept. 2004) <http://www.aei-brookings.org/publications/abstract.php?pid=853>.

Tabb, Charles J.: "Lessons from the Globalization of Consumer Bankruptcy." *Law & Soc. Inquiry*: 30 (2005): 763.

"Taiwan Takes Action over Credit Crunch Fears." *Cards International*: 319 (2004): 9.

Thaler, Richard. *Quasi-Rational Economics*. (1991).

"Turkish Card Growth Accelerates." *Cards International*: 321 (2004): 16.

Tversky, Amos, and Daniel Kahneman: "Availability: A Heuristic for Judging Frequency and Probability." *Cognitive Psychology*: 5 (1973): 207.

Tversky, Amos, and Daniel Kahneman: "Judgment Under Uncertainty: Heuristics and Biases." *Science*: 185 (1974): 1124.

UNICRI, Understanding Crime: Experiences of Crime and Crime Control. (1993).

U.S. Department of Commerce, Bureau of Economic Analysis, "Gross Domestic Product First Quarter 2005." <http://www.bea.doc.gov/bea/newsrelarchive/2005/gdp105a.pdf>.

"US State to Restrict Card Marketing on Campus." *Cards International*: 321 (2004): 11.

VandeHei, Jim: "Business Sees Gain in GOP Takeover; Political Allies Push Corporate Agenda." *Washington Post*: (27 Mar. 2005): A01.

Warren, Elizabeth, and Amelia Warren Tyagi. *The Two-Income Trap: Why Middle-Class Mothers and Fathers Are Broke.* (2003)

Warren, Elizabeth, and Jay L. Westbrook: "Contracting out of Bankruptcy: An Empirical Intervention." *Harvard Law Review*: 118 (2005): 1197.

Warren, Elizabeth: "The Phantom $400." *J. Bankr. L. & Pr.*: 13 (2004).

Wax, Amy L.: "Bargaining in the Shadow of the Market: Is There a Future for Egalitarian Marriage?" *Va. L. Rev.*: 84 (1998): 509.

Stuart E. Weiner, Stuart E. & Julian Wright: "Interchange Fees in Various Countries: Developments and Determinants." *Rev. Network Econ.*: 4 (2005): 290.

Weinstein, Neil D.: "Unrealistic Optimism About Future Life Events." *J. Personality & Soc. Psychol.*: 39 (1980): 806.

West, Mark D.: *Law in Everyday Japan: Sex, Sumo, Suicide, and Statutes.* (2005).

Westbrook, Jay: "Local Legal Culture and the Fear of Abuse." *American Bankr. Inst. L. Rev.*: 6 (1998): 25.

White, Alan M., and Cathy Lesser Mansfield: "Literacy and Contract." *Stan. L. & Pol'y Rev*: 13 (2002): 233.

White, James J.: "Autistic Contracts." *Wayne Law Review*: 45 (2000): 1693, 1700–01.

White, James J.: "Contracting Under Amended 2–207." *Wisconsin Law Review*: 2004: 723.

White, James J.: "Form Contracts Under Revised Article 2." *Wash. U.L.Q.*: 75 (1997): 315.

White, James J.: "The Usury Trompe L'Oeil." *S.C. L. Rev.*: 51 (2000): 445.

White, Michelle J. *Personal Bankruptcy: Insurance, Work Effort, Opportunism and the Efficiency of the 'Fresh Start.'* (unpublished 2005 manuscript) <http://econ.ucsd.edu/~miwhite/>.

White, Michelle J.: "Why Don't More Households File for Bankruptcy?" *J.L. Econ. & Org'n*: 14 (1998): 205.

White, Michelle J.: "Why It Pays to File for Bankruptcy: A Critical Look at Incentives Under U.S. Bankruptcy Laws and a Proposal for Change." *University of Chicago Law Review* 65 (1998): 685.

White, Robert: "The Impact of Australia's Credit Card Reform on the Nation's Payment Value Chain." (Aug. 2004 white paper) <http://www.edgardunn.com>.

Wilson, A. N.: *The Laird of Abbotsford*. (1980).

Wolf, Martin.: *Why Globalization Works*. (2004).

Wolters, Timothy: "Carry Your Credit in Your Pocket: The Early History of the Credit Card at Bank of America and Chase Manhattan." *Enterprise & Society*: 1 (2000): 315.

Worthington, Steve: "Down Under." *Eur. Card Rev.*: (Jan./Feb. 2005): 16.

"Your Debit Card Is the Key To Protecting Your Money." *USA Today*: (5 Oct. 1999): 14A.

Ziegel, Jacob S. *Comparative Consumer Insolvency Regimes: A Canadian Perspective*. (2003).

Zinman, Jonathan: "Debit or Credit?." (Oct. 2005), available at http://www.dartmouth.edu/~jzinman.

Zywicki, Todd J.: "An Economic Analysis of the Consumer Bankruptcy Crisis." *Northwestern University Law Review*: 99 (2005): 1463.

Zywicki, Todd J.: "Testimony Presented to the Judiciary Committee of the United States on Bankruptcy Reform." (10 Feb. 2005).

Zywicki, Todd J.: "The Economics of Credit Cards." *Chapman L. Rev.*: 3 (2000): 79.

* * * * * *

Web Sites

http://cgi.money.cnn.com/tools/debtplanner/debtplanner.jsp.

http://www.cardweb.com/carddata/charts/overlimit_fees.amp, (subscription only) (last visited May 27, 2005).

http://www.federalreserve.gov/boarddocs/press/bcreg/2003/20030108/.

http://www.wbs.ac.uk/downloads/research/sme-report-may-2005.cfm.

Index

CPSIA information can be obtained at www.ICGtesting.com
Printed in the USA
LVOW11s1019280716

498156LV00003B/82/P